Managing Archaeology Underwater

A theoretical, historical and comparative perspective on society and its submerged past

Antony Firth

BAR International Series 1055
2002

Published in 2016 by
BAR Publishing, Oxford

BAR International Series 1055

Managing Archaeology Underwater

ISBN 978 1 84171 435 6

BAR Publishing is the trading name of British Archaeological Reports (Oxford) Ltd.
British Archaeological Reports was first incorporated in 1974 to publish the BAR
Series, International and British. In 1992 Hadrian Books Ltd became part of the BAR
group. This volume was originally published by Archaeopress in conjunction with
British Archaeological Reports (Oxford) Ltd / Hadrian Books Ltd, the Series principal
publisher, in 2002. This present volume is published by BAR Publishing, 2016.

Printed in England

BAR
PUBLISHING

BAR titles are available from:

BAR Publishing
122 Banbury Rd, Oxford, OX2 7BP, UK
EMAIL   info@barpublishing.com
PHONE   +44 (0)1865 310431
FAX   +44 (0)1865 316916
www.barpublishing.com

Preface

This work is based on my PhD thesis, which was submitted in August 1996 and – following examination – finalised in February 1997. At the time of submission it was already an historical work, because some of the statutes, documents and policies referred to in the text had been superseded. As the purpose of these references was to highlight principles rather than to serve as a compendium, I did not regard the inevitable obsolescence of my evidence as a problem.

Unsurprisingly, the material used in my thesis is now even more outdated. Some major changes have occurred over the past five or six years in international and domestic spheres, and in the management of archaeology underwater. There are many examples within the following pages, from new names for departments to revised state constitutions. One long-anticipated change – the transfer of responsibility for marine archaeology to English Heritage (see Section 5.2) – is now imminent; another change that was hoped for but not expected was the conclusion of the *UNESCO Convention on the Protection of Underwater Cultural Heritage* (see Section 5.3).

As time passes the facts become less factual. Nonetheless, I still believe that the arguments I advanced are outliving the sources, so I have not sought to update any primary material in this publication. Some of the resulting inaccuracies may bring the reader up short, so I would like to apologise in advance for any indignation caused.

More problematic, perhaps, is the extent to which the secondary sources are now dated. My thesis drew upon a wide range of disciplines and perspectives, all with their own dynamics and expanding literatures. It is, of course, a concern that some of my arguments have been invalidated by other works published between then and now, but further review could only delay the point at which this thesis has to withstand critique in public.

In consequence, I have made no substantive alterations to the text. The only amendments are corrections of typographical errors and grammatical changes as I have sought to render some sentences less tortuous. The resulting work is 'of its time', even if that time is not long passed; please, reader, bear this in mind.

To the acknowledgements, I would like to add my external examiners, J.D. Hill and Timothy Darvill and, once more, I must thank Peter Ucko and Nick Gaskell for encouraging this publication. I am also very grateful to David Davison and Archaeopress/BAR for their patience and support in finally publishing this work.

Antony Firth
30 June 2002

Abstract

This study addresses the relationship between state-managed archaeology and control of the past, with particular attention to the rigid association of administration and identity, i.e. nationalism, as manifest in the nation-state. A critical approach is feasible because the management of archaeology underwater is implicated in the reproduction of two fundamental aspects of the nation-state – territoriality and nationality – by virtue of the frequent location of ancient material underwater on the fringes of territory, and of the inter-'national' character of ancient material of maritime origin.

Empirical material is drawn from a comparative analysis of managing archaeology underwater in France, Norway, Sweden, Denmark, the Netherlands, the UK and Ireland and from a historical analysis of the development of management in the UK from the mid 1960s to the mid 1970s. The theoretical basis is drawn from Anthony Giddens' work on modernity, structuration and locale.

Archaeology is shown to be an aspect of modernity that facilitates individuals' trust in the nation-state by presenting a 'reasonable' collective narrative that reconciles individual and abstract at an imaginable scale. The narrative takes effect, in part, through its physical manifestation in everyday environments and through people's behaviour towards ancient material.

Archaeologists and public dwell in preconceptions about the past through their practical experience of ancient material. These preconceptions can affect the introduction of management provisions, so that they become thoroughly structured within implementation, even if the provisions themselves appear 'neutral'. Furthermore, I show that the institutionalisation of preconceptions within management can constrain archaeological research, thus inhibiting the emergence of fresh interpretations.

In the case of the Protection of Wrecks Act 1973, the 'political' resources of parliamentarians, government and lobbyists were transformed into an 'archaeological' resource of protected wrecks. The character of the archaeological resource was, and still is, directly attributable to the mobilisation of resources in the legislative process. I also demonstrate that the use of specific statutory terms in a range of countries imposes particular characteristics upon the archaeological resource. Consequently, such terms are not to be considered simply in terms of their consistency or adequacy but also in terms of the presuppositions about the past embedded within them, which are subsequently impressed upon popular environments by differential conservation of ancient material.

The terms and phrases used in managing archaeology underwater also play a significant rôle in inculcating – and failing to inculcate – archaeological norms in the behaviour of non-archaeologists. Similarly, the structuring of interaction between archaeologists and non-archaeologists by procedure and organisation can encourage or discourage rule-following behaviour, as I show in respect of reporting marine finds. Furthermore, the way in which both positive and negative sanctions are formalised attests to the legitimacy of desired behaviour, even where those sanctions are implemented rarely. In the case of the Protection of Wrecks Act 1973, I demonstrate that the (in)effectiveness of management in trying to encourage non-archaeologists to behave archaeologically has been a product of various aspects of implementation relating to licensing of work on protected wrecks.

The model of the nation-state can be undermined by post-nationalist archaeological practices in domestic and international arenas. In considering the potential for translating innovative imaginings into applied management of archaeology underwater through the institutions of the European Union, I draw attention to the dangers that attend the construction of a super-national identity. Although the coherence of the nation-state may be reinforced by appeals to ancient material, the 'message' does not inhere in the material but in the practice that comprehends it. Consequently, archaeologists have an opportunity – and a responsibility – to engage in progressive practices in the course of their everyday activities.

This work is dedicated to Norman Stephenson
and to the memory of Christopher Thorne.

Contents

Tables

Acknowledgements

My greatest thanks must go to my fellow postgraduates at Southampton for their friendship, forbearance, humour and critique. I am deeply indebted to them all both collectively and individually. My special thanks go to Siân Jones and to Ben Alberti, Margarita Diaz-Andreau, Pete Durham, Cressida Fforde, John Glenn, Paul Graves, Kat Hall, Claire Jowitt, Katie Joyce, Ingareth MacFarlane, Quentin Mackie, David Roberts, Maggie Ronayne, Henry Stevens, Francis Wenban-Smith, David Wheatley and John Martin. I would also like to thank my colleagues in the Faculty of Law, especially Maria della Croce, Lincoln Wee, Courtney Davis and Emmanuel.

Turning to my supervisors, I am at a loss for words; Peter Ucko and Nick Gaskell deserve far more than my thanks in seeing this one through. What can I say?

Much of what follows has arisen from my work in archaeology underwater in the UK over a number of years. My thanks goes to my colleagues, notably in the formative Isle of Wight Maritime Heritage Project and in the Archaeological Diving Unit; though my thanks to Martin Dean, Ian Oxley, Steve Liscoe, Ben Ferrari and Kit Watson extends far beyond my time in St Andrews. I would also like to thank other friends and colleagues in maritime archaeology, notably Anne Allen, Mark Lawrence, David Gregory, Jon Moore, Phil Robertson and David O'Regan. My work has also benefited from experience of working with members of the Joint Nautical Archaeology Policy Committee, the Maritime Affairs Group of the Institute of Field Archaeologists, the Hampshire and Wight Trust for Maritime Archaeology and the Working Group on the ICOMOS Charter for the Protection and Management of the Underwater Cultural Heritage. I would also like to thank Sarah Dromgoole and Mike Williams for correspondence about the law affecting archaeology underwater in the UK, and Malcolm Cooper and John Carman for discussions about the character of management and archaeology.

I am very grateful for the support and stimulation given by the Department of Archaeology to this impostor from the very start of my time at Southampton. In many ways, it is unfair to highlight individuals in such a Department, as I am grateful to its entire staff, both 'academic' and 'administrative'. Nonetheless, my particular thanks must go to Jon Adams, Sara Champion, Tim Champion, Clive Gamble, Stephanie Moser and Julian Thomas. Special thanks go to Chris Goodier. Equally, considerable gratitude is due to staff throughout the Faculty of Law, especially Marion Dalton and Aloma Hack.

Particular thanks are due to my hosts during fieldwork for their interest, support and friendship, including: Thijs Maarleveld and the staff of Hoofd Afdeling Archeologie Onder water; Ole Crumlin-Pedersen, Flemming Rieck and the staff of the Institute of Maritime Archaeology, Roskilde; Henrik Christiansen, Hanne-Marie Myrhoj and students at Forhistorisk Museum/Arhus University, Moesgard; Jan Larsen (Bangsbo Museum); Carsten Lund, Birger Thomsen, Erik Aksig and the staff of the Danish Forest and Nature Agency; Christer Westerdahl (University of Copenhagen); Dag Naevestad, Michael Tiesen and Johan Klosters (Norsk Sjofartsmuseum); Marek Jasinski (University of Trondhiem); Carl Olaf Cederlund, Bert Westenberg and Goran Eckberg (Sjohistoriska Museet, Stockholm); Birgitta Johansen, Christian Meschke and Peter Norman (Riksantikvarambetet, Stockholm); Reinder Reinders (University of Groningen); Detlev Ellmers (Bremerhaven Maritime Museum); Beat Arnold (Canton of Neuchatel); Andre Marguet and the staff of CNRAS, Annecy; Professor Borker, Peter Winterstein, Markus Haist, Ilona Burger and other members of DEGUWA; Maik Springmann (Verein fur Unterwaserarchaologie Mecklenburg - Vorpommern); Christopher Grayson and Daniel Therond (Council of Europe); David Blackman (European Parliament); M. Lequerment, Jean Rongier, Michel L'Hour, Luc Long, Elizabeth Veryat and the staff of DRASM, Marseille; Patrice Pomey (University of Aix-en-Provence); Serge Ximenes (FFESSM); Eric Rieth (CNRS – Musee de la Marine, Paris); Patrick O'Keefe; Eamonn Kelly (National Museum, Dublin); Ed Burke and Fionnbar Moore (Office of Public Works, Dublin).

In addition, I must thank the following people for providing supplementary information and advice about archaeology underwater in Ireland, Denmark, Sweden, France, the Netherlands and Norway: The Irish Embassy, London; Elaine Kelly (Department of the Taoisigh); The Secretary, An Taisce; Con Manning (Office of Public Works); Seán Kirwan (Department of Arts, Culture and the Gaeltacht); Nessa O'Connor and Katherine Hyland (National Museum of Ireland); Colin Breen (Queens University Belfast); Claire Callaghan; Fiona Rooney; Donal Boland (Management for Archaeology Underwater); Graham Clynes; Matt Graham; John McCourt; Helle Hedegård Sørensen (Ministry of Culture, Copenhagen); Anne

Heidemann, Annelise Heidelberg and Katrine Sihm (Royal Danish Embassy, London); Lena Forsberg (Riksantikvarieämbetet); Edwina Simpson and Nancy Andersson (Embassy of Sweden, London); Bengt Grisell (Department of Vehicle Engineering, Royal Institute of Technology); Mr. G.W. Peters (Embassy of France, London); Mr. A. Bocquet (CNRAS, Annecy); Gwenaëlle le Gurun; Eric Frénée; The Netherlands Embassy; Katja C Nordgaard (Royal Norwegian Embassy, London).

Early in my research, I intended to collate information on the management of archaeology underwater in the widest range of countries bordering seas adjacent to the European land mass. Although this information was not used directly in the finished work, it formed an important context to the development of my ideas and I am very grateful to the following people for their assistance: L. Khelif (Embassy of the Democratic and Popular Republic of Algeria, London); Rezart Spahia (Instituti Arkeologjik, Tirana); Dagmar Hartl (Austrian Institute, London); Mr. Rauscher (Austrian Ministry of Justice); K. Dockx (Ambassade de Belgique, London); Christina Angelova (Centre for Underwater Archaeology, Sozopol); Milos Ruppeldt (Embassy of the Czech and Slovak Federal Republic, London); David Falada (Univerzity Karlovy, Prague); Peter Kresak (Univerzity Komenského, Bratislava); Hussein Sayed (Embassy of the Arab Republic of Egypt, London); Frank Hellstén (Embassy of Finland, London); Leena Sammallahti and Marja Pelanne (National Board of Antiquities, Helsinki); Cultural Department (Embassy of the Federal Republic of Germany); Dr. A. Hoffmann (Deutsches Archäologisches Institut); Michael Stoß; DEGUWA; Victoria Solomonidis (Embassy of Greece, London); Consular Department (Embassy of the Republic of Hungary, London); Helgi Ágústsson (Embassy of Iceland, London); Guðmundur Ólafsson (Head of Department of Archaeology, National Museum of Iceland, Reykjavík); Jo Andrews (Embassy of Israel, London); Ehud Galili (Marine Branch, Israeli Antiquities Authority); Elena Flavia Castagnino; Angelique La Spada; Clare Scannel (Lebanese Embassy, London); C. Asmar (Direction General des Antiquitiés, République Libanaise); Libyan Interests Section (Saudi Arabian Embassy, London); Mr. V. Pace (Malta High Commission, London); Dr. Tancred Gouder (Museums Department, National Museum of Archaeology, Malta); Agata Szumowska (Polish Cultural Institute); Andrzej Boyarowski (Polish Maritime Museum); the Portuguese Embassy, London; J.F. Martin de Silva (Museu de Marinha, Lisbon); Marianne Engler (Swiss Embassy, London); M. Bakir (Tunisian Embassy, London); Natasha Lebedere (USSR Embassy, London); Sasha Tulenev, Prof. V. Masson, Valerii Nikonorov and other members of the Institute of the History of Material Culture, St. Petersburg (I am especially grateful to the Tulenev family for hosting me in Vyborg); Alexander Okorokov (Russian Academy of Sciences); J. Petrinjak (Embassy of the Socialist Federal Republic of Yugoslavia); Anna Lebl; Mr. T.C. Sowden (Attorney General's Chambers, Jersey); Bailiff of Guernsey; Prof. T. St. J. N. Bates (Clerk of Tynwald, Douglas); Wendy Horn (Manx National Heritage).

Going yet further afield, I would like to thank the following: Wayne Cassidy (Department of the Arts, Sport, the Environment, Tourism and Territories (Australia)); Phillip Pendall (Legislative Assembly of Western Australia); Bruno Werz (University of Cape Town); Larry Murphy (Submerged Cultural Resourses Unit, NPS); Cheryl Haldane (Institute of Nautical Archaeology, Cairo); Clay Mathers (US Army Corps of Engineers); John Halsey (Michigan Department of State); Roger Smith (Florida Department of State); Peter Pelkofer (State Lands Commission (California)); Chris Olson and Anne Giesecke.

For my research in the UK I must thank, in addition to those already mentioned, the following people: Hillary Malaws (Royal Commission on Ancient and Historical Monuments in Wales); Sian Rees (Cadw: Welsh Historic Monuments); Alan Aberg (Royal Commission on the Historical Monuments of England); Diana Murray (Royal Commission on the Ancient and Historical Monuments of Scotland); Noel Fojut (Historic Scotland); Bill Startin (English Heritage); Brian Williams (Historic Monuments and Buildings Branch, DoE(NI)); Christopher Dawes, Graham Bond and Luella Barker (Department of National Heritage); the staff of the Archive Section, RCHME; Andrew Burr (Department of Transport); Veronica Robbins (Receiver of Wreck, Coastguard Agency); Mr. P. Williams (Foreign and Commonwealth Office); Christopher Mann (HM Customs and Excise); Stephen Douglass (Museums and Galleries Commission); Andrew Parker (House of Commons Library); Tam Dalyell, MP; Richard Morris (Council for British Archaeology); Toby Parker (University of Bristol); Colin Martin (Scottish Institute of Maritime Studies); Sean McGrail (Institute of Archaeology, Oxford); Barrie Andrian (Scottish Trust for Underwater Archaeology); David Hymans (Marine Archaeological Survey); Chris Dobbs (Mary Rose Trust); D.G. Law (Society for Nautical Research); Martin Bell (Severn Estuary Levels Research Committee); Gillian Hutchinson (National Maritime Museum); David Thackray and Philip Claris (National Trust).

The majority of my research would not have been possible without funding from the Economic and Social Research Committee in the form of a Postgraduate Research Studentship; I would like to thank ESRC for their assistance and support.

Finally, I would like to thank my family and my friends for their love, faith and patience.

My apologies go to anyone I have omitted to mention; thanks anyway!

Abbreviations

AAO	Afdeling Archeologie Onder water
ACHWS	Advisory Committee on Historic Wreck Sites
AHM	Archaeological Heritage Management
art(s).	article(s) (of convention)
CNA	Committee (later Council) for Nautical Archaeology
CNRAS	Centre National de Recherches Archéologiques Subaquatiques
CRM	Cultural Resource Management
CS	Continental Shelf
DNH	Department of National Heritage
DOT	Department of Transport
DRASM	Départment des Recherches Archéologiques Sous-Marines
DTI	Department of Trade and Industry
EEZ	Exclusive Economic Zone
EH	English Heritage
EU	European Union
HC	House of Commons
HL	House of Lords
IFA	Institute of Field Archaeologist
IJNA	International Journal of Nautical Archaeology
JNAPC	Joint Nautical Archaeology Policy Committee
MAP 2	*Management of Archaeological Projects* (English Heritage 1991)
MP	Member of Parliament
NAS	Nautical Archaeology Society
NATO	North Atlantic Treaty Organisation
nm	nautical miles
NMR	National Monuments Record
OJ	Official Journal of the European Communities
OPW	Office of Public Works
PPG 16	*Planning Policy Guidance: Archaeology and Planning* (Department of the Environment 1990 a)
RCHME	Royal Commission on the Historical Monuments of England
SMR	Sites and Monuments Record
s./ss.	section(s) or article(s) (of statute)
sch.	schedule (of statute)
UNCLOS III	Third United Nations Conference on the Law of the Sea
VOC	Vereenigde Oost-Indische Compagnie

Conventions, statutes and associated documentation referred to in the text by way of abbreviations (e.g. LOSC 1982, PWA 1973) are listed among the sources (Section 7).

1.   GHOSTS IN THE MACHINE?

1.1 Scope

This study has its origins in a desire to bring together information about the management of archaeology underwater throughout Europe in order to change the management of archaeology underwater in the UK. The inclination towards Europe was not, however, a search for exemplary statutes in other countries or for international decrees that could be used as levers to achieve domestic change. I was aware of both the failure of the Council of Europe to finalise a convention on archaeology underwater in the mid 1980s (see Firth 1988), and of the inappropriateness of attempting to transplant provisions from one national context to another. Rather, I believed that detailed comparative analysis of domestic legislation could reveal the basic purposes of managing archaeology underwater while demanding sensitivity to the peculiarities of local circumstance. These two elements could then be recombined in the context of change in the UK to arrive at aims that were at once fundamental and achievable.

Change can be sought through various media, but inclination and opportunity prompted me to pursue my investigation of the subject by way of academic discourse. Reasoning that is coherent, rigorous and contestable is, I believe, necessary to explain the nebulous character of 'management', conceived of initially as the provision and implementation of legislative and administrative measures in attempting to conserve ancient material underwater. Such reasoning also enables the incorporation of legal and socio-political approaches within research that is nonetheless archaeological in outlook.

My concern for change in the UK was linked closely to dissatisfaction with implementation of the Protection of Wrecks Act 1973 and the Merchant Shipping Act 1894, notwithstanding my own involvement in implementing those regimes and encouraging others to do likewise. To this exponent, archaeology underwater in the late 1980s/early 1990s seemed to be a coarse mix of good intentions, hard work and frustration. In many respects, this experience appears to be no different to that of earlier 'enthusiasts' in archaeology underwater twenty years earlier. Crucial changes have been achieved, but those changes – hard-won by dedicated people – are often the cause of present exasperation. In order to understand this paradox it became necessary to add a further aim to that of collating comparable information of management in the present; I sought to prepare an authoritative account of the experiences and endeavours of the past twenty years of managing archaeology underwater in the UK.

The notion that desirable objectives have been overcome by mediocre methods emphasises my interest in separating ends, however desirable, from the means of achieving them. The attempt to distinguish analytically between means and ends needs to accommodate their interaction while giving prominence to means rather than ends in attributing causality. Importantly, the notion that means can overwhelm desired ends – irrespective of the best efforts of the people concerned

– indicates that an inadvertent end might be achieved. In particular, I am concerned that archaeology may be contributing to the persistence of nationalism, even though most archaeologists would disavow the label 'nationalist'.

The juxtaposition of nationalism and the management of archaeology underwater is central to the following chapters. On land, archaeology and nationalism appear to complement each other; underwater, the concept of the nation-state seems incapable of accommodating material which now, as in the past, occupies a space that is conceptually and physically both between and beyond countries. As I show, the mutual reinforcement of nationalism and archaeology on land is not accidental, and appears to have made archaeology relatively resistant to critique. In contrast, archaeology underwater – which was effectively unknown at the emergence of the modern nation-state – problematises concepts fundamental to nationalism, such as territory, identity and origin. Once sensitised to this problematic, it is possible to turn fresh eyes on the nationalism that inheres in archaeology on land.

By way of definition, I take archaeology to mean both the activity and the material (artefacts, structures, and deposits) which is the focus of such activity, not least because material and activity are, as I show, mutually constitutive. By archaeology underwater, I mean activity and material which is predominantly submerged in water. Submergence has many implications; for example, it renders both activity and material impervious to unaided vision or visualisation, it alters the physical survival of material and it affects peoples' ability to approach and manipulate material. However, by archaeology underwater I do not mean 'marine', 'maritime' or 'nautical' archaeology. These terms all have their uses, but each carries a strong connotation of addressing the sea and/or ship(wreck)s alone. Insofar as my comments are directed at archaeology underwater they apply – unless otherwise specified – to the whole domain of activities and materials which are characterised by submergence, whether they be in fresh or salt water, or concerned with prehistoric landsurfaces or galleons. Nonetheless, both freshwater and landsurfaces are more easily reconciled with land, and with a nationalist paradigm, than saltwater and ships. Although much of what follows is directed to saltwater and ships as 'extremes' (and as the spheres in which most practice in archaeology underwater in the UK and in much of western Europe occurs) the explanations offered can be applied to archaeology underwater as a whole and, thereafter, to archaeology in all environments.

The attempt to distinguish means from ends requires the development of an explicit theoretical framework to classify significant factors and to describe the relationships between them. My initial attempts to theorise management, developed principally in the course of collating comparative material, depended on the separation of Form, Function, Context and Values (Firth 1995; Firth 1996). At that stage, I placed particular emphasis upon Form (the institutional matrix of management) rather than Function (abstract ideas about what ought to take place) as the driving force of archaeology. The ascendance of Form over Function led me to suggest that 'rather than acting as simple tools or conduits of decision-making, institutions are hosts to values embedded within their substance, like ghosts in a machine' (Firth 1995: 51). The framework facilitated a division of generalisable aims of management from institutional details which, however vital, hindered as much as they helped. In terms of my original aims, the framework allowed me to compile readily comparable information from countries with distinctive administrative traditions. In terms of my historical aspirations, the framework prompted me to question why – among all the possible administrative means of achieving some limited archaeological aims – the management of archaeology underwater in the UK had developed along such inadequate lines.

The homemade framework might have continued to work tolerably for the rest of my research, but in discussing my efforts with various others, I was directed towards the work of Anthony Giddens. Within a short period it became apparent – to me at least – that I could get far further using structuration theory and related work than I could with my own framework. In particular, the theory of structuration highlighted an enormous hole at the centre of my own theorisations; my own model lacked any explicit account of the role of the agent – the archaeologist – in reconciling (or changing) Form, Function, Context and Values. This omission was especially inopportune, as I believed my research to be grounded firmly in my own engagement in the constitution and transformation of archaeology underwater in the UK.

So many of Giddens' insights seemed fundamental to what I wanted to achieve that a major reorientation became unavoidable. This reorientation involved a thorough rewrite of my research using concepts from structuration theory and related work, and using a particular lexicon developed as I tried to draw from the management of archaeology underwater the types of sociological distinctions to which I was becoming sensitised. Although relatively little of this writing survives below, few of the discussions that I find insightful could have been written without the inspiration of Giddens' work. It should be noted that in devoting time and space to detailed analysis of specific aspects of managing archaeology underwater, earlier analyses of other aspects of the subject were discarded (cf. Firth 1996). In sacrificing breadth for depth, my earlier aims – to present comprehensive comparative and historical accounts of the management of archaeology underwater – became untenable.

Although motivated by a desire to change the management of archaeology underwater, both in terms of its nationalistic content and its archaeological efficacy, I do not prescribe any remedies. While the express ends of managing archaeology – although varied and dynamic – can be shown to be relatively homogenous, the means of management are relatively heterogeneous and correspondingly resistant to both generic analysis and to change. Analysis and change can be pursued in respect of specific circumstances, but emphasis on the historical and contingent detail of a particular mode of implementation precludes general statements about what should be done and how. As a result, readers searching for straightforward answers will be disappointed; such readers are advised to seek solace in applying the insights below – which *are* capable of general application insofar as they address the underlying character of archaeology underwater, its management and the nation-state – to their own specific concerns.

My reluctance to prescribe model statutes and procedures is also a product of my past and current involvement in trying to change archaeology underwater in the UK and internationally. Findings made in the course of research have already informed my attempts to generate change and will continue to do so. I feel that such attempts – pursued through routine work, education and lobbying, for example – are a more appropriate means of disseminating my findings than setting them out in a thesis. In the chapters below I elaborate the causal relationships between conditions and consequences, and emphasise the responsibility of archaeologists for engaging constructively in these relationships, but such engagement is better expressed by practice than by proclamation.

1.2 Rationale

My concern for the 'ghosts' that haunt archaeology underwater is sustained by two factors. First, Orwell's oft-quoted claim that 'who controls the past controls the future: who controls the present controls the past' (Orwell 1949 [1983]: 34; see Fowler, D. 1987: 229; Fowler, P. 1977: 154; Hodder 1992: 122). Second, the observation that most archaeology is managed by state institutions (see Cleere 1989: 5; Kristiansen 1992: 3; Smith, L. 1993: 56). I am concerned about the relationship between state-managed archaeology and the control of past, present and future because the legitimacy of contemporary states rests so heavily upon a rigid association of administration and identity, i.e. nationalism, as manifest in the nation-state. Apart from causing profound distress over the past hundred years, the model of social organisation presented by the nation-state leaves little room for the expression of identity as a contingent and situated characteristic of culture (see Jones, S. 1994: 63–81) or for the exploration of modes of social organisation that celebrate – rather than suppress – human diversity.

My concern, in focusing upon nationalism, is not how archaeology is used to prop-up a particular government or country, but how archaeology props-up the nation-state as a political form. By way of clarification, my argument is not with the formation of collective identities, nor with legal/rational forms of public policy-making and administration, but with the way that the links between the two are articulated. Notably, I am concerned with the assumption that legitimacy inheres in the union of one identity and one state. Dating the nation-state to the last decades of the Nineteenth Century (see Hobsbawm 1992) does not mean that neither nations nor states can be more than 100 years old, but that the justification of one in terms of the other dates only to that time. The same antiquity can be placed on nationalism, understood as 'a principle which holds that the political and national unit should be congruent' (Gellner 1983: 1, see also Hobsbawm 1992: 9; Smith, A. 1991: 73).

The recent development of the nation-state emphasises the contingent character of this form of social organisation – it is a particular arrangement that has developed in a particular epoch and will, one day, be no longer recognisable in its current form. This conception of the nation-state is, in itself, not contentious – all forms of organisation are dynamically constituted and subject to change. Slightly more contentious, perhaps, is the view that the nation-state is not simply changing, but that it is declining. Hence Hobsbawm has concluded that the history of the late twentieth and early twenty-first centuries 'will inevitably have to be written as the history of a world which can no longer be contained within the limits of "nations" and "nation-states" as these used to be defined' (Hobsbawm 1992: 191). Other commentators have challenged such optimism in the light of an apparent resurgence of nationalism (see e.g. Bowman 1994: 143; Smith, A. 1991: 1). My concern in trying to understand how archaeology is implicated in the constitution of the nation-state is to discover whether managed archaeology is hastening decline, or contributing to resurgence.

As a number of archaeologists have pointed out (see e.g. Jones, S. 1994: 111; Renfrew 1994: 156–157; Kristiansen 1992: 13; Rowlands 1994: 136), archaeology has played a notable rôle in promoting the illusion of primordial identity upon which the nation-state rests. Moreover, there are grounds for suspecting that state-sponsored archaeology will continue, as Orwell implies, to promote the illusion in future. To a cynical observer, 'nationalist' aspirations might seem to pervade archaeology underwater in many countries in north west Europe: the Swedish are preoccupied by memories of Seventeenth Century naval might, objectified in the *Vasa* and *Kronan* (see Cederlund 1994); the English have their royal *Mary Rose*, alongside *Victory* and *Warrior*, to recall centuries of combat with the French; the Dutch invoke an imperial golden age by reference to the vessels of the VOC; the Norwegians have housed the Gokstad and Oseberg Viking ships in a shrine rather than a museum (see also Olsen 1986: 34); the Danes also venerate their Vikings, and the war of 1863-64 still figures largely in accounts of boat archaeology (e.g. Crumlin-Pedersen and Rieck 1994: 39–45); in Ireland there are plans to raise *La Surveillante*, a French vessel lost in support of the republican uprising of 1798. 'Nationalist' overtones are less evident in archaeology underwater in France, though a certain 'national' conceit may inspire the *practice* of archaeology underwater; the activity only became possible through the invention of Gagnan and Cousteau, and the latter – together with Dumas and Taillez – played a pioneering rôle in application of the aqualung to the investigation of ancient wrecks (see Muckelroy 1978: 14).

I do not want to suggest, however, that there is any 'Big Brother' perpetrating the systematic misrepresentation of the past through archaeological practice. It is for this reason I refer to 'ghosts'; the 'machine' constituted by archaeological institutions is subject to forces and processes that are elusive, and remain resistant to analysis. Although some studies have – incidentally or intentionally – suggested that archaeology promotes nationalism, and that processes operating within management shape the way in which archaeologists work, few studies have indicated precisely how archaeology, its

management, and nationalism are linked in the course of everyday practice. Even fewer studies – if any – have suggested how archaeologists might counter their possible complicity at a practical level. I hope to show that a more critical approach is feasible because the management of archaeology underwater appears to be implicated in the reproduction of two fundamental aspects of the nation-state – territoriality and nationality – by virtue of the frequent location of ancient material underwater on the fringes of territory, and of the inter-'national' character of ancient material of maritime origin.

Insofar as there is no 'Big Brother', then it is to the rôle of the archaeologist that I turn to understand how nationalism might pervade archaeology. In particular, I feel it is necessary to temper the concern for nationalistic interpretations of the past – which have received some critical consideration – with increased attention to nationalistic practices in the present, i.e. to the everyday activities through which archaeologists reproduce the nation-state. Further, my concern for nationalistic archaeology encompasses the consequences of archaeologists' practices upon ancient material within environments inhabited by the public at large. I do not want to suggest, however, that interpretation can be separated from practice or from the impact of practice upon the environment, rather the opposite. Insofar as interpretation infuses practice and practice has material consequences, then the archaeological practices and ancient material that are implicated in interpretation have to be understood as thoroughly as the interpretations of the past that arise.

My interest in practice invokes concern for the state because it is the formalised repetition of archaeological practice – through regulation and organisation – that reproduces dominant institutions. Furthermore, state regulation and organisation are often focused on the object of archaeological practices – principally monuments and artefacts. As the management of archaeology comprises not only the institutionalised practices of archaeologists but also the institutionalised practices of non-archaeologists in respect of ancient material, then management links archaeologists, nation-state and society at large. These links occur in a flux of interpretation, materiality and practice.

At this point, it is necessary to resort to a more explicit theorisation of the problem in order to understand how the activities of individual archaeologists and members of the public can help to maintain the nation-state as a systemic phenomenon. My approach draws in particular upon the work of Giddens, for three reasons. First, Giddens is concerned explicitly with the interaction of individuals and systems, characterising his theory of structuration as an extended reflection upon Marx's observation that 'Men (*sic* – Giddens prefers 'human beings') make history, but not in circumstances of their own choosing' (Giddens 1984: xxi). Second, Giddens relates his work on structuration to the origins, development and profound transformations of modernity – the post-feudal order of Europe, which has acquired global relevance (see Giddens 1991: 14–15) – in a way that problematises the nation-state (see Giddens 1985). Third, in his references to 'locale' Giddens attributes a significant rôle to the place of material both in his account of structuration and in his account of modernity. Giddens is not without critics (see Craib 1992; Cohen 1989; Jary and Jary 1995; and papers in Clark, Clark and Modgil 1980; Bryant and Jary 1991; Held and Thomsen 1989) and my own use of his work is tempered by reference to a range of other scholars. Nonetheless, Giddens' work on structuration and modernity fosters a comprehensive approach to the complexities of managing archaeology underwater.

1.3 Evidence

My empirical material is drawn from two principal studies. First, I carried out a comparative analysis of managing archaeology underwater in France, Norway, Sweden, Denmark, the Netherlands, the UK and Ireland. This analysis was based largely on written sources such as statutes and policy documents – as listed among the sources – corresponding to the more formal and abstract characteristics of management. The documentary sources were compiled in Winter 1991/Spring 1992 and were correct at that time. However, numerous changes have occurred in management among the countries considered since then, and material that is more recent has been drawn upon where possible.

The comparative study also included analysis of a series of taped interviews with archaeologists involved in managing archaeology underwater in North West Europe, conducted in January and February 1992 – as listed in Section 7. Here, the emphasis was on individual perspectives of the system, on the individual's position within the system and on the more informal mechanisms of management. Taken together, the analyses were intended to generate a common framework for comparing management in each country by reference to management functions (see Firth 1995; Firth 1996).

In his recent work, Carman eschewed a comparative approach and argued that it would 'take a detailed knowledge of the history and nature of archaeology and of the legal system in at least two separate countries to compare their archaeological legislation meaningfully' (Carman 1993 b: 15). My answer to Carman is that notwithstanding the peculiarities of archaeology and its management in each country, the underlying structures are shared, pertaining to characteristics that the vast majority of countries experience in common, i.e. that they are nation-states and they are experiencing circumstances of global modernity. In contrast to Byrne, I do not attribute similarities in management to the hegemony of Western archaeology *per se*, but to the global scope of modernity and to the hegemony of the nation-state (see Byrne 1991).

Second, I carried out a historical analysis of the development of management in the UK from the mid 1960s to the mid 1970s. Particular use was made of questions and debates in the House of Commons and the House of Lords surrounding bills and amendments on historic wreck in 1970 and 1973, culminating in the introduction of the Protection of Wrecks Act 1973. I also drew on correspondence and documents from the archive of the Committee (later Council) for Nautical Archaeology (CNA), newspapers, books and published reports of investigations. The historical analysis is intended to illuminate the dynamics that run through management, notably at the time in which the system changed

in the early 1970s. This important period has its origin in the early activities of the CNA. The CNA started out as the British Nautical Archaeological Research Committee, established following a meeting called to set out the need for the co-ordination of ship research and to guide the work of archaeologists and divers in July 1964 (Marsden 1986). The minutes of the second meeting, on 12 October 1964, record that:

> It was also agreed that the legal position regarding the investigation of wreck must be established, and the Ministry of Works must be contacted in order to clarify the position with regard to the scheduling of some wrecks as ancient monuments.

(CNA Minutes 12/10/64)

However, legal matters were relatively incidental to the Committee's concerns until the summer of 1966 when enquiries were made about salvage law, notably in relation to the wreck of the *de Leifde*. By 11 October 1967 the Committee's attention had switched to looting at the site of the *Association*, though the first minuted suggestion that the Committee should investigate the preparation of an antiquities law dates only to 6 November 1968 (CNA Minutes 06/11/68). This suggestion concerned a draft antiquities bill prepared by the Council for British Archaeology (CBA) to which a paragraph on underwater antiquities was added. It was noted, however, that Mr. Sparrow QC, who had been advising the CBA 'was clearly of the opinion that we should have our own bill which would require much work' (CNA Minutes 19/03/69). The CNA commissioned a memorandum on Salvage Law and Ancient Wreck (CNA 1969: 1), and some suggestions on amending the Merchant Shipping Act were discussed in November 1969 (CNA Minutes 19/11/69). Shortly afterwards, John Nott MP approached the National Maritime Museum (and thereby the CNA) as he had an opportunity under the Ten-Minute Rule (see Marsh 1988: 12) to introduce a bill. At Mr. Nott's suggestion, the 1970 Bill was accompanied by an attempt to amend the Merchant Shipping Act 1894, which was being revised at the time. Neither the 1970 Bill nor the Amendments made it to the statute book, but the attempt was successful insofar as it prompted the then Minister, Mr. Goronwy Roberts, to set up a committee – the Wreck Law Review Committee – that would address the law relating to wreck (Table 1.1).

The Wreck Law Review Committee met for the first time on 24 July 1970 under a new, Conservative, administration. There was little apparent progress until 'banditry' at the site of the *Mary* during July and August 1971 led to the introduction, by the DTI, of a proposal for interim legislation. The proposal was set before the Wreck Law Review Committee in November 1971 and there was some hope that it would be introduced before summer 1972, but opposition from various interests led to negotiation and redrafting. The interim legislation was eventually introduced as a Private Member's Bill by Mr. Sproat (Table 1.2).

The Wreck Law Review Committee – returning to its principal task of reviewing the Merchant Shipping Acts – reported in 1975. At this stage, however, the Government was no longer of the opinion that further changes in the law

Table 1.1:   The attempt to introduce historic wreck legislation, 1970

4 March 1970	Commons	Historic Wrecks Bill, 1R (Ten-Minute Rule)	HC 797: 415-417
6 March 1970	Commons	Historic Wrecks Bill, 2R deferred	HC 797: 868
11 March 1970	Commons	Merchant Shipping Bill, Report: amendment on historic wreck introduced and withdrawn	HC 797: 1362-1378
13 March 1970	Commons	Historic Wrecks Bill, 2R deferred	HC 797: 1815
20 March 1970	Commons	Historic Wrecks Bill, 2R deferred	HC 798: 932
10 April 1970	Commons	Historic Wrecks Bill, 2R deferred	HC 799: 983
14 April 1970	Lords	Oral Question, Protection of Historic Wrecks: announcement of review committee	HL 309: 317-318
1 May 1970	Commons	Historic Wrecks Bill, 2R deferred	HC 800: 1715
8 May 1970	Commons	Historic Wrecks Bill, 2R no instruction	HC 801: 787
18 May 1970		Dissolution of Parliament announced prior to General Election	

Table 1.2:   Introduction of Protection of Wrecks Act 1973

29 Nov 1972	Commons	Presented, First Reading	HC 847: 426-427
2 March 1973	Commons	Second Reading	HC 851: 1848-1879
13 April 1973	Commons	Committed to a Committee of the Whole House	HC 854: 1756
4 May 1973	Commons	Committee of Whole House, Third Reading	HC 855: 1656-1707
8 May 1973	Lords	Brought from Commons, First Reading	HL 342: 256
17 May 1973	Lords	Second Reading	HL 342: 914-935
8 June 1973	Lords	Committee	HL 343: 306-317
28 June 1973	Lords	Report received	HL 343: 2173-2176
9 July 1973	Lords	Third Reading, passed	HL 344: 509
18 July 1973		Royal Assent	HC 860: 494; HL 344: 1161
5 Sept 1973		First restricted area (Cattewater) came into force	DTI 1973 c

were required, and the Secretary of State for Trade made a statement to this effect on 4 March 1976 (HC 906: 707-708w). Consequently, the interim bill – as the Protection of Wrecks Act 1973 – became the central pillar of managing archaeology underwater in the UK for over 20 years. In view of the influence of this period, I use the term 'the 1973 regime' to refer collectively to a) the 1973 Act, b) the arrangements made for the Act's implementation, and c) associated administrative changes in implementation of the Merchant Shipping Act 1894.

In attempting to understand the influence of the early history of the 1973 Act upon subsequent management of archaeology underwater I have drawn particularly on the accounts of debates in 1970 and 1973, and of other relevant debates and Parliamentary Questions, as recorded in Hansard. My recourse to the debates is partly a response to the lack of information about implementation of the 1973 regime. The reports prepared by licensees of wrecks protected by the 1973 Act and the reports of the Archaeological Diving Unit are for the eyes of the Department and its Advisory Committee alone, and the minutes of the Advisory Committee are confidential. The lack of official information necessitates an interpretative approach based on indirect sources.

Although Hansard is a relatively transparent source in the sense that debates are recorded *verbatim*, the substance of debates has to be treated with caution; parliamentary procedure is highly constrained by tradition, time and the

party of government. Even when individual MPs do act independently of their party whip their intentions are often diverse and hard to divine (see Searing 1995: 419–427). Furthermore – and notwithstanding constitutional theory concerning the sovereignty of Parliament – Parliament is not, in practice, a decision-making body; it has but a limited effect on legislation that the executive – i.e. the government – seeks to have enacted (see, e.g., Burton and Drewry 1981: 267). Although the Protection of Wrecks Bill was a Private Members Bill, introduced by Mr. Sproat, it was a Government Bill 'in all but name' (see Marsh 1988: 41) as it had been drafted by the Department of Trade and Industry. Given the minimal impact of Parliament upon legislation, the parliamentary stages have to be seen as one of the final stages of a legislative process that starts long before a bill is announced (see Burton and Drewry 1981: 256; Drewry 1988: 122–127).

Nonetheless, Hansard remains an important source, for several reasons. First, it sets out the progress of bills through each House from First Reading to Royal Assent. This is important in understanding the impact of the procedural character of the 1973 Bill – a Balloted Bill in this case – upon both its content and, in particular, upon the arguments voiced to facilitate its passage. I shall argue below that such arguments had a substantial effect upon implementation of the 1973 Act, even though they did not impinge upon the provisions enacted. Second, as Burton and Drewry argue, 'parliamentary proceedings provide a small window into the secret places of an essentially closed system of government'

(Burton and Drewry 1981: 256). They suggest that '... in studying the parliamentary stages of the legislative process ... it may be possible ... for a major part of the policy-making process to be reconstructed' (Burton and Drewry 1981: 42). Certainly, in the case of the Protection of Wrecks Bill, the parliamentary debates serve as a key to concerns of the Government and of various interests that were largely resolved in pre-parliamentary consultation and negotiation. Third, as Burton and Drewry state, 'parliament's principal role is a legitimating one' (Burton and Drewry 1981: 27). Hence, in Section 4.2.2 I argue that the effort made in debate to accommodate various interests – notably salvors and divers – was not just to ensure that the 1973 Bill passed through Parliament unopposed, but also to secure the compliance of such interests in the absence of policing once the Act was implemented.

My suggestion that Mr. Sproat, who introduced the 1973 Bill, may have served primarily as a vehicle of the Government's intentions rather than as a free agent prompts an elaboration of the rôle of the various characters involved in the debates, and of the importance to be attributed to their contributions. Mr. Onslow played a very important rôle, both as Minister and as an MP with a persistent interest in archaeology underwater. Burton and Drewry summarise the importance of Ministers' speeches in general as follows:

> ... the minister's statement at second reading has to be compiled to anticipate ... scrutiny and also must reflect the various discussions that have taken place during the pre-parliamentary stages of the legislative process in order to reassure participants in that process that their views have been heeded ... It may, of course, through accident or design, contain distortion, omission or falsehood, but ... [it] constitutes a unique source for uncovering the substantive intentions behind, and the content of, government legislation.
>
> (Burton and Drewry 1981: 43)

It was, perhaps, unusually fortuitous to have a Minister that had a personal interest in the subject of the 1973 Bill. Onslow had – as a backbench MP – been among the supporters of Nott's Historic Wrecks Bill in 1970, and had spoken in debate in support of Nott's proposed amendment on historic wreck to the Merchant Shipping Bill 1970. As Under Secretary of State for Trade and Industry his rôle may have been crucial in causing DTI to draft a bill, and he gave the Protection of Wrecks Bill ample support when it eventually entered Parliament. Furthermore, Mr. Onslow continued to take an active rôle in lobbying for improvements in administration of archaeology underwater, raising questions into the 1990s (e.g. HC 253: 676-677w; HC 255: 216w). Sproat's importance is, perhaps, less than his success in sponsoring the Protection of Wrecks Bill might suggest. However, it might be presumed that his contribution to the debates was endorsed – if not prepared – by DTI, hence his comments can be given due weight. Similarly, Mr. Stewart was the only one of the 1973 Bill's original sponsors – other than Mr. Sproat – to contribute to the debates and he too may have been primed by DTI, though he also had a constituency interest in the Tobermory Galleon. The contributions made by Mr. MacArthur and Mr. Money in Committee might also be treated seriously as their remarks were fairly substantive

and may have been prompted by the DTI, possibly in an attempt to filibuster the following bill (see Section 3.2.1). Turning to the remarks by Labour members, again I am inclined to consider them noteworthy. Mr. Mason, Dr. Owen and Mr. Faulds spoke during the Second Reading debate. Mr. Mason had been President of the Board of Trade when his Minister, Mr. Roberts, set up the Wreck Law Review Committee, and both Dr. Owen and Mr. Faulds had taken an interest in archaeology underwater on earlier occasions. Similarly, Mr. Hamling – who spoke at Third Reading – and Mr. Dalyell – who spoke elsewhere and raised Parliamentary Questions – seemed to have an abiding personal interest in archaeology underwater. In short, the principal participants in the debates demonstrated either a reasonable knowledge of archaeology underwater, or at least an intelligent grasp of their brief. I feel it is valid, therefore, to assume that the various contributions were a fair representation of contemporary views on archaeology underwater, both within and outwith Westminster.

Although I have carried out comparative and historical studies, it is not my intention to produce a comparative analysis or a history of the management of archaeology underwater. Rather, I have used these studies to pursue my argument that the persistence of nationalism can be challenged, by comprehending and manipulating the management of archaeology underwater. Particular studies drawn from comparative and historical research are used to illuminate an analysis of the relationship between archaeology, society and the nation-state by way of the theory of structuration, to which I now turn.

1.4 Structuration

I use the term 'archaeology' to refer to a collection of human practices directed towards ancient material (cf. Shanks and Tilley 1992: 21). Archaeology exhibits certain patterns when viewed through time; it is these patterns that I refer to as 'management', i.e. managed archaeology consists of more-or-less institutionalised behaviour that shows a degree of repetition and routine and is, therefore, susceptible to analysis of its underlying structures. Archaeology is not, moreover, accidental; it depends on the directed involvement of people engaging with ancient material, though the conditions and consequences of management actions may not be apparent even to those who direct such activities themselves.

Giddens' theory of structuration addresses the debate within the social sciences about the relative influence of individuals and structures in impelling activity. The debate has tended towards polarisation with arguments supporting voluntarism or determinism that are poorly equipped to explain the rôle of structure or of individuality respectively (Giddens 1976 [1993]: 26–27). Giddens suggests that the difficulty can be overcome by focusing on the point at which structure and individual come together in recurrent social practice. He refers to the lived-through process of everyday conduct as 'agency' (Giddens 1976 [1993]: 81). Agency is the process whereby social practice is constituted by acts carried out by individuals as they pursue various aims. In the course of acting, individuals make use of and add to the context within

Table 1.3:   Three dimensions of structure (from Giddens 1984: 31)

Structure(s)	Theoretical Domain	Institutional Order
Signification	Theory of coding	Symbolic orders/modes of discourse
Domination	Theory of resource authorisation	Political institutions
	Theory of resource allocation	Economic institutions
Legitimation	Theory of normative regulation	Legal institutions

which they find themselves, and the relationship between individual and context is manifested in the instant of action ('instantiated') as 'structure'. Together, structure and individual constitute a system that cannot be reduced to either the voluntarism of individuals or to the determinism of structure. The interrelationship of structure and individual is referred to as the duality of structure, hence:

> By the duality of structure I mean that social structure is both constituted by human agency and yet is at the same time the very medium of this constitution

(Giddens 1976 [1993]: 128–129)

Structure is considered to enable agency as well as to constrain agency (Giddens 1979: 69–70) as structure indicates a framework that allows an act to take place as well as a framework that places limits on the act. The possibility that new practice can spring from a structured position means that structure's propensity to be reproduced is complemented by the capacity of structure to be transformed: 'Every act which contributes to the reproduction of structure is also an act of production, a novel enterprise, and as such may initiate change by altering that structure at the same time as it reproduces it' (Giddens 1976 [1993]: 134). However, the notion that structure can be produced, reproduced or transformed does not imply that these properties are inherent in structure. Structure is not self-replicating; rather, production, reproduction and transformation come about only in the instant of practice as a result of the action of individuals, who are 'the only moving objects in human social relations' (Giddens 1984: 181).

Structure is difficult to analyse because it only exists in instants. However, it is possible to observe patterns that are formed from repeated instants of structure over time. The starting point of analysis is Giddens' observation that structure has three dimensions: signification, domination and legitimation, which he links to theoretical domains and institutional orders, as set out in Table 1.3.

The notion that practice always has these three dimensions is a useful antidote to theories that deal with one dimension and then have to bolt on aspects of the others. Such a charge that can be levelled at, for example, semiological or base-superstructure models that privilege signification and domination respectively (see Giddens 1984: 31).

Although Giddens notes that structure has three dimensions, he sees it as comprising only two elements, resources and rules (Giddens 1979: 64; Giddens 1984: xxxi). However, he notes that two aspects of rules are implicated in social practice – meaning and sanction (Giddens 1979: 82; Giddens 1984: xxxi). In view of this division, it seems appropriate to hold the constitution of meaning – the semantic component – separate from the normative component (which involves sanctions) as a third element of structure, 'signs'. This conceptual reorganisation gives due weight to signs as equal partners of resources and rules in constituting structure and, in dissolving the privileged relationship between rules and signs, gives greater scope for analysing things that are signs and resources simultaneously. In this configuration, resources, rules and signs – the components of structure – match domination, legitimation and signification as the dimensions of structure, as set out in Table 1.4.

As archaeology is a social practice, then the same dimensions of structuration can be discerned in management: archaeology is constituted by signs, resources and rules that can be analysed in terms of signification, domination and legitimation. In terms of practice, the reciprocal invocation of signs, resources and rules by individuals, groups or societies can be regarded as a negotiation of meaning, power and trust. The conception of management in terms of signification, domination and legitimation is one of two principle axes that constitute the model upon which this study is elaborated.

In contrast to theories that consider structures to be 'real' things that underlie all human action, Giddens insists that structure exists only in the instants of action. The transitory existence of structure means that it can only be analysed in the historically contingent circumstances of its instantiation (Giddens 1979: 64-65; Giddens 1981: 26; Giddens 1976 [1993]: 127; 134). As structure is continuously produced and

Table 1.4:   The components and dimensions of structure

Giddens 1979		Components	Dimensions
Resources		Resources	Domination
Rules	Sanction	Rules	Legitimation
	Meaning	Signs	Signification

re-produced, agency has to be seen as an inherently dynamic and historically situated process (Giddens 1981: 36). The central rôle of time and space in structuration arises from the mediations that they impose on interaction. Action that occurs when people are face to face is different in character to action when people are far apart. Giddens refers to the distinction between interaction in circumstances of presence from interaction in circumstances of absence as a difference between 'social integration' and 'system integration' (Giddens 1979: 16–78; Giddens 1984: 28). The distinction between social and system integration is not one of scale – i.e. micro vs. macro (Giddens 1984: 139–144) – but of differences in the pattern of relations in time and space; the types of practice that hold systems together diverge from the practices involved in immediate relations between individuals. Although the two levels are analytically distinct they are also inseparable because the acts that constitute (and are constituted by) *social* practices are simultaneously involved in *systemic* practices. There are immediate links between the way in which individuals conduct themselves in face to face interaction and the maintenance of society as a whole (Giddens 1979: 77).

The specific circumstances of time and space are incorporated within interaction because each individual monitors these conditions – together with other types of knowledge – and alters their behaviour accordingly. Such individual reflexivity extends to monitoring the consequences of the individual's own actions and the actions of other individuals (Giddens 1984: 3; 5). However, the complexity of interaction is such that no single individual can take account of everything that has already happened, or of everything that might happen as a result of subsequent acts. Each act, therefore, is based upon unacknowledged conditions and unintended consequences (see Giddens 1981: 28), where the consequences of one action become the conditions of the next.

One of the ways in which, according to Giddens, individuals cope with the complex conditions and consequences of daily life is by generating routines. Routinisation – 'a fundamental concept of structuration theory' (Giddens 1984: xxiii) – results in the repeated instantiation of similar structure that appears, over time, as a 'constraint', i.e. an unintended consequence of action becomes an unacknowledged condition. Notwithstanding such constraints, individuals act in a routinely creative fashion by virtue of their knowledgeability and reflexivity, prompting Giddens to state that 'the production of society ... is always and everywhere a skilled accomplishment of its members' (Giddens 1976 [1993]: 133). Consequently, structuration theory requires an account of individuality that will explain how people can be skilled and knowledgeable, and yet responsible for consequences that they did not intend. To this end, Giddens offers a 'stratification model of consciousness' which focuses upon the different forms of attention that people commit to the activities in hand, namely discursive consciousness, practical consciousness and the unconscious (Giddens 1984: 5–7).

Both discursive and practical consciousness are said, by Giddens, to accompany acts that are 'intentional' or 'purposive', in contrast to the unconscious, which prompts actions for which individuals cannot account other than through therapy. However, whereas discursive consciousness requires 'real-time' concentration, practical consciousness may only receive attention 'after the fact', if at all. The recognition of different levels or forms of consciousness facilitates Giddens' emphasis on the reflexive character of human action; individuals can monitor their actions, their surroundings, and the actions of those around them continuously without such monitoring impinging unnecessarily upon their discursive faculties. Hence, it is entirely possible for two people to participate in an abstract debate through polite conversation while walking along a corridor and into a room. An important element of such monitoring is the individual's effort to maintain coherent behaviour from activity to activity at entirely different times and places through their lifetime; Giddens refers to this process as 'rationalisation' (Giddens 1984: 4). Rationalisations are monitored by others as 'competence', such that any individual may be prompted to give a 'reason' for their actions. Reasons need not be accurate or truthful, they need only satisfy the questioner of the individual's competence, i.e. reasons have to be reasonable (Giddens 1979: 57–58; Giddens 1984: 6). The maintenance of a continuous, coherent rationalisation of one's activities – a 'narrative of self' – is, according to Giddens, a major factor in the construction of identity (Giddens 1991: 52–54) – a matter to which I return in Section 1.7.

In view of the central rôle of the self-reflexive individual in structuration theory it is appropriate, I believe, to regard rationalisation as a form of integration – of each individual with themself – that complements social and system integration. As with social and system integration, rationalisation is not a different 'level' of integration, but is intimately related to the constitution of groups and of societies. Moreover, in speaking of the integration of the individual, as with social and system integration, 'integration' is not synonymous with 'cohesion' – people are often inconsistent in their behaviour – simply that action and reflection are interdependent aspects of agency (see Giddens 1979: 76).

The analytical separation of individual rationalisation, social integration and system integration forms the second of the two principle axes that constitute the model upon which this study is elaborated. Hence, the three dimensions of structure – domination, legitimation and signification – that were introduced above can be applied across the transformations described – individual, social and system – to produce a model of managing archaeology arranged along two intersecting axes (Table 1.5). In brief, when individuals engage with ancient material, their agency in respect of that material can be analysed in terms of all three structuring principles, i.e. as the instantiation of signs, resources and rules. Similarly, the three principles can be discerned as the experience of archaeology is shared in the course of face-to-face interaction, generating meaning, power and trust. Finally, as archaeology is abstracted to a systemic level – beyond the realm of immediate experience – it ties in with the structuration of society as a whole, with its patterns of significance, dominance and legitimacy. Importantly, it is

Table 1.5: **Two axes of managing archaeology**

	individual rationalisation	social integration	system integration
signification			
domination			
legitimation			

through individual instantiations that social and system integration occur, and it is the structuring of the societal system that frames the experience of groups and individuals. Hence, the intersection of the two axes produces a matrix of terms that can be used in analysing the different structuring principles in different circumstances of integration (Table 1.6).

Analysis using this matrix can proceed 'horizontally' – i.e. by considering the transformations that occur between individual rationalisation, social integration and system integration – or 'vertically', to examine the constitution of signification, domination and legitimation within each form of integration. While Chapters Two, Three and Four are separated vertically, the narrative within each chapter proceeds horizontally from individual to system. Similarly, Section 1.7 proceeds horizontally in considering the relationship between the formation of individual, collective and abstract identities. Notwithstanding the analytic divisions of the three structuring principles and the three forms of integration, their joint instantiation as 'structure' should always be borne in mind.

1.5 The trouble with archaeology

Since the mid-1980s a number of publications have drawn attention to the complicity of archaeologists in creating pasts that are oppressive. The critique of 'scientific' archaeology has been accompanied by a fear that archaeology has lost its relevance to society, either because the public is not interested, and/or because of the exclusivity fostered by archaeologists. The critiques have noted that not only is archaeology unavoidably political, but that archaeologists should harness their political beliefs to an archaeology that – though no less rigorous – is relevant and interesting to the public, and contributes directly to the alleviation of society's ills (see e.g. Bond and Gilliam 1994; Gathercole and Lowenthal 1994; Hodder 1992; McDonald et. al. 1991; Pinsky and Wylie 1989; Roskams 1988; Rowlands 1994; Shanks 1992; Shanks and Tilley 1992; Trigger 1984; Ucko 1987; Ucko 1989 a; Ucko 1990 [1994]; Ucko 1995).

Many of the critiques cited describe the complicity of archaeologists in patriarchal, racist, imperialist and ethnocentric subjugation (see, in particular, papers in Cleere 1989 b; Layton 1989; Gathercole and Lowenthal 1994). These critiques tend to concentrate on the effects of western archaeologies upon non-western groups in colonial and post-colonial settings (including the USA, Australia and New Zealand, Ucko 1989 b: xiv; but also the UK – e.g. Belgrave 1994; Hasted 1990; Visram 1990; and see e.g. Olsen 1986 and Fawcett 1986 on suppression of Saami and Ainu histories by archaeologists in Norway and Japan respectively). With the exception of gender-based critiques (e.g. Jones, S. and Pay 1994), studies of Nazi archaeology (McCann 1994; Mikolajczyk 1994; Veit 1989) and accounts of 'misuse' in eastern Europe (Slapsak 1993; Brown 1994; Kohl 1993), there have been fewer accounts of such subjugation of 'Europeans' by 'Europeans'.

Such accounts as are available of 'European' misuse concentrate on academic interpretation (Hodder 1991; papers in Graves-Brown, Jones and Gamble 1996), the symbolism of particular sites (Dietler 1994; Fleury-Ilett 1993; Fleury-Ilett 1996; Woodman 1995) and/or public presentation (e.g. Addyman 1989; Addyman 1994; Shanks 1992; Kristiansen 1992: 19–28; Piccini 1996). Criticism levelled at the hegemonic role of the 'heritage industry' in the UK (e.g. Shanks and Tilley 1992: ch. 4; 258) is generally limited to the presentation of ancient material in museums and heritage centres. The writing analogy that Shanks and Tilley develop (Shanks and Tilley 1992: 254) seems to concentrate upon archaeology as the production of specialised texts – reports and books – rather than as the production of ancient material within everyday environments.

While all archaeological practices – survey, excavation, analysis, presentation and so on – have a rôle in the constitution of ancient material, I wish to concentrate upon archaeological practices directed to ancient material *in situ* rather than with practices in the office, study, laboratory or display room. Such practices have received little attention, though Mackay's discussion of the landscape of Highland clearances (Mackay 1990; Mackay 1993) and Solli's account of fieldwork in Norway (Solli 1996) are important exceptions

Table 1.6: **A matrix of terms for analysing the management of archaeology**

	individual	social	system
signification	**signs**	**meaning**	**significance**
domination	**resources**	**power**	**dominance**
legitimation	**rules**	**trust**	**legitimacy**

(and see Hodder 1992: 128–129 on relations with metal detectorists). Nonetheless, archaeological activities directed towards ancient material *in situ* are among the most thoroughly institutionalised practices, subject to laws and organisational arrangements that may be quite exacting and with which archaeologists are often unwilling or ill-prepared to engage (see Ucko 1989 a : xii –xiii; Ucko 1989 b: xiv). Such accounts of archaeological institutions as are available tend to be technical descriptions that barely touch upon the effects of institutions on the constitution of ancient material itself (e g. Cleere 1984; Cleere 1989 b; Hunter and Ralston 1993; Hutt et al. 1992; though see Carman 1990; Carman 1993 b; Carman 1995).

Arguably, this gap in the literature might imply a presumption that the management practices involved in producing ancient material are objective or apolitical, at least in western societies. Shanks and Tilley, however, believe management to be a hegemonic exercise, typifying all management as commodification and marketing: 'The language of cultural resource management might be termed the language of cultural capitalism' (Shanks and Tilley 1992: 24–25; Tilley 1989). While this might be an apt characterisation of management texts in the 1970s and 1980s (see e.g. Cunningham 1979, Walka 1979), the suggestion that management and the 'cult of professionalism' is inherently alienating and restrictive (Shanks and Tilley 1992: 24–25; 263; see also Tilley 1989: 279) actually serves to distance archaeologists from their social context. In contrast to Shanks and Tilley, therefore, I suggest it is necessary to address management sympathetically, not least because management documents such as PPG 16 (Department of the Environment 1990 a), MAP 2 (English Heritage 1991) and the Institute of Field Archaeologists' codes and standards (e.g. Institute of Field Archaeologists 1988; Institute of Field Archaeologists 1990; Institute of Field Archaeologists 1994) are – by making practices explicit – dragging archaeologists' unspoken ethics, predispositions and philosophies into the open. Management obliges archaeologists to confront their place in the world, so it is unsurprising that they resist. Paradoxically, criticism directed at management might be seen as a defence mechanism employed by archaeologists to perpetuate the 'cloistral seclusion of archaeology from real political processes' that Shanks and Tilley, among others, claim to wish to escape (Shanks and Tilley 1992: 263).

1.6 Towards a critical perspective

Arguably, the lack of a critical perspective on the management of ancient material *in situ* has arisen because few scholars have articulated satisfactorily the relationships between individual archaeologists and the society within which they work (though see Chapman 1989; Chippindale 1983, and Murray 1989 on the institutional context of British archaeology in 1860s-1880s; also Champion 1991; Jones, B. 1984; Hudson 1981; Roskams 1988 on more recent times). The relationships that have been articulated – presentation in print and display – are important because the 'author-archaeologist' has considerable control over the 'reader-public', but as these relationships are also relatively transparent there has been some success in highlighting the most blatant excesses. Similarly, the complicity of western archaeologies in the subjugation of non-western societies has

been propelled onto the agenda. There is a danger, however, that the persistence of a gap in a proliferating literature will confirm that abuse occurs *somewhere else* – in museums, abroad, in Nazi Germany, in the nineteenth century – and not in the domestic, daily practices of archaeologists *here*, *now*. Cleere provides a striking example of such complacent extroversion:

> With older nations which have survived as discrete political entities for many centuries, such as France or England in Europe, the innate awareness of cultural identity is such that material symbols ... are perhaps hardly needed. The average French or English man or woman does not need archaeological or historical monuments as a reminder of his or her Frenchness or Englishness; this is inborn and reinforced daily in many ways ... The secure cultural identity of such nations contrasts with others, such as the Poles or the Jews, for whom monuments are potent symbols of nationhood.

> (Cleere 1989: 8)

In disturbing this complacency, I want to focus on the ephemeral – though thoroughly institutionalised – avenues between archaeologists and society that operate at a 'practical' level, i.e. precisely the matters that Cleere appears to dismiss as 'daily reinforcement'. These avenues could involve a contestable discourse between archaeologist and public, but as the avenues are opaque, they are largely unrecognised by public or archaeologists. This lack of recognition suggests a hegemony in which all sides are complicit. Although archaeologists' coercion of the public may be an unintended consequence of their activities, those activities are no less purposive – and archaeologists are no less responsible – for that coercion. I hope, therefore, to articulate the way in which ancient material connects archaeologists to society, thus rendering the link transparent. Although I agree with Shanks and Tilley that management manifests hegemony, I believe that such hegemony can only be challenged by mastering management, not by dismissing it. In short, I am in sympathy with Smith's position in respect of Archaeological Heritage Management (AHM):

> Any study of AHM should provide post-processual theory with the links it so desperately lacks between the political realities of archaeological practice and the post-processual call for, what is so far, highly abstract political action.

> (Smith, L. 1993: 68)

I also believe that archaeology can only regain its relevance in society by re-absorbing management as an integral concern, hence the need to confront the notion that distance from management absolves responsibility for the reproduction of reactionary hegemonies. As Carman indicates (Carman 1993 a), the relationship between archaeology, its management, and its social relevance has to be approached historically, where the history of archaeology is the history of modernity (see Rowlands 1994).

1.7 The trouble with modernity

Modernity is – according to Giddens – driven by certain dynamics, notably the separation of time and space, chronic institutional reflexivity and, importantly, the proliferation of *abstract systems*. Abstract systems are mechanisms that remove social relations from their local context, comprising 'symbolic tokens' (such as money) and 'expert systems' (including the institutions of the modern state, such as state-sponsored archaeology). These dynamics are wrapped up in a number of other aspects of modernity, notably the overthrow of tradition, the emergence of chronic revision (so that all knowledge is uncertain), and the possibilities of nuclear, ecological or economic catastrophe. Although modernity has given rise to a world that is 'troubling' to inhabit, modernity has also resulted in a separation of day-to-day life from matters that cause anxiety. Giddens refers to this separation as a 'sequestration of experience' which brings the source of anxiety within the realm of secular control and conceals any external point of reference, hence sequestration tends to 'repress a cluster of basic moral and existential components of human life' (Giddens 1991: 167). Sequestration has direct benefits insofar as it serves to contain many forms of anxiety by putting them aside institutionally (Giddens 1991: 185) but the tranquillity attained is fragile due to the general climate of uncertainty and to the diversity of crisis situations that may arise.

Modernity is also characterised by the development of the nation-state as a universal political form (cf. Giddens 1985: 291). The specific character of the nation-state can be understood by reference to the more general definition that Giddens gives to 'society':

> A social system may be said to be a society ... if it embodies an intermingling of the following criteria:
>
>> The association of the system with a ... 'social space' or 'territory of occupation'... the sustaining of a legitimated series of prerogatives over occupied social space: especially the prerogative of the use of the material environment ... an 'institutional clustering' of practices among the participants in the social system ...
>>
>> An over-all awareness ... of belonging to an inclusive community with a certain 'identity'.
>
> Giddens 1981: 45-46 (see also Giddens 1984: 163–165)

Giddens offers an account of the development of societies from traditional states, through absolutist states to nation-states (Giddens 1981; Giddens 1985). Although Giddens considers capitalism to mark the major discontinuity between modern and traditional societies, capitalistic enterprise is seen as only one of four 'institutional clusterings' associated with modernity. The other three clusters are heightened surveillance, industrial production, and the consolidation of centralised control of the means of violence (Giddens 1985: 5; Giddens 1991: 14–15). Historically, the constitution in time and space of these four clusters has stretched (i.e. they exhibit increasing 'time-space distanciation', see Giddens 1984: 377). Consequently, the onset of modernity has seen changes in the predominant form of social organisation, resulting in the institution known as 'the nation-state', hence: 'modern "societies" are nation-states, existing within a nation-state system' (Giddens 1985: 1). The nation-state is defined as follows:

> The nation-state ... is a set of institutional forms of governance maintaining an administrative monopoly over a territory with demarcated boundaries (borders), its rule being sanctioned by law and direct control of the means of internal and external violence.
>
> (Giddens 1981: 190, Giddens 1985: 121)

Giddens' definition of the nation-state reflects most of the criteria set out in his definition of 'society', with one important exception. His definition of the nation-state does not refer to any sense in which people within a nation-state consider themselves to belong to an inclusive community. Hence Giddens' concept of nation is 'political' rather than 'cultural': 'A "nation" ... only exists when a state has unified administrative reach over the territory over which its sovereignty is claimed' (Giddens 1985: 119). Breuilly has argued that Giddens' failure to grapple with the specific role of nationality excludes:

> ... many of the central problems for the analyst of the modern state, above all the connections between the expansion of state power, the active political community, the institutions which handle those expansions of both power and participation, and *the political ideologies which justify these developments and help people handle them effectively.*
>
> (Breuilly 1990: 287, my emphasis)

The way in which the state helps people to handle modernity by invoking the ideology of nationalism is of particular interest here. On an individual level, modernity has transformed self-identity from something that was oriented according to external points, to ways of life that are internally referential (Giddens 1991: 74–80). The net effect of accompanying institutional developments is that 'mastery substitutes for morality' (Giddens 1991: 202) but again, the tranquillity which self and society attain is very brittle. The fragility and brittleness of individuals and society is exposed by 'the return of the repressed'. There are a number of existential and moral issues that refuse to go away and which are prompting significant social phenomena. These phenomena include 'fateful moments' (decision-making points at which certain existential issues must be confronted – society's relationship to the past and to the future, for example) and the emergence of new social movements. Arguably, the nationalist movements of the eighteenth and nineteenth centuries are prototypical of the social movements that have accompanied the onset of modernity, hence:

> What is clear is that nationalism became a substitute for social cohesion through a national church, a royal family or other cohesive traditions, or collective group self-presentations, *a new secular religion...*
>
> (Hobsbawm 1983: 303, my emphasis)

The coincidence of archaeology and nationalism is apparent in Trigger's *A History of Archaeological Thought*, as he repeatedly juxtaposes the development of the two phenomena. Trigger cites examples in sixteenth and seventeenth century Scandinavia, seventeenth and eighteenth century France, eighteenth century Romanticism, the pioneering work of Thomsen and the culture-history of the nineteenth century and later (Trigger 1989: 49–51; 60; 73–75; 148–150). Moreover, in setting out to examine archaeology as an expression of the ideology of the middle classes (Trigger 1989: 14–15), Trigger indicates a link between archaeology and nationalism that seems to be borne out by Hobsbawm, who continues the phrase quoted above as follows:

> ... the class which required such a mode of cohesion most was the growing new middle class, or rather that large intermediate mass which signally lacked other forms of cohesion.
>
> (Hobsbawm 1983: 303)

Nonetheless, the juxtaposition of the development of archaeology with the nationalism of existentially troubled middle classes does not in itself explain how or why the institutionalised practices of archaeology have taken on their contemporary form. For this, it is necessary to develop a theory of identity formation that can link individual experience of modernity to its systemic expression in the nation-state.

1.7.1 Individuals and identity: rationalisation

Structuration theory uses the stratification model of consciousness to explain how people can be skilled and knowledgeable, and yet responsible for consequences that they did not intend (see Section 1.4). Although the stratification model suggests *how* individuals shape and are shaped by structure simultaneously, it does not explain *why*. In Giddens' scheme, activity is driven by the need to maintain 'ontological security'. After Laing, he regards 'ontological security' as a '"basic security system" largely inaccessible to the consciousness of the actor...' (Giddens 1976 [1993]: 124). Ontological security provides the individual with 'security of being', which is 'largely taken without question in most day-to-day forms of social life' and consists in part, of 'sustaining ... a cognitively ordered world of self and other' (Giddens 1976 [1993]: 124). Ontological security emerges in the course of each infants' development as they cope with existential differences between 'self', 'other (people)' and the 'object-world', and as they come to terms with 'being' itself (Giddens 1991: 47–55). Ontological security is lessened by anxiety, i.e. a sense of indefinable worry (Giddens 1991: 45). Consequently, motivation can be understood as the perpetual effort to manage anxiety in the course of everyday life. Giddens suggests that anxiety is managed through trusting others, maintaining a coherent narrative of self, and mastering the environment.

Giddens' work on trust – which draws from Erikson (see Giddens 1984: 51–60) – starts with infants' acquisition of the ability to trust early in their development. In the course of that development and thereafter, trust serves as an inoculation that screens the individual from fears and anxiety that might otherwise engulf them (Giddens 1991: 39). Trust among small numbers of individuals may arise through the development of intimacy and of 'pure relationships' between each person (Giddens 1991: 94–98). Trust in the broad range of people encountered in day-to-day life, however, is pursued through 'tact'; each individual acts in accordance with 'common conventions' (i.e. rules) to promote conditions of trust within which neither their own nor other people's security is threatened (Giddens 1984: 64). Importantly, trust always involves mutuality, i.e. expectations of reciprocity (Giddens 1984: 53) and can, therefore, be distinguished from 'faith'. The character of trust is especially clear in Giddens

references to 'active' trust as 'trust in others or in institutions ... that has to be actively produced and negotiated' (Giddens 1994: 93–94; see also Giddens 1994: 14).

The relevance of a coherent narrative of self to the management of anxiety arises from Giddens' emphasis on individuals' reflexivity, that is to say their ability to monitor themselves, people around them, their surroundings and so on in demonstrating 'competence' (cf. Section 1.4). Each individual must demonstrate the reasonableness to others and to themself of their activity through time and space – from group to group and from locale to locale. For example, an individual may be prompted to give one reason for being coarse at the pub, another reason for being polite at home, and a further reason that assimilates the two previous reasons as a unitary account of evidently schizoid behaviour. Giddens suggests that such overall reasonableness is established by way of a narrative of self, hence 'the reflexive project of the self ... consists in the sustaining of coherent, yet continuously revised, biographical narratives...' (Giddens 1991: 5, see Section 1.4). According to Giddens, the biographical narrative equates with self-identity, which is 'the self as reflexively understood by the individual in terms of his or her biography' (Giddens 1991: 244). This formulation effectively reconciles continuity with contingency in the formation of self-identity, resolving the apparent opposition between 'primordialists [who] see identity as deep, internal and permanent [and] interactionists [who] see it as shallow, external and contingent on social circumstances' (Rowlands 1994: 132).

Lyon has pointed out the impact of individuals on the development of nationalism – the 'Herder Syndrome' – in several quite distinct contexts, rooting their efforts in an attempt to create a sense of identity for themselves (Lyon, J. 1994: 224–225). Smith suggests the thesis that nationalism is the resolution of intellectuals' 'identity crises' should not be generalised to other strata or classes (Smith, A. 1991: 96). However, he emphasises the importance of such intellectuals ('poets, musicians, painters, sculptors, novelists, historians and *archaeologists*, playwrights, philologists, anthropologists and folklorists' (my emphasis)) in proposing, elaborating and disseminating the concepts and language of nationalism (Smith, A. 1991: 91–93). The apparent hiatus between the individual crises of the élite and an essentially stable (but uninspired) consuming mass might be filled by Hobsbawm's middle classes. However, society cannot be reduced to such a simplistic spectrum because, after Giddens, society is the achievement of the skilled, knowledgeable and reflexive activities of all of its members, all of whom are – nevertheless – equally susceptible to conservative routinisation.

The recognition that all individuals, of whatever class, have some rôle in constituting 'a nation' directs attention away from individual self-identity towards identity formation in a relationship between individual and collectivity; the sense of belonging to 'a nation' depends upon each individual considering themselves to be 'more than' an individual. However, the notion that people start to think of themselves as an *imagined* community (Anderson 1983 [1991]: 5–6) raises the following question: how do people come to think in terms of *community*? Surely, the conception of several million people, of who you are only one, does little to bolster a sense of self? Confino has highlighted this problem, noting that – following Anderson's work – 'we need a method that can tell us about the way people devise a common denominator between their intimate, immediate and real local place and the distant and abstract national world' (Confino 1993: 44).

1.7.2   Collective identity: social integration

The linking of identity to narrative, and of narrative to the maintenance of ontological security, provides a mechanism for identity formation that is rooted in the individual but which can be adapted to circumstances of social and system integration. Although brief encounters on the street or in a corridor which are not generally threatening can be dealt with through behaviour based on low-level expectations (i.e. tact), the less casual encounters that are required to go on in life successfully require greater 'exposure', i.e. increased dependence on each party's behaviour. The willingness to accede to a transaction will depend upon an estimate of the other person's propensity to sustain trust during the transaction. The behaviour of the other cannot be predicted because the other is not self, but the other has to be sufficiently similar to self that behaviour can be anticipated. The propensity to sustain trust may be gauged in three ways. First, by iterative interaction in which each party 'learns' by monitoring the extent to which the other party reciprocates. Second, the parties may recall previous successful transactions. Third, the parties may recognise general characteristics that permit the parties to consider themselves alike.

This third means of gauging trustworthiness is particularly interesting because it concerns outward displays upon first encounters, which might include dress, mannerisms and behaviour towards people and material in the vicinity. However, it is not the outward show as such that indicates the propensity to sustain trust but the 'reasonableness' evinced by it, i.e. trust can be assumed if each party manifests a common conception of reasonableness through their outward appearance and behaviour. As each party's conception of reasonableness is linked to their narrative of self then apparent trustworthiness indicates commonality in biographical narratives. As narratives are the basis of identity, then trustworthiness implies joint or collective identity; in short, trustworthiness is assumed when people identify with each other. This explanation highlights two important points. First, biographical narratives are fundamental not only to the construction of self-identity, but – by virtue of their rôle in facilitating trust – also to the construction of group identity. Second, group identity is constituted by the assumption of trust on the basis of people's behaviour towards other people and to their material surroundings. In this sense, group identity is not simply displayed; it is practised.

Importantly, collective identity does not reside in the group as such, as if the group is a self-reflexive entity in itself. Rather, collective identity arises from each individual's constitution of self-identity through common features that facilitate the assumption of integrity by other individuals.

Trust in other members of the group is linked to recognition of self in the other, that is to say, in the comparability of individual and group narratives.

This formulation of identity formation suggests that identity is constituted through similarity. The formulation is, therefore, in conflict with accounts of identity that emphasise the rôle of difference, such as Eriksen's explanation of ethnic identity:

> The first fact of ethnicity is the application of systematic distinctions between insiders and outsiders; between Us and Them.
>
> (Eriksen 1993: 18)

The conception of identity constituted principally in relation to 'otherness' is found in both theoretical and empirical studies (e.g. Colley 1992: 5; Handler 1988: 51; Hobsbawm 1983: 274–278; Neumann and Welsh 1991; Said 1978 [1995]: 54; see also Goddard, Llobera and Shore 1994: 27; Schlesinger 1991: 181). It appears to go back to Saussure's *General Course in Linguistics*: 'what characterises each most exactly is being whatever the others are not' (Saussure 1916 [1983]: 115). Difference can play a crucial role in bringing a sense of common identity to the fore. However, theorisations of group identity founded principally on the basis of collective otherness seem deficient because – insofar as the overriding 'other' to any individual is anything that is not 'self' – such theories do not explain why individuals choose to associate themself with one 'other' as opposed to another 'other'. Difference may play a major role in delimiting similarity, but it seems that the fundamental reason why one individual chooses to associate with another individual or with a group is that the individual perceives sufficient similarity in the other to assume trustworthiness and to engage in non-threatening interaction.

My argument can be illustrated by reference to individual interaction with crowds. The circumstances of a crowd rarely permit the level of interaction required for each individual to deal with each other tactfully and, collectively, a crowd does not constitute a single 'other' with whom trust can be developed by reciprocity. The inability to distinguish between the many 'others' in a crowd would be a nightmare to the ontologically insecure individual. Arguably, the existential differentiation of self from other that occurs at the earliest stages of infant development must incorporate a further distinction between 'like other' and 'unlike other'. 'Like others', though 'other', are sufficiently 'like' to trust. In contrast, the integrity of 'unlike others' is wholly suspect. Hence, trustworthiness can be seen as a measure of 'likeness' intended to resolve a delicate balance of like and unlike. If this is the case, then either agent in prospective interaction may demonstrate 'likeness' in order that interaction may commence. This conception of identity formation is sympathetic to observations such as that by Handler, who discusses difference *after* similarity, e.g.:

> These incarnations of 'not-Quebec' *complement* the positive vision of a Québécois nation endowed with definite political, cultural and historical boundaries
>
> (Handler 1988: 47, my emphasis)

Collective identification overcomes the hiatus between individual identity and the nation-state indicated by Confino because the formation of groups enables people to conceive of a collectivity without exposing them to their all-too-probable insignificance. The rôle of groups in the social integration of modern society is indicated by the mutual development of the modern state and civil society (e.g. Giddens 1991: 151–152; also Giddens 1984: 197). Insofar as Giddens characterises modernity in terms of the separation of social and system integration through the stretching of space-time, so that state co-ordination no longer depends on presence (Giddens 1984: 181–185), then civil groups seem to pack out the absence and render the shower of printed abstractions – newspapers, novellas, pamphlets, laws (Anderson 1983 [1991]: ch. 3; Colley 1992: 21–22; Giddens 1985: 178–179; 210–211) – 'reasonable'. In Confino's study of the rôle of Heimat in the constitution of German nationalism between 1870 and 1914, for example, the generation of the idea and its reinforcement in images, histories and museums cannot be divorced from the Heimat-related groups that existed locally, regionally and nationally (Confino 1993: 51).

Confino stresses the capacity for the Heimat idea to appeal to the whole population of Germany – traversing the religious, political and social divisions of the time – but he lays particular emphasis on the impetus attributable to the German bourgeois:

> who ... stood at the crossroads of German society after 1871: modernity and nation-building. In Heimat memory they found a way to reconcile local with national identity, and local and national pasts with modernity.

> (Confino 1993: 53)

Although group formation is not limited to the middle classes, Colley's work on British identity also suggests that bourgeois voluntary associations in particular – 'breaking out like measles over the face of Britain and the rest of Europe' in the mid-Eighteenth Century – played a significant role in the development of nationalism (Colley 1992: 90–98), recalling Hobsbawm's emphasis on the new middle class. The formation of voluntary associations is relevant to more abstract, systemic integration because 'merely by existing, the societies challenged the way that the British state was currently organised' (Colley 1992: 93). Not only did the groups help people to associate on an imaginable scale but in so doing they could see themselves fulfilling activities that the state ought to carry out on behalf of the population. This realisation may have contributed to the conceit that such associations were representative of the population, or of its 'best interests'. Groups are, therefore, composed of individuals with their own motives or interests and yet encouraged to generalise their experience by companionship that, collectively, yields political clout. Analysis of such groups is relevant both to the development of nationalism (cf. Hutchinson 1987, in which groups figure prominently) and to the development of archaeology (see, e.g., Chapman 1989).

1.7.3   Trust in abstract systems: system integration

Interaction between individuals and abstract systems such as state institutions involves reciprocity; insofar as the relationship is not violently coercive nor wholly deceptive then the core of the relationship is based upon trust (Giddens 1991: 18):

> All forms of expertise presume active trust, since every claim to authority is made alongside those of other authorities, and experts themselves often disagree with one another ... expertise can never sustain the claims to legitimacy possible in more traditional systems of authority ... an expert has no more than a provisional claim to authority, because the expert's views may be contested by others with equivalent credentials

> (Giddens 1994: 95)

Giddens states that abstract systems help foster day-to-day security (Giddens 1991: 185, also Giddens 1991: 167) and that trust is a medium of interaction with abstract systems, which allows the 'leap into faith' that practical engagement demands (Giddens 1991: 3). However, such juxtapositions imply that abstract systems are only trusted because they work, and only work because they are trusted. Although he accepts that a leap to commitment is inherent in all forms of trust (Giddens 1991: 19), abstract systems do not allow the incremental, monitored leaps that are the foundation of personal trust. Notwithstanding the integral role of clients and practitioners in their constitution, abstract systems lack a reciprocating individuality of their own that might allow trust between system and individual to develop. Giddens refers to the problem of formulating trust with respect to abstract systems as follows:

> The forms of social solidarity which [the domain of personal relations] can generate ... cannot be directly interpolated within wider institutional or political orders, the reason being that the trust mechanisms involved depend on the recognition of personal integrity ... In the other areas mentioned – abstract systems, the state and more global interconnections – *the means of developing active trust have to be different...*

> (Giddens 1994: 131, my emphasis)

Generally, trust in abstract circumstances is ascribed to definition by opposition to an 'other'. The problems with such arguments have been rehearsed above, and their weakness is compounded if the chosen 'Us' is not another individual but an abstraction such as the nation-state, especially as individuals can have no immediate experience of an abstract 'Them' to which they are opposed. In contrast, the contention that identification is based fundamentally on similarity, rather then otherness, facilitates the argument that an equivalent mechanism allows individuals to regard themselves as similar to abstract systems, i.e. that trust in abstract systems may develop on the basis of presumed similarity.

Abstract systems cannot display 'likeness' at a distance in the same way as a crowd, or an individual. Three possibilities might be postulated. First, emphasis is placed on the rôle and responsibility of the individuals (e.g. bureaucrats) that constitute the system (representation). Second, the system projects an individuality that is assimilable by the individual as a 'like other' (personification). Third, the need for trust is

Table 1.7:   **Relationship between trust in abstract systems and forms of narrative**

Manner of inviting trust	Form of narrative
representation	constitution:- an account of the relationship between trustworthy representatives and the system as a whole
personification	personality cult:- a biographical account akin to an individual narrative
reification	religious or scientistic cosmology: - a treatise upon the nature of the world

subverted by the implication that the rules of interaction cannot be broken because they obey natural laws (reification).

It was suggested above that ontological security is maintained through the construction of biographical narratives that rationalise inconstant behaviour and thereby constitute self-identity. Furthermore, social integration was linked to recognition of self in others, by way of a group narrative. At the level of system integration, I argue, legitimation rests on an equivalent process whereby abstract systems demonstrate a capacity to be 'like' and therefore worthy of trust. Legitimation might arise through three forms of narrative, corresponding to the three ways that abstract systems invite trust referred to above, as set out in Table 1.7.

The importance of representation, personification and reification in facilitating trust with respect to abstract systems by way of a narrative is thus reflected in Weber's three ideal types of legitimacy: legal/rational, charismatic and traditional (Gerth and Wright Mills 1991: 78–79). Although these types of legitimating narrative are rarely found in their pure form, the 'ideal types' provide a framework for addressing the narratives of collectivities – such as nation-states – and the contribution that archaeology makes to such narratives.

1.8 Archaeology and modernity

The rôle of archaeology is significant because the narratives of abstract systems have, by definition, a temporal component. By analogy to personal and group narratives, the rationalisation of nation-states as abstract systems requires a collective biography, which can be carved from the past. Hence, archaeology serves to constitute a national past with which to negotiate the national future. This is not to suggest that the abstract system is an entity – an individual writ large – that has a biographical narrative of its own. Rather, the individuals that subscribe to an abstract system posit a common history that they can draw upon in relating to each other and in rationalising their own activities within the context of the system. Consequently, archaeology can be seen as one of the 'social movements' that characterised the onset of modernity. Individuals, associating in local groups, generated an abstract system of antiquities laws and heritage agencies that provide the sponsoring state with a narrative to which all citizens can expect and are expected to subscribe. The coincidence between the development of managed archaeology and the development of the nation-state is illuminated by Giddens' account of surveillance, which refers to:

> ... the supervisory control of subject populations, whether this control takes the form of 'visible'

supervision in Foucault's sense, or *in the use of information to co-ordinate social activities.*

> (Giddens 1991: 15, my emphasis)

Archaeology may not have been developed instrumentally to fulfil the rôle of a state surveillance service, but Giddens' reference to surveillance as the accumulation and storage of coded information serves equally as a description of archaeology (Giddens 1991: 14). The correlation of archaeology with surveillance is particularly apparent in the causal link that Giddens sees between the collection of official statistics and the development of disciplines that elaborate and analyse such information, hence:

> Social science [read 'archaeology'] ... has from its early origins in the modern period been a constitutive aspect of that vast expansion of the reflexive monitoring of social reproduction that is an integral feature of the state.

> (Giddens 1985: 181)

The qualities of archaeology as surveillance may not seem so direct as Giddens implies for other official statistics, which relate to the activities of individuals that are to be administered, rather than individuals that are long dead. However, the principal focus of archaeology is the present; i.e. however agèd the material upon which archaeology is focused, that material is considered in terms of a problem conceived and held relevant in the present. In this way archaeology is implicated in '"smoothing of the rough edges" such that behaviour which is not integrated into a system – that is, not knowledgeably built into the mechanisms of system reproduction – becomes alien and discrete' (Giddens 1991: 150). The complicity of archaeologists in the exercise of state surveillance has been described by Fotiadis in the context of regional archaeology in Greece:

> Compared again and again to the census taker, tax assessor, state bureaucrat, we are taught something about the political parentage of our regional project: regions are not the natural, geographical entities we thought. They are also a strategic means for the exercise of state power, for committing the social world to state order ... when the local people show suspicion or defiance to our presence, that is the same suspicion and defiance they show to the state.

> (Fotiadis 1993: 161)

Importantly, the relationship between archaeologists and the state is not limited to the collation of information and the formulation of interpretations; two further points follow from the recognition of a national narrative within which individuals rationalise their own activities. First, individuals will draw upon their surroundings as locale in constituting their narrative of self in relation to the narrative of the nation-state. Second, individuals' behaviour towards their surroundings will be an index of both self-identity and of abstract identity. Insofar as archaeologists concern themselves with the remains of putative pasts in the environment, then they are implicated in creating ancient material upon which people draw as locale, and in determining the behaviour towards ancient material – keeping off the grass, not climbing on the walls, forming a neat queue – that identifies an individual with an abstract system. Consequently, close attention to people's *physical* engagement with the past is required.

1.9 Materiality

Insofar as all interaction is situated in time and space, then all institutions have a concomitant physical component. However, the institutions through which archaeology is managed enjoy a particularly close relationship with the material world, as archaeology is *intended* to entail physical intervention – drawing attention to otherwise unnoticed features of the landscape, facilitating the survival of particular monuments, and overseeing the destruction of others. This purpose is not lessened by the invisibility of ancient material beneath turf or turbid water, though such circumstances generate certain practical difficulties. Differential treatment of ancient material – either directly or through regulation of others' activities – means that archaeologists' actions can have a persistent effect on social life. It is necessary, however, to elaborate a theory of materiality to explain how such acts may impinge upon society and, thereby, upon the maintenance of the nation-state despite the intangibility of fleeting instants of structure, as emphasised above.

Archaeology is based upon two assumptions about human activity: first, that past human activity involved ongoing interaction between individuals and social structures; second, that such interaction involved physical material as an integral element. These two assumptions are sufficient to postulate that ancient material results from the work of humans – rather than geological processes, extra-terrestrials or faeries – and that such material retains traces of the social systems in which these humans were situated. These assumptions may be challenged, as occurs when the 'natural' or 'artificial' origins of a feature are disputed, but most archaeology is directed to ancient material in order to find out about humans whose activities left physical traces of the societies in which they lived.

Notwithstanding the central rôle of material in archaeology, ancient material does not 'exist' before archaeology but is created by it (see Barrett 1994: 168–169; Shanks and Tilley 1992: 106). This claim may seem difficult to reconcile with the notion that material persists physically, upon which – following the argument above – archaeology depends. The apparent contradiction can be resolved by reference to Edgeworth's conception of discovery:

> ... in the act of discovery, objects emerge and *take* form in our perception only as we *give* form to them, by *acting* upon the material field in particular ways ...
>
> (Edgeworth 1990: 244, original emphasis)

Although material persists physically, it can only be known in the course of human agency; the capacity of archaeologists to reconcile idea and material, i.e. to offer ideas about past lives on the basis of physical traces, depends on what archaeologists can give to those traces through interpretation. Equally, those traces are relics of what people gave to material in the past. Consequently, the physical existence of ancient material cannot be comprehended before archaeological practice; it only becomes comprehensible through practice, at which point the material might be termed 'ancient material'. As used here, then, 'ancient' does not imply age as such, simply that the material has become the subject of archaeology.

In order to distinguish between material and idea without implying an essential dualism (cf. mind:body, culture:nature, subject:object, see Massey 1993: 147–149) it is helpful to invoke a metaphor: 'idea' and 'material' can be seen as two inseparable faces of one coin. The coin is, however, spinning on its edge, describing a sphere of 'agency' as it moves in time and space. The sphere of agency – the management of archaeology underwater in this case – is not itself reducible to either of the faces, but the coin can be arrested analytically. I shall attempt such an arrest in the following paragraphs in considering materiality.

Three points have to be made about material. First, in contrast to the instants of agency, material is relatively persistent. While material is often physically resistant to transient agency it can, nevertheless, be wrought. Hence, material may leave impressions of its engagement in agency in its physical form. Second, alterations to the physical form of material tend to obey rules that appear unchangeable. One consequence of the persistence and obedience of material is that its 'response' in the course of agency can be anticipated. Third, material cannot be manipulated by an unmediated effort of 'mind'; while I can tap my fingers on the desk I cannot move the pen just beyond them simply by thinking about it. In this respect, material is 'external'.

One effect of these characteristics of material is that there is a tendency to locate structure within material, rather than in the agency through which structure was instantiated. Consequently, materiality becomes synonymous with objectivity and material appears to have an independent existence of its own that can partner 'ideas' in the dualism referred to above. It is important, therefore, to recall that material – notwithstanding its persistence and externality – only 'exists', i.e. it can only be comprehended, through agency. Importantly, agency is not something that is applied to material; rather, material and its comprehension interact in the course of agency. In this respect material is not a mere reflection of action but integral to it, hence the importance of 'locale' as the physical setting of interaction in structuration theory (Giddens 1984: 118–119). Consequently, structuration comprises both the structuring of the material and of the activity: the hand picks up the pen, but the pen shapes the hand around it.

In the course of agency, material may be wrought and its physical form altered such that the physical form of the material is 'structured' by action. However, notwithstanding the persistent physical consequences for the material, the structure impressed upon it in the course of agency does not, in itself, linger; structure dissipates as soon as action stops, leaving only incidental traces that persist because of the robustness of the material. Hence, material is a 'container' of structure only insofar as it is in use. Once material has been discarded or its use has changed, any physical impressions can only indicate relict structure, not structure itself.

The notion that material is only comprehensible insofar as it is instantiated in the course of agency must, however, be reconciled with the evident persistence of material in time and space due to its physical robustness. If I leave my pen on the desk this evening, will I be shocked to find it there tomorrow? The contradiction can be resolved in two ways. First, the persistence of material between instantiations can be regarded as a residue of the structure manifest in the most recent activity. The residue of previous structuring, i.e. relict structure, is drawn upon in subsequent instantiations, constraining and/or enabling any fresh activity that takes place. In this respect I structure the relationship between pen and desk last thing before leaving, and the relics of such structuring enable me to engage the pen in the course of agency the following morning with a minimum of searching.

Second, the persistence of material permits its future 'existence' to be anticipated. Relics can be 'held in mind' while their external existence cannot be known. My earlier experience of pens leads me to suppose that the one I leave on my desk will not decay overnight. Moreover, insofar as its persistence can be anticipated I will not bring another pen from home, and in this respect the pen on the desk can structure my actions – i.e. it can 'exist' – even though it is physically absent. Importantly, however, the pen on the desk is not an imaginary pen; the pen on the desk exists physically in the action of not picking up a pen at home.

The notion of uninstantiated material as a relic both in the mind and in the world is expressed quite well in Edgeworth's description of discovery as '*the practical meeting-ground of an expectation and its material conditions of satisfaction*' (Edgeworth 1990: 247, original emphasis). However, material conditions do not always satisfy expectations, and a discovery may be even more thrilling for the puzzle that ensues. Subsequently, some material may be apprehended experimentally; in Edgeworth's words, an unfamiliar object 'can be practically constituted in terms of ... *potentialities* and *possibilities* (Edgeworth 1990: 249, original emphasis). Edgeworth draws particular attention to experiment by reference to the human body, such as testing the weight, balance etc. of an object to see what it *could* have been used for. However, such experimentation is difficult to reconcile with the argument that structure dissipates upon disuse, referred to above; the use of the body as a referent assumes that the interaction of object and body in the present will be structured in the same way as such interaction in the past. While the present form of the object might be accepted unproblematically because of the robustness of material, no such assumption can be made about the discoverer's body. Other assumptions may be even less tenable.

Consequently, every discovery requires an effort to re-establish a link between structure in the past and structure in the present without the aid of a referent of which the finder has direct experience. The effort to make this leap in the course of archaeological practice constitutes 'interpretation'.

Insofar as discoverers' apprehension of material draws upon their expectations, then the engagement of material in agency has a paradigmatic character. If the discoverer is an archaeologist, working within an archaeological paradigm, then the material will be constituted as something quite different to ostensibly similar material discovered by someone working within an alternative paradigm. For example, archaeologists' treatment of human remains that they regard as ancient are often at odds with people who regard those same remains as ancestral (see, e.g., papers in Layton 1989). The paradigmatic character of people's relationship with ancient material arises from the more general character of the integration of individuals, groups and societies – as discussed in Section 1.7 – in respect of their environments in circumstances of modernity.

At the level of the individual, Giddens has emphasised mastery of the environment as a means of managing anxiety: 'acquired routines are ... constitutive of an emotional acceptance of the reality of the 'external world' without which a secure human existence is impossible' (Giddens 1991: 42; see also Giddens 1991: 54; 167). The juxtaposition of locale and the maintenance of ontological security through mastery of the environment may go some way to resolving criticisms that Giddens' theory of material is weak (Barrett 1988: 9). Giddens considers individuals to draw upon and transform their environment *as a part* of day-to-day life, not *as a result* of day-to-day life. Consequently, each individual's day-to-day interaction with their environment is constitutive of self – a notion that sits happily with Gibson's insistence that 'to perceive the environment is to co-perceive oneself' (Gibson 1979 [1986]: 141). For example, Bowman quotes Sayigh:

> The village ... was built into the personality of each individual villager to a degree that made separation like an obliteration of the self.
>
> (Sayigh, R. (1979) *Palestinians: from peasants to revolutionaries*, p. 107, quoted in Bowman 1994: 148)

The rôle of the environment on perception is all the stronger because the link is not articulated discursively. In *The Third Way*, Shehadeh describes a discussion with Robert Stone, who claims to be baffled by Palestinian national rhetoric which seems shallow compared to the richness of Jewish claims to the same land. Shehadeh takes Stone to visit a Palestinian, Abu-'Isa, and recalls the episode as follows:

> When we left Abu-'Isa I felt a bit apologetic – the old man hadn't said very much. But Robert interrupted me excitedly and said that it was precisely Abu-'Isa's inarticulate, silent love that couldn't be relayed in any rhetoric, because he himself had no words for it.
>
> (Shehadeh 1982: 86)

The unspoken effect of the environment upon individual identity recalls Gibson's refutation of memory, '... information does not have to be stored in memory because it is always available' (Gibson 1979 [1986]: 250, see Chapter Two). As 'the environment is the embodiment of past activity' (Ingold 1992: 50), then the past is structured within the present. Hence, ancient material within the environment constitutes a physical narrative as it is drawn upon subliminally by individuals in the course of day-to-day life. As Rowlands puts it, 'the production of past material cultures has the spontaneity of a kind of unconscious speech, a taken-for-granted, common-sense existence that simply demonstrates that a people have always existed in that place' (Rowlands 1994: 136).

Similarities in locale may figure in similarities in narrative, so material can play a role in communicating likeness, and in the assumption of trust. Consequently, material may be drawn upon in articulating social integration. For example, Harevan and Langenbach note that:

> Beyond their individual experiences, buildings were so sign-ficant to people's memories because of their *associations with other people*, such as family members, friend, neighbours, and fellow workers, *with whom they had shared these experiences*.
>
> (Harevan and Langenbach 1981: 116, my emphasis)

Beyond the group, material surroundings can serve as familiar, physical manifestations of abstract institutions, thereby facilitating system integration. Hence Hobsbawm makes the following observation about monuments in France: 'Such monuments traced the grass roots of the Republic – particularly in its rural strongholds – and may be regarded as *the visible links between the voters and the nation*' (Hobsbawm 1983: 272, my emphasis).

The close relationship between the environment and the persistence of an abstract system can be mobilised instrumentally, hence Bowman quotes Trotsky on the importance of establishing the place of the 1917 Revolution in history:

> He [Lenin] was anxious to have as many revolutionary monuments erected as possible, even if they were of the simplest sort, like busts or memorial tablets to be placed in all the towns, and, if it could be managed, in the villages as well, so that what had happened might be fixed in the people's imagination, and leave the deepest possible furrow in memory.
>
> (Trotsky, L. (1975) *My Life: An attempt at an autobiography*, quoted in Bowman 1994: note 14)

The rôle of 'statuomania' in impressing national 'traditions' upon the landscapes of late nineteenth century France and Germany has been detailed by Hobsbawm (Hobsbawm 1983) and Johnson has shown how both historic and contemporary statuary impinges upon the construction of 'community' in Ireland (Johnson 1995). The importance of material surroundings to the success of systemic historical narratives has also been harnessed in museums. Papadakis' observes that the contrast between the religious overtones of Greek nationalism and étatist, army-orientated Turkish nationalism is underlined by the siting of their respective 'national struggle' museums in Nicosia, Cyprus: 'the Turkish Cypriot museum being next to an army camp, and the Greek Cypriot

one next to the Archbishopric...' (Papadakis 1994: 404). He also notes of the Turkish Cypriot museum:

> The museum's last section ... is ... designed to make the visitor feel the '... air of freedom and peace breathed by the Turkish Cypriots...'. This effect is architecturally accomplished by placing this section in a large well-lit room which contrasts with the comparatively darker corridor housing the previous exhibits.
>
> (Papadakis 1994: 409)

Equally, Piccini's analysis of the way visitors are obliged to experience 'celtic' heritage centres shows that 'the physical structure of these heritage representations affirms historically specific images of Welshness' (Piccini 1996: 8).

Such instrumental manipulation of the environment is not limited to building monuments and exhibiting artefacts; it encompasses attempts to legitimise domination by framing entire landscapes. McGuire demonstrates that housing patterns in certain US towns were intimately related to the sociological beliefs of the entrepreneurs that founded them in the late Nineteenth Century/early Twentieth Century so, for example, development of new sites outside Binghamton...

> ... allowed Johnson to construct a new cultural landscape, to create the surface necessary for his industrial democracy ... He argued that workers and employers should live as friends and neighbors in a community of mutual interest; he thus created a cultural landscape that mystified the reality of class relations at Endicott-Johnson by denying the existence of class differences and class interests.
>
> (McGuire 1991: 115)

In contrast, the fortifications around Derry have been repeatedly embellished both materially and conceptually for over three hundred years to affirm the distinctiveness of 'besieged' Protestants from their Catholic foe, though recent 're-writes' are eroding sectarian monopolies on the historic environment (Mac Giolla Chriost 1996). Consequently, the 'discovery' and differential treatment of ancient material may impinge upon the formulation of individual, collective and systemic narratives, contributing thereby to imbalances of signification, domination and legitimation in people's everyday environments. Importantly, however, political abuse does not inhere in ancient material, but in the 'act that comprehends it' (Polanyi 1967: 55, see Chapter Two). That is to say, the material has no structure in itself – it is structured in its re-instantiation in the course of day-to-day life in the present. Moreover, there is always a gap between the way in which archaeologists structure material in their interpretations, and the public's structuring of the same material as they draw upon it. In this sense, ancient material can 'escape its author'. Musil illustrates this escape:

> ... the most striking thing about monuments is that you do not notice them. There is nothing in the world as invisible as monuments. Doubtless they have been erected to be seen – even to attract attention; yet at the same time something has impregnated them against attention. Like a drop of water on an oilskin, attention runs down them without stopping for a moment ... The virtually drive off what they would attract. We cannot

say that we do not notice them; we should say that they de-notice us, they withdraw from our senses...

(Musil, R. (1936) 'Denkmale' in *Nachlass zu Lebzeiten*, Zurich: 87–93, translated in Warner 1985: 21)

The notion that a monument is not noticed suggests one of two things. Either the monument is irrelevant to the observer, i.e. there is no connection between it and the structuring of the observer's life, or the monument is *so* closely tied up with the structuring of the observer's life that the monument inheres in the observers' practical experience. Such a close relationship is implied in Warner's description of women's responses to living in cultures pervaded by monumental female allegories:

We are living now among female forms who have adopted ... the allegorical language of the past, but are not reproducing it in stone or plaster or copper, but enacting it live in order to take up tenancy of the hollow monuments...

(Warner 1985: 37)

Warner is not suggesting that women dwell in the ideas that past authors built into their monuments, rather she implies that women are instantiating new resources, rules and meanings through those same monuments in the present, though at a subliminal level. Although the robust remains of relict structure may have a constraining effect, the monument is effectively recreated. Musil may be right that monuments seem impervious to interest, but such irrelevance may disguise a more pervasive re-creation of monuments in the image of contemporary identities.

Insofar as archaeologists do not determine how monuments are interpreted, then greater sensitivity to the inhabitants of a particular environment is warranted. As Harevan and Langenbach note, 'industrial slums' are not only a material imposition that determines what their inhabitants can think or feel:

The assumption of social reformers and planners that the working-class past in these industrial settings must be eradicated because it symbolizes poverty, grimness and exploitation, misses what the workers themselves feel about their world.

(Harevan and Langenbach 1981: 116)

The authors do not deny that the industrial landscape was constitutive of domination in industrial towns, but they do suggest, quoting Marris, the need for a greater sympathy for the creation of positive environments and identities within such constraints by the inhabitants: 'They identify with the neighbourhood: it is part of them, and to hear it condemned as a slum is a condemnation of themselves too' (Marris, P. (1974) *Loss and Change*, p. 55, quoted in Harevan and Langenbach 1981: 115). The recognition that structure does not reside in material but in the way that is instantiated is important because all ancient material will, in its original use, have exhibited some imbalance of power, trust or meaning. Such imbalances do not, however, inhere in the material; the problem lies in finding ways to draw out the relics of structure in such a way that the imbalance is not re-produced. It need not be the case, as Shanks and Tilley (Shanks and Tilley 1992: 86) say of Beamish Open Air Museum, that 'a sticky, slimy past sucks the present into the mire'. Notwithstanding any 'original' inequity evident in ancient material, the management of archaeology can be an emancipatory project.

I have shown that archaeology is an aspect of modernity that facilitates individuals' trust in the nation-state by presenting a 'reasonable' collective narrative that reconciles individual and abstract at an imaginable scale. The narrative takes effect, in part, through its physical manifestation in everyday environments and through people's behaviour towards ancient material. Identification of a dubious process is, however, without merit if it does not provoke change. Change, to be successful, depends upon a thorough understanding of the problematic mechanism – in this case, the management of archaeology underwater – and of likely responses to attempted alteration. It is to a detailed analysis of the management of archaeology underwater that I now proceed.

2. SIGNIFICATION: MANAGEMENT AND THE PRODUCTION OF MEANING

In the following three chapters I consider how people interact with ancient material in the environment, how such material comes to warrant preferential behaviour, and how preferential behaviour is assured. These matters are analysed with reference to Giddens' three dimensions of structure – signification, legitimation and domination. In this chapter, I consider the articulation of signs, meanings and significance through institutions that – although constituted by the aggregation of individual actions – structure the way in which individuals understand their world.

2.1 Signs

The identification, by an individual, of a link between material and a concept illustrates the quality of ancient material as a 'sign'. For example, if an archaeologist uncovers a piece of metal and regards it as evidence of a wreck from the Second Century AD, then the combination of metalwork and Second Century is 'a sign' to that individual (cf. Saussure 1916 [1983]: 67; Barthes 1957 [1972]: 111–117). The metal is not a sign in itself; if no association is made, then the metal is just a bit of scrap on its way to the skip. In this sense, a sign cannot be divorced from what it is a sign *of*. The metal is recalled to life by the act of association, which interrupts the metal's journey to the spoil heap and elevates it to the status of a discovery. I will argue that such signs within the environment can be perceived directly, i.e. that associated physical and ideational components are noted together without the explicit attention of any party. Insofar as 'relevance' is noted unwittingly, then the presence of ancient material may serve as a subliminal prompt to individuals in the course of daily activity and, as I shall argue, ancient material may have a pervasive influence precisely because it is so little remarked.

2.1.1 Practical perception

Gibson's ecological psychology offers a theory of perception in which observers enjoy an integral relationship with the environment by way of 'affordances'. Affordances are what any medium, surface or object in the environment gives to – 'affords' – the inhabitants of the environment. Affordances can be known directly because their structure is revealed in their appearance: 'the basic properties of the environment that make an affordance are specified in the structure of ambient light, and hence the affordance itself is specified in ambient light' (Gibson 1979 [1986]: 143). Gibson is intent on destroying any notion that perception is based on a retinal image that is communicated and translated by the brain. Instead, he offers an account of observers as integrated perceptual systems – 'between observation and judgement lies no shadow of thought', as Fenton expresses it in discussing navigation by direct perception (Fenton 1993: 44). In dismissing a mind/body dualism Gibson also assaults any dualism of subject/object or culture/nature. In his view, the observer is *in* the environment: 'to perceive the environment is to co-perceive oneself' (Gibson 1979 [1986]: 141).

Gibson's theory can be illustrated by reference to archaeologists' perception of their environments, such as factors affecting the preservation of ancient material underwater. All the archaeologists that I interviewed in the course of my research demonstrated familiarity with the processes that affect preservation, citing salinity, biological action (especially by *teredo navalis* – shipworm), weather and sea-level change. Factors that relate to the geology of the sea bottom received particular attention. The presence or absence of silt was an important point to Naevestad, Jasinski, Rieck, Thomsen and Maarleveld. Thomsen and Christiansen described the destruction attributable to the movement of sand waves, with reference to the west coast of Jutland (Thomsen pers. com.; Larsen pers. com.). In these cases, it seems that preservation was perceived directly. In short, the archaeologists' environments consisted of certain physical processes that prompted automatic responses about the likelihood of preservation. Hence, Thomsen's statement of a site located in sand – 'I was *surprised* really at finding it preserved' (Thomsen pers. com., my emphasis) – suggests the disruption of a direct perception that sand affords deterioration.

Direct responses may become deeply embedded within management policies. A reference by Naevestad to oxygen, sediment and salinity reflected research intended to prioritise areas according to these factors (Naevestad pers. com.). Such research will be drawn upon in the course of management practice, so that certain areas may be given little priority, irrespective of the actual presence of material (Naevestad 1991; Naevestad 1992; see also Maarleveld 1995 b). As the practice becomes more entrenched, the perception that, for instance, 'sand does not afford preservation', may be acted upon directly. In this respect the affordance may be seen as a 'natural law' akin to gravity, inducing a sense of powerlessness, as evinced by a comment made by Christiansen:

> But you can do nothing against the sand ... you can say 'that's how it looked in 1989 and see how it looks in 1991' – it's torn apart, so what? You can do nothing about it.
>
> (Christiansen pers. com.)

Notwithstanding 'natural laws' such as those affecting preservation, people adopt different ways of accommodating affordances in the course of action. Archaeologists' references to working practices, for example, illustrate their active engagement with the 'natural laws' that govern tides, weather and divers' physiology. The work of archaeologists who concentrate on ancient material located underwater is, unsurprisingly, structured by the difficulties of living and working in water. Although the history of archaeology underwater is not wholly explicable in terms of the development of the aqua-lung, SCUBA and associated technologies have played a strong rôle in structuring the discipline. Breathing underwater is an achievement on a par with human flight, but as none of the interviewees mentioned their carefully-learned skills it might be assumed that being underwater no longer merited attention. The technology and techniques that keep them alive are so much a part of their being underwater that they are rarely discussed. The archaeologists did, however, refer to several other factors, notably the weather and underwater visibility – which were highlighted repeatedly – and low water temperatures and depth. The responses that archaeologists describe are notable because they demonstrate that practice is not structured by working conditions as such, but by anticipation of those conditions. This statement is not as banal as it may seem, as it implies that – notwithstanding the influence of environmental factors – there is no such thing as a 'natural law' in managing archaeology underwater. Insofar as archaeological practices are structured by anticipation of the working environment rather than physical factors *per se*, the 'facts' of these archaeologists' environments – destruction by sand waves, weather and gas laws, for example – are no more 'given' or 'external' than any other variable. Although such phenomena are unalterable, the environment is constructed socially because the archaeologists fit their activities around the regularities that they perceive. Hence, Maarleveld's frustration with the weather was not directed at the wind as such but at the need to set aside 12 to 14 weeks rather than timetabling a project for a particular month (Maarleveld pers. com.). Equally, if Naevestad has to survey a site in 25 metres he does not perceive the water depth, but the infrastructure necessary to get him down there. Two dives to 20-22 metres would require – by law – a decompression chamber, which in turn requires an air-bank and a container, and consequently a supply-ship to support the dive (Naevestad pers. com.). In this case, Naevestad is not anticipating the likely effects of breathing pressurised air on his own physiognomy; rather, he is anticipating the state's generalised anticipation – manifest in health and safety regulations – of the plant most likely to mitigate any ill-effects that might occur. These examples of the ways in which diving archaeologists comprehend their environment are notable because such comprehension also structures relations between archaeologists. Hence Christiansen commented on the difficulty that traditional (land) archaeologists had in understanding why an underwater archaeologist could spend 10 hours in the field but only a couple of hours on site (Christiansen pers. com.).

The notion that the world is socially constructed even in relation to 'natural laws' underlines the routinely creative character of archaeologists' engagement with their environment – even though such creativity may not be considered explicitly. Hence Gibson comments: 'I realized that perceiving is an act, not a response, an act of attention, not a triggered impression, an achievement, not a reflex' (Gibson 1979 [1986]: 149).

Notwithstanding this reference to the skill of individuals in perceiving the environment, some of Gibson's statements indicate a degree of environmental determinism. He clearly regards the environment as a singular 'given', something 'out there' that animals – and humans – perceive similarly and fit into or fit around themselves. Gibson's determinism is perhaps most evident in his characterisation of the environment in terms of 'invariants': 'the affordance of something does not change as the need of the observer changes ... the affordance, being invariant, is always there to be perceived' (Gibson 1979 [1986]: 139). It follows that: ' ... the environment as a whole ... existed prior to animals ... [it] had to be invariant for animals to evolve' (Gibson 1979

[1986]: 128). Even though he refers to perception as an active pursuit, Gibson appears to limits the creative abilities of observers to relatively passive 'tuning':

> Knowledge of the environment, surely, develops as perception develops, extends as the observers travel, gets finer as they learn to scrutinize, gets longer as they apprehend more events, gets fuller as they see more objects, and gets richer as they notice more affordances. Knowledge of this sort does not 'come from' anywhere; it is got by looking, along with listening, feeling, smelling and tasting.
>
> (Gibson 1979 [1986]: 253)

He is similarly dismissive of memory and the past:

> Evidently the theory of information pickup does not need memory. It does not have to have as a basic postulate the effect of past experience on present experience by way of memory. It needs to explain learning, that is, the improvement of perceiving with practice and the education of attention, but not by an appeal to the catch-all of past experience or to the muddle of memory.
>
> (Gibson 1979 [1986]: 254)

Gibson makes such provocative statements to demolish the retinal image approach to perception (see Gibson 1979 [1986]: 53–57). He does not deny, however, that 'higher processes' (Gibson 1979 [1986]: 255) or 'extended perceiving' (Gibson 1979 [1986]: 250) – remembering, thinking, inferring, imagining and so on – take place. He only contends that they cannot be understood as operations of a disembodied mind. Ingold – whose work, in drawing upon Gibson, seems to share some of its determinism – concurs with Gibson's position on higher processes in discussing the differences between animals and humans:

> I do not deny the importance of knowledge-sharing practices in human society; my point is that the discursive representation of the environment ... is not a precondition for our contact with it ... or for our contact with one and other ... The cultural construction of the environment is not so much a *prelude* to practical action as an (optional) *epilogue*.
>
> (Ingold 1992: 52, original emphasis)

The difficulty with this view is that it is unclear how the ideational and physical components of a sign come to be associated in the first place. Personal experiment may provide people with a basic grasp of the differences between walls and doorways, for example, but it is hard to see how 'tuning' alone could lead an archaeologist to associate a piece of bent metal with second century seafaring, or a depth contour with a support ship, or a sediment sample with the absence of ancient material. Yet, such associations are an unremarkable (and unremarked) aspect of routine archaeological practice. While Gibson's theory may explain *how* the environment is perceived, it fails to account for the constructed character of *what* is perceived. The challenge is, therefore, to start exploring 'the ways in which direct perception has itself been transformed through historical change' (Costall and Still 1989: 439; see also Heft 1989; Meacham 1993; Noble 1981; Noble 1993; Reed 1993).

2.1.2 Discursive interpretation

The strengths of ecological psychology can be rescued from determinism by assimilating Gibson's ideas about perception with Polanyi's theory of knowing. Polanyi suggests that all knowing draws on tacit knowledge, characterised as 'knowing more than we can tell' (Polanyi 1967: 4). In the course of understanding, individuals necessarily make assumptions in order to find out something new. Consequently, Polanyi suggests that all understanding takes place by attending *from* a term *to* a term, referring to this as working from a 'proximal' (near) term to a 'distal' (distant) term (Polanyi 1967: 10). Importantly, the proximal term is generally known only through its use in rendering the distal term comprehensible, i.e. 'we are aware of the proximal term of an act ... in the appearance of its distal term' (Polanyi 1967: 11). Consequently, 'all meaning tends to be displaced away from ourselves' (Polanyi 1967: 13), exacerbating the tendency to locate structure in material, rather then action (see above, Section 1.9).

This perspective on knowing is useful in understanding the comprehension of materiality because Polanyi regards the individual's body as an irreducible proximal term: 'our body is the ultimate instrument of all our external knowledge' (Polanyi 1967: 15; cf. Edgeworth 1990: 249, discussed in Section 1.9). Insofar as individuals can only know about the world through tacit acceptance of the proximal terms that constitute their bodies, then knowledge is based on 'dwelling'. As each distal term may subsequently become the proximal term upon which further acts of understanding are based, 'knowing' can be seen as a progressive extension of the body into the assumptions that knowledge is based upon. Polanyi likens this progression, which he refers to as 'interiorization', to the process involved in learning to use a tool such as a probe. Initially, an individual may concentrate on the sensations of the probe on the hand, but these sensations become tacitly accepted as attention is focused upon the end of the probe, i.e. the individual comes to dwell in the probe as an extension of the body (Polanyi 1967: 12–13). The same process applies to all other distal terms that become proximal through their application: 'we keep expanding our body into the world' (Polanyi 1967: 29). Pálsson, drawing upon Polanyi, expresses this notion very well in his account of Icelandic fishing:

> ... experienced skippers often speak of knowing the details and the patterns of the 'landscape' of the sea bottom 'as well as their fingers'. This indicates that for the skilled skipper fishing technology – the boat, electronic equipment and fishing gear – is not to be regarded as an 'external' mediator between his person and the environment but rather as a bodily extension in quite a literal sense.

> (Pálsson 1994: 910)

The contention that all explicit knowledge is based upon tacit knowledge sets up a complex duality. The proximal term can only be understood in its effects upon the distal term, but the distal term can only be addressed by dwelling in the proximal term. Hence 'we are attending from the theory to things seen in its light, and are aware of the theory ... in terms of the spectacle that it serves to explain' (Polanyi 1967: 17). Insofar as it is necessary to dwell in a proximal term in order to approach any distal term, then 'what is comprehended has the same structure as the act that comprehends it' (Polanyi 1967: 55). This conception of the relation between pre-conception and comprehension can be illustrated by reference to Ingold's characterisation of 'nature' as an 'interpretative stance'. Ingold contrasts 'nature' with 'environment', suggesting that whereas environments are known through engagement, 'nature' is only knowable at a distance: 'thus an animal cannot engage with nature, or enter into an active relationship with neutral objects, since the neutrality of nature is given only in *dis*engagement' (Ingold 1992: 44). Nature is, therefore, constituted as a distal term by the way in which disengagement is achieved; the 'nature' of the Earth's pull on other objects at its surface is known to be 9.8 ms^{-2} because of the abstract notation for acceleration and intangible 'laws of gravity' in which physicists dwell. Similarly, the 'laws' governing the solution of nitrogen in blood are known by tables that place a 30 minute limit on dives to 20 metres, and the 'nature' of ancient material in the Netherlands is known by bathimetric and sedimentological maps.

2.1.3 Perception and interpretation

Gibson's ecological psychology explains how people may carry on in life using direct perception, without paying special attention to their surroundings. Polanyi's account suggests how perceptions are acquired, i.e. by interpretative extension into ever more complex 'dwelling'. The relationship between the two forms of cognition – perception and interpretation – can be expanded by reference to Giddens' 'stratification model of consciousness'. According to Giddens, individuals' awareness consists of three layers: the unconscious, practical consciousness and discursive consciousness (Giddens 1984: 5–8; see above, Section 1.4). It is the differentiation of practical and discursive consciousness that is most illuminating here. Practical consciousness is the realm of thoughts and actions that take place without specific attention but can be explained on request, and might be seen as the realm of Gibson's direct perception and Polanyi's dwelling. Discursive consciousness refers to the thoughts and actions that the individual thinks about explicitly, i.e. the distal terms to which 'knowing' is directed. Inherent in the stratification model is the notion that ideas can move between the different forms of consciousness; individuals can direct attention to their habitual dispositions, rendering them discursive, while things that were once known discursively can subside into practical knowledge. The permeability of the practical/discursive boundary (Giddens 1984: 7) accords well with Polanyi's notion of interiorisation, and also suggests an opposite process of introspection in which proximal terms are progressively fractionated into contested assumptions – a notion that will be considered in more detail below.

The analytical differentiation of discursive and practical consciousness is particularly relevant to explaining why people can accept social constructs, such as archaeological interpretations, as being 'natural'. Interpretations, formed discursively, may subside into practical consciousness as, in Polanyi's terms, people come to dwell in such knowledge; insofar as the interpretation has a physical aspect, then Gibson's theory suggests how people then perceive directly the 'truth' in their surroundings. Whereas, for example, the

Table 2.1:   Two phases of interpretation

	1st Phase		2nd Phase	
methodological presupposition	proximal ⇓ distal	ancient material in the present	proximal ⇓ distal	knowledge about past lives

association of bent metal with second century seafaring may have developed only slowly through analysis of numerous discoveries, once the explicit interpretative project has attained such a degree of repeatability that the material is 'diagnostic' of the idea then (re-)interpretation upon subsequent discoveries may seem unnecessary. At this point the association of material and idea subsides into practical consciousness: second century seafaring is perceived directly from a piece of bent metal; the association of one with the other is unremarked and its truth is unquestionable.

2.1.4   Archaeological interpretation

The focus of archaeologists' endeavour is not ancient material as such but the people who – in the course of living – left physical traces of their activity. Insofar as these past lives are the distal term that archaeologists are attempting to approach, then archaeologists have to dwell in a proximal term, namely the ancient material that retains the relics of past structuring. However, as the structure associated with material dissipates when engagement ceases, relevance resides not in the relics but in the perception of the traces of past structuring by a fresh 'observer'. It follows that archaeologists cannot dwell in material directly – the archaeologist cannot perceive what past individuals perceived. Consequently, all efforts to understand the past demand careful attention to the persistent traces of relict structures, hence the material itself has to be approached as a distal term. The proximal term from which archaeologists attend to ancient material is the methodology of archaeological practice. The two phases of interpretation are, therefore, as follows: archaeologists dwell in the methodologies and techniques of archaeology in order to know ancient material, which is the distal term; they then expand into that material as it becomes a proximal term, attending thereby to the new distal term – past lives (Table 2.1).

These two phases approximate to Wylie's distinction between 'vertical tacking' and 'horizontal tacking' respectively, if the vertical tack is seen to occur between methodological presupposition and 'data', and the horizontal tack to reach out to past ways of life (see Wylie 1989: 8–10. NB Polanyi's metaphor of progressive dwelling is more appropriate than Wylie's vertical and horizontal tacks because, to my mind, Polanyi better expresses the way in which presuppositions become embodied in everyday practice). Furthermore, the need for an interpretative leap in each phase undermines any lurking suspicion that the effort to re-construct past lives is a 'theoretical' endeavour whereas method is 'atheoretical', or that archaeology can be safely

divided into 'technical' and 'interpretative' branches (see also Champion 1991; Barrett 1994: 155–157).

The first phase – the process of coming to know ancient material – can be seen in archaeologists' interest in artefacts. For example, Christiansen – citing the case of Tybrind Vig, a submerged Neolithic site – drew attention to the propensity of archaeology underwater to present organic evidence of artefacts and of skills that has not survived on land, including clothes, fishhooks and knots (Christiansen pers. com.). The enthusiasm that diving archaeologists display for artefacts might be read as a naïve, empiricist preoccupation with objects that land archaeology has grown out of. However, such concern for artefacts might warrant a more interesting explanation: insofar as the ancient material absorbs their attention, then there must be a proximal term from which archaeologists attend to the material; here, the proximal term is the successful transfer of archaeological methodologies to an underwater environment. Further to the discussion above, the archaeologists' practical consciousness accommodates the skills to stay alive and to 'do' archaeology, thereby allowing them to direct their attention to the material. Such successful dwelling in archaeology underwater may explain diving archaeologists' exasperation with land archaeologists who continue to regard their clammy colleagues as somehow different – not proper archaeologists. Polanyi's observation that meaning is expelled into the distal term is also informative in this case; the archaeologists wonder at the artefacts when it is the practices that make their observations possible that are wondrous. Furthermore, as Polanyi points out, the structure of meaning in the distal term arises from the structure of practice, i.e. the ancient material is known in terms of the methodologies that are brought to bear upon it – distances, measurements, radiocarbon dates, context numbers and so on.

There is a tendency in underwater archaeology to linger on the wealth of preservation and to allow the density of minutiae to draw further analysis to small-scale particularism. Such particularism, which may barely extend beyond one wreck at a time, is linked to a fascination with shipwrecks as characteristically closed finds. There is sometimes a tendency to suppose that minutiae means that ships are 'society in miniature' (cf. 'you have a snapshot of everyday life, of working life' (Johansen pers. com.)). Although Naevestad acknowledged that ship sites never reflect the whole society of the time, he remarked that ' ... it's close ... they have everything with them' (Naevestad pers. com.). Such perspectives illustrate the danger that accompanies the success of archaeological methodologies; as relevance is felt to lie in the material rather than methodology, the archaeologists assume that their perception of the material is unproblematic. The tendency of archaeologists to proceed directly to an interpretation of past lives – rather than paying due care to the interruption that occurs when material ceases to be used – might be a greater problem for underwater archaeologists because of the well-preserved 'every day' artefacts whose purpose seems all too clear.

Renders, a maritime archaeologist in the Netherlands, indicated a similar material-driven particularism, but his interest broadened out into a more general concern. Starting with the inventories recovered from wrecks found in the IJsselmeer Polders, Renders became interested in how people lived aboard small vessels. Noting how these vessels involved whole families living and working on board, he moved on to compare ship-based society with land society. In Polanyi's terms, Renders can be said to be 'dwelling' in the ships' inventories, as he approaches shipboard society as a distal term. In interiorising the ancient material that makes up the inventory, the investigative approaches, methodologies and techniques that were used are obscured. Moreover, relevance is expelled into the distal term – knowledge of ship-board societies – and it is these interpretations that are seen to be 'real' rather than the material, and still less the practices through which the material was first approached.

The conflation of relevance into material and, thereafter, into interpretations of the past gives the impression that such material and such pasts have an existence that is external to the archaeologist. One symptom of externalisation is a tendency to regard the archaeologist's rôle as a servant of those external realities. This tendency can be seen in relation to the strong interest expressed by many of the archaeologists interviewed in ship construction. Such interest seems attributable to the perceived proclivities of ancient material – a 'fact' of preservation. Maarleveld noted that one of the benefits of the deep sediments of some areas of the Netherlands seabed is that there is a large proportion of relatively coherent wrecks which facilitate detailed study of construction (Maarleveld pers. com.). Equally, Rieck remarked that the extensive chronological spread of wrecks gives Danish archaeologists an advantage in comparing ships from different periods (Rieck pers. com.). The impression given by such statements is that it is the material that demands interest in construction – and that the archaeologists are bound to serve those demands – not that the archaeologists are themselves choosing to concentrate on methodologies of timber recording.

Furthermore, the tendency to compare constructional details seems to be rationalised as a *response* to trends in ship design attributable to 'cultures' and 'traditions'. For example, Rieck stated that the aim of wreck studies was to learn how ships have developed through dugouts to plank-built sailing vessels (Rieck pers. com.). Similarly, Rieth commented that it was becoming possible to identify the influence of the eastern Mediterranean on wrecks found off the south coast of France, while noting that knowledge of construction techniques on the Atlantic coast was very uneven (Rieth pers. com.). Maarleveld identified the development of a distinct northern European carvel building technique as the main research

focus of his institution (Maarleveld pers. com.). At first sight, such research agendas seem to ascribe the importance of ship construction to an externalised culture-history, i.e. relevance lies not in the material, but in an evolutionary past. These perspectives deny the agency of the makers and users of the ships – a point that Maarleveld has underlined (Maarleveld 1995 a: 6)) – and of the archaeologists that have chosen to place their studies of shipbuilding within a culture-historic paradigm. It should be noted that in denying their own agency, archaeologists evade responsibility for decisions about approach and methodology – they are only following orders handed down from the past by the material.

Further comments by Maarleveld and by Rieck suggest an attempt to escape culture-history, though they imply contrasting paradigms. Maarleveld drew upon an economic framework in suggesting that carvel-built ships were more attractive to corporate investors than clinker ships, the success of which depended largely on the skill of a single shipwright. Moreover, clinker and carvel techniques have different implications for the division of labour, hence the mode of construction can be related directly to interpretation of the social system (Maarleveld pers. com.). Rieck offered a communication/transport-based framework, as he linked Scandinavian successes in the Viking age to 'excellent ships which could move people around' (Rieck pers. com.). Both interpretations have their own agency-denying pitfalls, but insofar as they posit alternative relevances to historical changes in ship construction, they draw attention back to the material upon which their interpretations are based. Conflicting interpretations disrupt archaeologists' dwelling in ancient material, but such contestation must also take in the earlier stage of dwelling, i.e. the 'truth' of any interpretation does not lie solely in the ancient material, but also in the methodologies through which such material was approached. Conflicts about interpretations of the past are interesting because they reveal the preconceptions within which archaeologists have come to dwell. Notwithstanding the verbal fencing that characterise disputes about, for example, techniques and terminology, such disputes clarify the assumptions upon which archaeologists invent the past (see for example, the 'replication' debate in the *International Journal of Nautical Archaeology* – Westerdahl 1992; McGrail 1992; Fenwick 1993; Goodburn 1993; Westerdahl 1993; Marsden 1993).

2.1.5   Introversion, loss and co-perception

Whereas Polanyi is concerned to offer a model of the progress of science, sociological projects often move in the opposite direction; rather than extending themselves into increasingly advanced assumptions, techniques and technology, sociologists may seem preoccupied with querying the 'obvious' in a progressive introversion. Insofar as a presumption is questioned, then an anterior distal term is drawn out of a hitherto familiar proximal term; in Giddens' terms, practical consciousness is rendered discursive. This process of challenging assumptions arises from occurrences and observations that cause people to question a presumed familiarity with their environment. In this sense, and notwithstanding their constructedness, environments offer a 'network of resistances' to their inhabitants (Shanks and Tilley 1992: 104) who are obliged to rethink their presuppositions (see Wylie 1989: 16). Introversion occurs in archaeology underwater as in other spheres of life, hence my suggestion that the earlier traditions of Swedish archaeology constrained any critical engagement with people's knowledge of the past prompted a strong reaction: 'The sources are not controlled. It's a question of having an open mind and seeing things which haven't been seen before...' (Cederlund, pers. com.). Similarly, Jasinski turned around a question about what could be learned from sites underwater in the following manner:

> We as archaeologists ... are limited in our philosophy, perspective, with our questions, with our research capacity. Not the sites. They are unlimited.

(Jasinski pers. com.)

As introversion involves the separation of distal from proximal terms, then relevance is displaced outwards, i.e. the unspoken relevance that pervades a person's environment is seen to lie in the object of attention. Hence, although relevance is identified it is at the loss of having known such relevance inherently. Polanyi's theory can thus be assimilated with Barthes' characterisation of myths, insofar as Barthes uses 'meaning' to refer to that which is practically experienced, and 'form' to refer to the displaced, but now-noticed relevance:

> When it becomes form, the meaning leaves its contingency behind; it empties itself, it becomes impoverished, history evaporates, only the letter remains.

(Barthes 1957 [1972]: 117)

This process is exemplified by Shehadeh's account of his increasingly discursive appreciation of the landscape due to Israeli settlement:

> Sometimes, when I am walking in the hills ... unselfconsciously enjoying the touch of the hard land under my feet, the smell of thyme and the hills and trees around me – I find myself looking at an olive tree, and as I am looking at it, it transforms itself before my eyes into a symbol of the samedin, of our struggles, of our loss. And at that very moment I am robbed of the tree; instead there is a hollow space into which anger and pain flow.

(Shehadeh 1982: 87; see also Bowman 1994: 158–159)

The fascination with organic preservation cited above might be explained in these terms. The sense of wonder that discovery of well preserved organic material ignites is a source of feeling that can compensate for the loss that occurs as relevance is displaced into the distal term. The knot may end up as a radiocarbon date, an account of its composition and as a fraction in a statistical analysis by the time that the site is published. As Barrett puts it, 'the fascination of discovery along with the techniques that make it possible is ... soon replaced by the tedium of display' (Barrett 1995: 6). It is to be hoped that such a dry account will not eclipse the archaeologist's amazement that such a fragile manifestation of some person's dexterity can survive for six or seven thousand years. Marsden, recounting a visit to the site of the *Amsterdam*, illustrates the competing appeals of 'professional' detachment and a more humanistic appreciation:

> Archaeologists deal with facts, and are not supposed to be carried away on journeys into the past, but on that night those events of a long-gone age were disturbingly near to me.

(Marsden 1974: 120; see also Marsden 1974: 182)

Earlier, I argued that ancient material can be relevant both to past people and to archaeologists, but that such relevance is interrupted, thus preventing direct perception of the past by archaeologists. However, if the environments of archaeologists and of past people are similarly structured then the archaeologist may be able to overcome the interruption. This possibility underlies the contention that archaeologists can, by visiting places once occupied in the past, 'empathise' with long-dead inhabitants. Arguably, the persistent structure of weather and tides may give seafaring archaeologists privileged access to the perceptions of past seafarers, hence Throckmorton remarked 'nautical archaeologists ... must be seamen' (see Blackman 1973: 520). Similarly, Parker notes (disapprovingly) a lecture in which the demand was made for maritime archaeologists to be Master Mariners (Parker 1995: 93; see also McGrail 1995: 331). However, co-perception may be entirely misleading, even though both the ancient mariner and the archaeologist may sense the same roll of the deck beneath their feet. The distal term of the mariner might be a port, a deal or a fight whereas the distal term of the archaeologist is more likely to be past communications, economics or warfare (or, perhaps, future publications, salaries and personal advancement). Such differences can only be drawn out by interpretation; the experience of being at sea does not generate insight unless the archaeologist is prompted to question that experience. The pitfalls of co-perception can be illustrated by reference to the recollections of Morrie Young – a shipwright – who acted as an adviser to the Mary Rose (1967) Committee in the early 1970s:

> I had started measuring a large deck carling from the port side of the wreck, when I noticed something odd about it. Closer examination revealed that one of the dozen or so 'housings' ... had been incorrectly cut at five inches, and a one-inch graving piece inserted to reduce it to the right size. This, of course, was in no way damaging to the strength of the hull and I must admit to having corrected my own errors in a similar manner when working on wooden ships. Until that moment, however, it had never occurred to me that a shipwright working in one of Henry VIII's dockyards could have had the same human failings as I.

(Morrie Young, quoted in McKee 1982: 97)

Young is routinely involved in measuring something he seems immediately familiar with, using a contemporary term to name the timber, until he notices 'something odd'. Such recognition is an act of introversion; a distal term is fractionated out of the previously familiar proximal term and Young is propelled out of his environment into 'nature', which he must consider discursively. Once the repair is regarded as a distal term, he finds relevance in it, i.e. the human failing of making a mistake that he and the shipwright share. Their commonality actually lies in the earlier familiarity – the co-perception of two shipwrights, dwelling in similar environments – but had perception not given way to interpretation, such common humanity may never have been recognised. This example suggests that assumed co-perception may actually deaden archaeologists to the past, simply because in dwelling they do not notice things. Hence although co-perception across the ages is not inconceivable, it might be discouraged; contrary to Throckmorton's contention, being a seafarer does not offer insights to the maritime archaeologist, it obscures them. As Westerdahl notes, 'it would not be of benefit for ... an archaeologist to be too immersed in present day maritime culture' (Westerdahl 1994: 266; and see Parker 1995: 93).

2.2 Meaning

The problem of co-perception across the ages introduces the more general problem of co-perception in the present, and the establishment of meaning between people. Reconsidering the determinism of Gibson's theory, it should now be clear that affordances do not exist in an external environment. Rather, they become known initially by interpretation and thereafter by practical expression in the course of dwelling. Once the human character of the environment is acknowledged, then Gibson's notion of direct perception can be used to explain how individuals go about their lives on the basis of practical consciousness. All the time, however, humans retain the ability to interpret – to challenge perceptions by discursive attention – hence individuals may select and shape their environments creatively. Insofar as the environment is known only in the context of each individual's activity, then there are as many environments as there are individuals. Moreover, each individual's environment is structured by the way in which they come to know its affordances for them. This point raises the question of how any two individuals, each inhabiting a distinct environment, can communicate. The problem can be dealt with by considering Gibson's distinction between variance and invariance, and by returning to the transformations that occur between varying circumstances of presence and absence.

Gibson's theory of direct perception depends upon the individual's sensitivity to invariance in the stream of variance caused by their movement; an individual's visual array changes as they move around, but the elements of the array that correspond to surfaces (things) do not change – they are invariant. As Gibson insists that there is only one environment, then such invariants will be the same for each individual, and on such a basis they can communicate. However, if environments are constructed in the embodied mind of each individual, there is no basis upon which two individuals can perceive the same thing – there is no invariance. Consequently, Gibson's view that individuals detect *invariance against variance* is better understood as a process of detecting *relative variance*; individuals constitute their environment from the less-variant (things exhibiting structural properties) as compared to the more-variant (such as occlusions and changes arising from their own movement). The contention that variance is structured gives grounds for communication; although no two individuals can perceive the same environment, their own environments may be sufficiently similarly structured for meaning to be established between them, as becomes evident when two parties manage to communicate successfully. Insofar as the structure of learning appears in the structure of an individual's

environment, then meaning is supported by common education or 'socialisation'. Interruptions in the structure of learning will inhibit communication, as the environments of each party will not coincide, hence the impossibility of establishing co-perception through time simply through being aboard a boat or observing the same material. In the following section I will consider how archaeologists put their interpretations across to the public, suggesting that a gap arising from the different structuring of their respective learning can be overcome by reference to features that are shared, notably locality, the tangibility of certain artefacts, and identity. However, all three of these bridges between archaeologists and the public carry their own dangers.

2.2.1 Dwelling in interpreted material: archaeologists and the public

The distinction between archaeologist and non-archaeologist (cf. 'professional' and 'amateur', Taylor 1995) is principally one of degree; there can be very few individuals within a society who are not at least casually aware of ancient material through television programmes, visits to museums, reading or some other medium. Equally, all archaeologists are laypeople outside of their discipline; the more attuned that an archaeologist becomes to their own area of expertise, the less time they have to devote to other areas of interest, even within their own discipline. Hence 'all experts are themselves laypeople most of the time' (Giddens 1991: 138). Nonetheless, a distinction can be made in archaeology between the 'more discursively aware' and the 'less discursively aware', i.e. between 'archaeologists' who spend large parts of their life developing and practising a particularly close interest in ancient material and 'non-archaeologists' whose principle expertise lies elsewhere.

The existence of 'archaeologists' and 'non-archaeologists' makes the constitution of meaning between the two difficult, because of the different circumstances in which archaeologists and non-archaeologists experience ancient material; the dissimilar structuring of their respective environments inhibits communication. Archaeologists and non-archaeologists dwell in different presuppositions; in Wylie's terms (see Section 2.1.4), archaeologists and non-archaeologists are engaged in different 'vertical tacks' (see also Barrett 1994: 11–13, 33–35; Fotiadis 1993: 159-160).

Polanyi's theory of knowledge and the identification of two interpretative phases, discussed in Section 2.1.4, provides an insight into the difference between archaeologists' experience of ancient material and the public's experience of the same material. Ancient material is generally presented as a single, self-evident reality, divorced from the initial proximal term – the assumptions of archaeological methodology – that made any form of interpretation possible. Although the public may be invited to partake of the knowledge that archaeologists produce, they are discouraged from dwelling in archaeology as such; archaeology is an 'expert system' (Giddens 1991: 29; 243) that the public may find difficult to enter. Rather, the public is required – in order to understand archaeologists' interpretations of the past – to internalise both ancient material and its relevance to past lives as a single proximal term. Consequently, archaeologists' efforts to present ancient material to the public may obscure the methodologies through which such material gained its relevance. Insofar as the public is not given access to such methodologies, the environments of public and of archaeologists will remain dissimilarly structured, inhibiting the attainment of meaning; the public will not share the relevance of an artefact to an archaeologist.

The difficulty of attaining meaning between archaeologists and the public is intensified by the loss that may be felt when practical experience is rendered discursive. Whereas archaeologists may happily support such loss due to intellectual stimulation and the enhanced knowledge of the past that results, public enjoyment may be compromised by archaeological 'enlightenment' that holds no compensation for them. Of two interpretative paths identified by Barrett, only archaeologists can tread the first as only they are allowed the means to remain intrigued and attracted; non-archaeologists are expected to tread the second, where ignorance is expelled by certainty and the unusual becomes familiar (Barrett 1995: 5–7). The dubious benefits of 'enlightenment' to the public seem to be reflected in the responses of the archaeologists who I interviewed to questions about public interest in archaeology underwater. Although the interviewees generally believed that archaeology underwater is 'of interest' to the public, the notion that archaeology underwater is 'important' to the public in all of the countries was not accepted unanimously. Johansen, Maarleveld and Rieth thought that the interest was principally in treasure, Klosters referred to public nostalgia (Klosters pers. com.), and Christiansen alluded to 'the great octopus and the cannons sticking out of the side of the ship' (Christiansen pers. com.). All these archaeologists were suspicious of the depth of attention underlying superficial interest. Christiansen mentioned the disappointment that accompanied the revelation that archaeology underwater also required hours of study in libraries and archives. He linked this disappointment to the fall-off in numbers that follows initial enthusiasm: ' ... you have ... 20 people in one night, telling them about marine archaeology, and you go to it and you have 10 people, and after a few months you have 4 or 5 left ... those you can count on. That's the public interest' (Christiansen pers. com.).

Although it was generally accepted that the past was quite important to the public – if only at a superficial level – there was some divergence among the interviewees when asked whether archaeology underwater had changed people's views about the past. Some archaeologists were certain, such as Rieck and Jasinski, whereas some were more circumspect, such as Naevestad and Cederlund. Rieth included a caveat that limited the scope of perceived change to the specialists: 'at the moment it's only at the level of research ... archaeologists and historians, more than the general public' (Rieth pers. com.). Reinders started his answer 'it's changed my mind a little bit' but went on to suggest that in 20 years the material that he knew about would result in substantive changes to maritime and shipbuilding history, though such changes might only affect a limited public (Reinders pers. com.). A couple of the interviewees felt that archaeology underwater would not change peoples' minds about the past. Christiansen linked the lack of change to popular notions of archaeology underwater: 'I think if you talk to scientists you can say yes, they have changed their minds ... But if you ask the general public, they're probably out with Jacque Cousteau, and they still have their dream' (Christiansen pers. com.). Johansen did not think that archaeology underwater had changed anybody's mind about the past, or suggested any new interpretations: 'it doesn't change your world, finding a ship and excavating it' (Johansen pers. com.).

These comments suggest that archaeologists have often failed to establish meaning with the public. My contention that such failure is attributable to the dissimilarity in the structure of their respective environments is supported by the following 'exceptions', where environments have been shared through apparent familiarity with a locality, with the material discovered, or with the presumed character of the past society.

Larsen challenged Christiansen's disenchantment with popular interest with reference to a fourteenth century vessel excavated in a field that had once been a harbour: 'some people came and said "Now I understand why they found this old ship in the countryside" ... I think a lot of people on the local level may ... have changed their minds about their own history' (Larsen pers. com.). He stressed, in particular, the way in which an earlier familiarity was confronted: 'they had been driving along this place 20,000 times and suddenly there is a piece of history there'. Naevestad made a similar point in respect of the discovery of the slaver *Friedensburg*:

> Suddenly 25 elephant tusks are coming out of the water at this place on the south coast. Imagine what that meant to the local community. And pieces of mahogany, and a whole story coming out of the sea ... next to where you swim in summer, or have your lobster pots.
>
> (Naevestad pers. com.)

Rather than demystifying some element of the public's environments, with the resulting loss described by Barthes and Shehadeh (see Section 2.1.5), the archaeologists are adding to such environments by enhancing their relevance. Importantly, the addition is not based on the hidden assumptions of archaeology; it extends from the public's earlier familiarity with the places where the material was discovered. Whereas archaeologist and public do not share the assumptions of archaeology, they do share the place in which work is carried out; consequently, their environments are similarly structured in terms of place, and similarity furnishes meaning.

In Section 2.1.4 I argued that the high quality of preservation underwater may encourage archaeologists to presume that the ancient material that they encounter is interpretatively unproblematic, and that they can proceed directly to interpretations of past lives. Although high quality preservation constitutes a danger to the archaeologist, it may ease the establishment of meaning with the public. In the same way that familiarity with a place establishes common ground between archaeologist and public, the apparent familiarity of an object can also facilitate communication. Naevestad, for example, referred to the discovery of a battle-axe, complete with shaft – a 'beautiful find which you wouldn't make on land' – by a diver (Naevestad pers. com.).

The discovery caused substantial media interest that unearthed the story of a battle in c. 1200 AD, researched by local historians. Although the story of the battle was not new, it was not until the discovery of the axe that the story was, in Naevestad's terms, 'actualised' for the local community. Moreover, the public was given 'something more, actual proof of a historic event, which always means something' (Naevestad pers. com.). In this case, the axe was readily assimilated by the community as a proximal term that allowed its members to attend to the old story as a distal term worthy of attention. Given the danger noted above, however, archaeologists have a responsibility to problematise the character of ancient material if the public's eagerness to dwell in such material yields facile interpretations of the past.

A further example of a similarity in the structuring of environments that facilitates the establishment of meaning between archaeologists and public was drawn out by archaeologists in Norway and Sweden. Jasinski and Klosters suggested that the close link between the population and the sea in contemporary Norwegian society resulted in a close interest in underwater archaeology. Jasinski stated that every Norwegian family included someone employed in fishing, or included someone who owned a boat. He also referred to the focus of Norwegian industry upon the sea. Together, such factors influenced 'the mental connection between the population and the sea'. Jasinski claimed that, as a result, 'it's no problem to *make* people interested in what we are doing, they *are* interested' (Jasinski pers. com.). Klosters made a similar point, claiming that Norwegians have a common interest in everything connected to maritime conditions, because 'they all ... have an uncle or a brother or father – or ... are themselves – involved in ... maritime activity' (Klosters pers. com.). Cederlund attributed a general interest in maritime history to Swedish citizens' integration with their maritime surroundings but, in contrast to Norway, such integration arose from leisure boating rather than economics (Cederlund pers. com.). Again, it can be argued that familiarity with the sea structures the environments of all members of Norwegian and Swedish society – irrespective of whether they are archaeologists or not – and such structured similarity furnishes meaning. Moreover, it might be implied that such familiarity with the sea extends back in time, that the current population perceives the same world as past populations. The dangers of claiming such affinity across time have already been alluded to; if the interest in maritime history is explained as a consequence of the 'maritime' character of contemporary society, then it might be presumed that such character is 'essential' rather than historically contingent. Furthermore, an 'essential' view of society's character might encourage the transposition of other characteristics of contemporary society onto the past. Hence Klosters' reference to uncles, brothers and fathers as the principle participants in maritime activity today (a suggestion that can surely be questioned) might foreclose perspectives that suggest that women played a significant or primary role in past maritime societies.

Although these 'exceptions' suggest ways to encourage the constitution of meaning between archaeologists and the public, they are hazardous. The hazards can be overcome by drawing the public's attention to the methodological difficulties that attend the interpretation of ancient material. In short, archaeologists must invite the public into the assumptions in which they dwell. By this, I do not mean simply that the public is taught to survey and record, as such techniques are simply conduits that may shape archaeological methodology but do not constitute methodologies themselves. The need to engage the public in archaeological methodologies means that not only do archaeologists have to examine their own assumptions explicitly – as has occurred, to some extent, as a result of the increased awareness of 'theoretical' archaeology – they also have to carry out such examinations 'in public'. If the public is allowed to become familiar with the ways in which archaeologists construct their interpretations, then archaeologists may find that the public's interest in their findings is more profound than the preoccupation with cannons, octopus and treasure of which the interviewees complained.

2.2.2 Salvage: problem and solution

The introduction of the Protection of Wrecks Act 1973 presents an interesting case study in establishing a shared environment among archaeologists and legislators about a specific set of circumstances. The interest arises because it is quite clear that the way in which the circumstances were conceptualised had a major impact on the solution that the varied and disparate parties came together to endorse. The 'nature' of the problem facing archaeology underwater in the early 1970s was addressed in terms of salvage – rather than, for instance, by extending the principles of terrestrial antiquities law – because the problem had come to be comprehended through familiarity with salvage law. This particular conception of the problem prompted a specific solution as legislation was prepared and passed through Parliament, resulting in a regime that might be characterised as a statutory version of 'salvor in possession'.

The archaeologists lobbying for improvements were afflicted by the preoccupation with salvage as much as the legislators. The only people excepted from this preoccupation were – it seems – the civil servants involved in the initial drafting of the Protection of Wrecks Bill. These civil servants drew upon land antiquities legislation, notably the Ancient Monuments Consolidation and Amendment Act 1913 (AMCA 1913), the Ancient Monuments Act 1931 (AMA 1931 s. 15) and the Historic Buildings and Ancient Monuments Act 1953 (HBAMA 1953 ss. 10, 11) (Department of Trade and Industry 1971 b). Although the substance of the 1973 Act differs from the measures being discussed in 1971, many of its provisions are comparable to terrestrial protection (Table 2.2) (see also AMAA 1979 ss. 1(3), 2(1), 2(3)).

This is not to say that salvage was inimical to the 1973 Bill; a number of salvage-related terms do appear within its provisions (notably in s. 1(3) and s. 1(5)(a)). However, it appears that these sections may have been introduced to defuse resistance to the draft bill from salvage interests prior to the bill appearing in Parliament (see CNA Minutes 20/07/72; Department of Trade 1974). I would argue, therefore, that the emphasis on salvage and recovery is not intrinsic to the bill as originally conceived by the Department of Trade and Industry, nor – notwithstanding ss. 1(3) and 1(5)(a) – to the general arrangement of the 1973 Act.

Table 2.2:   A comparison of underwater and terrestrial protection

Protection of Wrecks Act 1973	Historic Buildings and Ancient Monuments Act 1953
If the Secretary of State is satisfied with respect to any site in United Kingdom Waters that ... on account of the historical, archaeological or artistic importance of the vessel ... the site ought to be protected from unauthorised interference ... he may by order designate an area around the site as a restricted area (PWA 1973 1(1))	Where in the case of a monument which appears to the Minister to be an ancient monument - the Ancient Monument Board report to him that the monument is in danger of destruction or removal or damage ... and that the preservation of the monument is of national importance ... the Minister ... may ... serve a notice ... stating that the monument will be under the protection of the Minister (HBAMA 1953 s. 10(1))
... a person commits an offence if, in a restricted area, he does any of the following things otherwise than under the authority of a licence granted by the Secretary of State ... (PWA 1973 1(3))	While an interim preservation notice or a preservation order is in force ... the monument shall not be demolished or removed, nor ... shall any work carried out in connection therewith, except with the written consent of the Minister ... (HBAMA 1953 s. 12(1))
A licence granted by the Secretary of State for the purposes of subsection (3) above shall be in writing and ... may be granted subject to conditions or restrictions ...(PWA 1973 1(5)(b))	... the written consent of the Minister granted either unconditionally or subject to such conditions as the Minister may think fit. (HBAMA 1953 s. 12(1))

However, land-derived concepts such as scheduling and temporary protection came to be discussed within a salvage paradigm. My concern is, then, not with the substance of the 1973 Act but with the presumptions that surrounded its introduction, which saw the imposition of a salvage mentality that subsequently informed implementation of the 1973 Act. The preoccupation with salvage did not arise solely from a pragmatic effort to tailor the 1973 Bill to a marginal legislative opportunity; rather, the legislators and lobbyists were 'dwelling' in salvage to the extent that the alternatives to a salvage-based system were barely considered.

The preoccupation with salvage that characterised the legislative process is apparent in the debates in 1973, an environment characterised particularly by perceptions of competing salvors, recovery, the *Girona*, the *Association* and the *Mary*. This shared environment furnished common meanings between disparate parties that facilitated the passage of the 1973 Act. However, it also spawned administrative undertakings by the Government, voiced in the course of debates, which perpetuated the very circumstances that the 1973 Act was intended to overcome.

The failings of salvage law had been rehearsed in debates in 1970 (HC 797: 1362–1377) and 1972 (HC 834: 888–889; 924–925; 960–962; 976–978), and the Government had established the Wreck Law Review Committee to present recommendations for comprehensive revision of the law (HL 309: 317–318). The 1973 Bill came about as a temporary measure to prevent the depredations likely to occur in the time that the committee took to complete its review and for amendments to the Merchant Shipping Act to be introduced. Mr. Mason set out the grounds upon which the 1973 Bill was welcomed: 'Meanwhile the Bill is a useful interim measure ... I hope it will be only the beginning of further legislation which will be needed even when it becomes law' (HC 851: 1854). Similarly Mr. Faulds remarked: 'I understand that this is interim legislation and that longer-term legislation will not be too long in coming ... I hope that the long-term legislation which is envisaged as a follow-up to this interim measure will get to grips with the operation of salvage law' (HC 851: 1863-1864). The Government seems genuinely to have been of the same view, as Mr. Onslow stated:

> I wish at the outset to say that the detailed review of
> wreck legislation mentioned by the right hon. Member

for Barnsley is still continuing in consultation with the interests concerned. Its object is to introduce comprehensive legislation to bring up to date the wreck provisions of Part IX of the Merchant Shipping Act 1894 in their general operation and to make provision for historic wrecks ... the Government agreed that a relatively short Bill ... should be prepared to give some measure of interim protection to selected historic wrecks pending the introduction of comprehensive legislation.

> (HC 851: 1865, see also HC 855: 1673 and statements
> for the Government by Earl Ferrers HL 342: 928)

Given its interim character, the weaknesses of the 1973 Bill were recognised and dismissed in the interests of speedy enactment. Mr. Onslow commented 'I think it would be a mistake to expect too much of this Bill ... there are many things which have to be left to be dealt with...' (HC 855: 1703-1704; see also the Earl of Cork and Orrery HL 342: 916-917). Mr. Onslow stated that the limited intention of the 1973 Bill was 'to secure the protection of wrecks from interference from unauthorised persons'. He added: 'it may, incidentally, lead to a more orderly exploitation of wrecks, but that is not the prime aim of the Bill' (HC 855: 1705). However, it is clear from the debates, and from implementation of the Act, that 'orderly exploitation' was central to the perceptions of the Government; protection was to be pursued through regulated destruction.

While many MPs regarded the Merchant Shipping Act 1894 as being fundamentally incompatible with archaeology (e.g. Mr. Mason, HC 851: 1853; Mr. Faulds, HC 851: 1863–1864), some comments suggest that the salvage regime was not thought wholly inappropriate. For example, Mr. Sproat contrasted the provision for preventing disorder during shoreline salvage (MSA 1894 s. 514 – subsequently repealed, MSA 1993 sch. 4 s. 21) with the lack of such a provision offshore (Mr. Sproat HC 855: 1665; see also HC 829: 262w). The implication is almost that the 1894 Act could be used, if only it applied equally to the seabed. Furthermore, Mr. Sproat presented a history of salvage law which implied that the system used to be adequate – that a fresh bill was required simply to recoup the position lost following advice in 1965:

There are cases on record which show that at one time the Board of Trade and the Ministry of Transport granted licences to dive on ancient wrecks and to recover items irrespective of whether the Crown or a United Kingdom Government Department was the original owner ... In these cases it was believed that the Crown had the title to derelict vessels lying on the sea bed in United Kingdom territorial waters ... In 1965 the Board of Trade was advised that it should not be taken to be a principle of United Kingdom law that all ancient wrecks lying in United Kingdom territorial waters were vested in the Crown, as they lie irrespective of their original ownership ... It followed that licences to dive on such wrecks had no validity and would not keep other persons away.

(Mr. Sproat HC 855: 1662-1663)

Concern for licensed salvage seems to have blinded both lobbyists and parliamentarians to other alternatives, so although the Protection of Wrecks Bill was conceived and debated with particular scenarios in mind, the scenarios did not extend to the full range of circumstances known at the time. For example, the *Amsterdam* and the *Mary Rose* were cited on a number of occasions during the debates, but they had little influence on discussions about protection. Both wrecks were in areas where infringements could be easily monitored, in contrast to the distant reefs that had trapped the *Association* and the *Mary*. Most importantly, perhaps, neither the *Amsterdam* nor the *Mary Rose* was a 'treasure' ship of the same class as the *Girona* and the *Association*. Moreover, it was possible to extend relatively effective protection over the *Amsterdam* and the *Mary Rose* without recourse to primary legislation, by way of seabed leases and the powers of local authorities (Marsden 1973: 492; HC 866: 274w; McKee 1982: 67, 86).

In contrast, the scenario presented by the *Association* and the *Mary* of conflict between salvors was particularly influential, to the extent that the provisions of the Protection of Wrecks Bill seem to have been tailored precisely to protect the *Mary*. In the case of the *Association*, the Ministry of Defence had concluded contracts with two teams to salvage material from the wreck (Mr. Sproat HC 855: 1664). Competitive salvage on that site – to the detriment of archaeological interests – was responsible for the earlier lobbying and attempts to introduce a Ten-Minute-Rule Bill and amendments to the Merchant Shipping Act in 1970 (see HC 797: 415–417; HC 797: 1362–1377). When the *Mary* was discovered a repeat occurrence seemed likely – another vessel of archaeological and historical relevance would be fought over. One of the groups involved – which was closely linked with the CNA and bore their 'archaeological seal of approval' – sought to acquire a contract from MoD. It was hoped that this group could acquire an 'exclusive' contract and, thereafter, be able to seek a civil injunction against other groups interfering on the site. However, the Ministry of Defence was unwilling to grant any such contract. In January 1972 Mr. Faulds asked the Minister of State for Defence, Mr. Kirk, if he would reconsider his refusal to grant the CNA exclusive rights of recovery from the *Mary*, and if he would give the reasons for the initial refusal. Mr. Kirk replied 'it is not the practice to grant exclusive rights of recovery from historic wrecks' (Mr.

Kirk, HC 829: 212w). The CNA pressed the case in correspondence in March 1972, but again the MoD refused, stating:

It is the view of the Ministry of Defence that having regard to the existing law governing historic wreck, the granting of any form of salvage contract to work on a historic wreck would not by itself prevent other persons diving on or recovering items from the wreck.

(MoD to CNA 29/03/72)

This explanation was repeated in response to pressure applied by Dr. Owen, among others, during a Royal Navy debate in 1972 (Dr. Owen HC 834: 119; 977; Mr. Kirk HC 834: 977) and also in a subsequent letter from Kirk to Dr. Owen (Mr. Kirk to Dr. Owen 16/05/72). Other reasons for not granting an exclusive contract were that the MoD could not adjudicate between claims for exclusive contracts made by several groups who discovered a wreck at about the same time (Croome to Kirk 15/3/72; Mr. Kirk HC 834: 977), and that no action could be taken while the Committee on Wreck was still deliberating (Croome to Kirk 15/3/72). Although the correspondence and debates suggest that Kirk was sympathetic, though constrained, the MoD's stance and the Government's position generally was ridiculed in the media (*The Observer* 16/01/72; *The Guardian* 18/04/72; *The Daily Telegraph* 28/04/72).

Arguably, the Protection of Wrecks Bill presented the Government with an opportunity to overcome its inability to grant exclusive contracts. Moreover, the concept of 'salvor in possession' offered a model solution that had been applied to wreck on the seabed and was being adopted to deal with ancient wrecks. Hence, Mr. Sproat cited the case of the *Tubantia* (*The Tubantia* [1924] P 78). This case demonstrated that 'a salvor who could show that he was in possession of a derelict vessel and its contents lying on the sea bed might in certain circumstances obtain a High Court injunction restraining other salvors from interfering' (Mr. Sproat HC 855: 1665). The lesson had not been lost on salvors of ancient material:

Sténuit obtained an opinion of the Northern Ireland court to this effect in an action concerning the *Girona*. A similar action has been initiated by Roland Morris to restrain the Lyonesse Salvage Company from interfering with the wrecks of the 'Association' and the 'Romney'.

(Mr. Sproat HC 855: 1665)

In contrast to activities at the sites of the *Association* and the *Mary*, Sténuit managed to investigate the *Girona* relatively unhindered, claiming to be 'salvor in possession' and turning away another group of divers after a confrontation (Sténuit 1969: 775). MPs and archaeologists alike generally regarded the outcome as favourable. Interesting, attractive and valuable material was recovered and passed to the Ulster Museum by an 'archaeologist' (see Mr. Sproat, HC 855: 1658). Davies – who was heavily involved in the CNA's attempts to protect the *Mary* – contrasted the two scenarios in a note to an article on the *Mary*:

The acquisition of all the artefacts from the *Girona* by Belfast Museum provides a fine example of what can be achieved.

(Davies 1973: n. 4)

Thus, the *Girona* appeared to offer a desirable model for archaeology underwater, comprising effective, uninterrupted salvage by one salvor leading to acquisition of the complete collection by a museum. Establishing a claim to be salvor in possession is, however, a question of fact and degree in each case (see *The Association and The Romney* [1970] 2 Lloyd's Rep 59: 61). Even if established, possession may not present sufficient grounds to support an injunction against other divers. Whereas Wignall was successful as 'salvor in possession' in appealing to the Irish courts in preventing interference on the *Santa Maria de la Rosa* site (Wignall 1975 a), Morris' attempt to extend an injunction – as referred to by Mr. Sproat – failed even though the judge found in favour of his case for possession (*The Association and The Romney* [1970] 2 Lloyd's Rep 59: 61). Such drawbacks in the regime of salvor in possession may have contributed to Kirk's insistence – noted above – that MoD contracts could not be used to prevent other divers from interfering in a site, and encouraged the notion that an unambiguous, statutory version of salvor in possession was required.

Returning to the vaunted case of the *Girona*, it could be argued that if there had been less preoccupation with the need to acquire the collection – and more interest in interpretation and preservation – then the example, and the salvage regime upon which it drew, might have been viewed with less enthusiasm. Sténuit's own account, published in the *National Geographic*, gives a clear picture of his methodology:

We are proud of our 2,800 hours of labor under the sea. There where we have toiled for five months, the disturbed terrain is no longer recognizable. The bottom is pitted with the deep wounds of our digging.

(Sténuit 1969: 777)

The immediacy of the link between salvage and destruction manifest in this phrase, and the emphasis on recovery that inheres in the concept of 'salvor in possession' seem to have caused no difficulty to the MPs debating the 1973 Bill. Moreover, salvors' interests were regarded sympathetically by the Government. When Mr. Money sought to introduce a provision for national museums to have the option to purchase material at a reasonable price, rather than await auction (HC 855: 1688), Mr. Onslow refused to countenance any constraint of salvors' interests: '... in many cases the costs involved in recovery are such that there is a case to be made that the owner is entitled to get the best price he can ... I should hesitate to suggest that an artificial limit should be placed on that price...' (HC 855: 1693). Such support for salvage interests can also be seen in the following statements made by the Government's spokespersons:

We must recognise that the rights of an owner or salvor in possession of a designated wreck may be affected by the order ... We recognise, therefore, that the owner or salvor has the prior claim to salvage the wreck provided he can meet the conditions required for a licence necessary for the protection of the archaeological value of the site.

(Mr. Onslow, HC 851: 1869)

It is therefore right that such a person should have prior claim to be allowed to inspect and salvage the wreck, provided he is willing and able to meet the conditions of the licence necessary for the protection of the archaeological value of the site. It is hoped that such conditions will not be unduly onerous.

(Earl Ferrers, HL 342: 932)

It might be noted that these statements amounted to a substantial undertaking about the adjudication of competing applications for the 'right' to work a site – precisely the type of judgement that Kirk had avoided in 1972. The most telling comment was, however, made by Mr. Sproat in relation to enforcement:

Probably our greatest aid in enforcing the provisions of the Bill is that there is an authorised salvor on the spot looking after his own interests ... we can be certain that the salvor who has the licence will protect his own interests absolutely.

(Mr. Sproat, HC 851: 1877)

Admittedly, the sympathy with which salvage interests were handled was attributable in part to the fragile legislative opportunity (see Section 3.2.1). However, irrespective of tactical purposes, the explicit dependence of the passage of the Protection of Wrecks Act upon salvors' defence of their interests indicates the degree to which the perceptions of the 1973 Bill's sponsors had been pervaded by salvage. The preoccupation with salvage had a substantial effect on implementation of the 1973 Act, as demonstrated by the constitution of designated sites as a resource (Section 3.2.2) and licensing of work on such sites (Section 4.1.2).

2.3 Significance: the Protection of Wrecks Act 1973 and research interests

Having shown that a particular conception of a problem prompted a specific response as legislation was prepared and passed through Parliament, I would like to pursue the matter as to what happens when such conceptions structure subsequent activity. My particular concern is the way in which ideas about shipwrecks current in the early 1970s, as articulated in the course of introducing the 1973 Act, seem to have impressed themselves on subsequent research. Grenville has argued that archaeology is 'a profession in which curation and research are largely decoupled, to the very great disadvantage of both' (Grenville 1994: 127). I share her general view that the relationship between research and curation has to be examined closely, but here I argue that research and curation are too closely coupled, though at a near-invisible level. Whereas Section 2.2.2 considered the establishment of common meaning among the various parties, this section considers the way in which – in the course of the legislative process – these opinions became abstracted into a generalised conception of the 'significance' of shipwrecks.

The debates in 1973 served as an exposition to the citizenry of the UK of the relevance of shipwrecks and the need to protect them. This expository aspect of the debates equates with abstraction, and with the expression – perhaps imposition – of society-wide relevance. Although presented by individuals with affiliations to particular group interests (see Section 3.2.1), the MPs' views were expressed as self-evident truths that applied throughout UK society. Arguably, the MPs were encouraged to assume that their views had societal relevance because of the non-contentious character of the bill under discussion (e.g. Mr. Stewart, HC 851: 1861–1862; Mr. Maclennan, HC 855: 1699; Mr. Onslow, HC 855: 1703). In the course of debates, therefore, individual and group interests became an abstract expression of the relevance that wrecks *did* have, of the relevance that wrecks *should* have – hence the need for legislation – and, insofar as these interests were carried over into the administration of the 1973 Act, of the relevance that wrecks *would* have.

It might be argued that criticism is unwarranted; the 1973 Act was a temporary holding measure to conserve sites and its success is to be measured in terms of preservation rather than any contribution to new knowledge. Such a defence is inadequate. As I showed above, the 1973 Act was not – at least in the minds of the legislators – introduced to preserve sites, it was introduced to regulate their excavation by individual salvors (notwithstanding Mr. Onslow's assertion that the Act was not intended to lead to more orderly exploitation of wrecks (HC 855: 1705; see Section 2.2.2)). Consequently, the legislators' expectations about what the wrecks would produce in terms of artefacts and/or knowledge was fundamental to their concern that certain wrecks should be regulated; i.e. the whole legislative project was prefigured by some conception of significance.

Reference was made both in 1970 and in 1973 to the qualities of wreck sites as 'time capsules'. Hence in 1970 Mr. Onslow spoke of '... something unique - a time capsule which we have only just begun to know how to open, the past locked up underwater round our shores' (HC 797: 1372). In 1973, as Minister, he was to repeat the importance of wrecks as closed finds (HC 851: 1870) though he also pointed out that essentially intact sites such as the *Amsterdam* 'are by no means in an untouched state' (HC 855: 1704). Mr. Mason, Mr. Tilney and Mr. Faulds all referred to wrecks as 'closed finds' (HC 851: 1854; 1857; 1864) and the Earl of Cork and Orrery used the analogy of a stopped clock (HL 342: 915-916). To a certain extent, these comments may have reflected the excitement felt by archaeologists in relation to newly discovered sites such as the *Mary Rose* and the *Amsterdam* that seemed remarkably coherent. Marsden, for example, referred to the self-evident relevance of the *Amsterdam* as a receptacle as follows: 'Clearly the wreck was important as it contained a very large, dated group of antiquities...' (Marsden 1972: 73). However, the 'time-capsule' analogy is both erroneous in theory (cf. the 'Pompeii premise' discussed in Binford 1981) and inaccurate in practice. Nevertheless, the time capsule analogy remains a popular misconception that is difficult to undo; for example, current publicity for the *Mary Rose* still makes prominent use of a quote from the Washington Post: 'It's a perfect time capsule' (Mary Rose Trust n.d.). More worrying, perhaps, is the apparent acceptance of the 'time-capsule' analogy in 'academic' archaeology; a commentary in *Antiquity* refers to 'shipwreck assemblages, providing closed capsules of contemporary material', stating that 'this is the major and *the intellectually unifying feature* of the discipline' (Gibbins and Chippendale 1990: 334, my emphasis). While the longevity of the misconception cannot be attributed solely to debates in 1973,

such debates indicate its currency at the time that the 1973 regime was established as the principal focus of management in the UK.

Resistance to the 'time-capsule' analogy has come from two sides. First, divers have stressed oceanic forces that leave wrecks as a jumble bereft of archaeological relevance. Hence, Morris poked fun at 'modern marine archaeologists' and their penchant for 'pre-disturbance surveys': 'the survey of any wreck site on the Atlantic fringe off south-west Cornwall and the Scillies would merely show the latest rearrangement of the debris by the most recent ground-sea disturbance' (Morris 1979: 117; see also 159–160). The transparency of intention – to justify recovery without recording – is equalled by the transparency of the argument's inaccuracy. Notwithstanding his assertions about the power of sub-sea phenomena, Morris' account of his investigation of *Colossus* includes several references to close spatial associations, which he used to interpret the lie of the wreck and the probable location of its ceramic cargo (see Morris 1979: 161–163; 171–175). The second direction from which the time-capsule analogy has been criticised is associated in particular with Muckelroy's work in the late 1970s. Muckelroy contested the static notion of wreck sites (see, e.g. Price and Muckelroy 1974: 260) and set about demonstrating that the spatial relationships of material on the seabed could be interpreted archaeologically (see Muckelroy 1978: esp. ch. 5) thus emphasising the need to record sites in their entirety. Both sets of criticisms refute beliefs expressed at Westminster in 1973; nonetheless, the debates endorsed an agenda – close attention to formation processes – which has remained a primary concern of investigations in the UK to the present day (see, e.g., Ferrari and Adams 1990; Gregory 1995).

Another important focus in 1973 was the high level of preservation of ancient material on sites underwater. Mr. Sproat, for example, referred to the 'extraordinary state of preservation' (HC 851: 1876), and both Mr. Tilney and Mr. Faulds drew attention to differential preservation, such that finds from underwater included things (e.g. wood and leather) that were not generally found on land (HC 851: 1857; 1863). The high level of preservation – particularly of organic material – on wreck sites has been borne out by many investigations in UK waters. Preoccupation with the high quality of preserved artefacts might be seen in the concern for materials conservation on designated sites (e.g. Priestman 1973; Gawronski 1986; Gawronski 1987). This is not to say that materials conservation is not an important adjunct to investigation, simply that concern for the survival of the artefacts may eclipse the interpretation of such artefacts. The circumstantial grounds for this argument are reinforced by an evident interest in 1973 in recovery, collection and display. For example, Mr. Mason commented '... our museums have been denied many valuable pieces' (HC 851: 1855). Mr. Sproat proclaimed that 'anyone who has not seen what is brought ashore from old vessels would be astounded by the variety, richness ... of many of the articles that are found' (HC 851: 1875). Mr. Sproat also focused on the recoveries from sites in describing the *Amsterdam*, *Association*, *Girona*, and the *Mary* (e.g. HC 851: 1848; HC 855: 1657–1658).

Table 2.3: Headings used in publications relating to PWA 1973

Kennemerland	ship's armament, ship's equipment, personal possessions, cargo	(Price and Muckelroy 1974).
	coins, jewellery, clay pipes, stoneware, pottery, earthenware, glass, pewter objects, lead objects, iron objects, bronze and brass objects, navigational and scientific objects, armament, wooden objects, rope, leatherwork, bone etc., objects of stone	(Price and Muckelroy 1977; Price and Muckelroy 1979).
Amsterdam	Parts of the ship and her armament, ship's stores, VOC equipment for use on board, personal belongings, cargo	(Marsden 1972)
	ship structure, functional groups of finds	(Gawronski 1990)
Anne	cannon balls, grenades, musket ball, barrels	(Marsden and Lyon, D. 1977)
Invincible	sandglasses, buckets, barrels, magazine tools, messdeck utensils, shovels, cannon accoutrements, small arms, grenades, buttons, blocks, fids, parrels and trucks, bullseyes, deadeyes and coils of rope	(Bingeman 1985)
Hazardous	artefacts, guns, exposed timbers	(Owen 1988)
Duart Point	objects of wood, ceramics, objects of stone, objects of metal	(Martin, C. 1995)

The MPs' interest in the quality of finds has been closely matched by the evident interests of authors who have published investigations of wrecks protected under the 1973 Act. The preoccupation with the intrinsic relevance of artefacts is evinced by the tendency to 'publish' investigations in the form of a catalogue of finds. Such catalogues usually consist of a brief description, illustrations and reference to other examples, but there is rarely any interpretative effort to relate the finds, in isolation or as assemblages, to the lives of people in the past. Such interpretations as are implied are usually functional 'descriptions' that are neither problematised nor justified. Table 2.3 summarises the 'catalogue headings' used in a number of publications relating to designated sites.

Such a catalogue style is adopted for the series of publications relating to the *Dartmouth*; the following specialist reports have been printed in IJNA: 2. Culinary and related items (Holman 1975); 3. The guns (McBride 1976); 4. The clay pipes (Martin, P.F. de C. 1977); 5. The ship (Martin, C. 1978). Although the *Dartmouth* articles are more inclined to discussion than the articles listed in the table, there remains a danger that a catalogue structure will omit uncategorised material and might prevent interpretative synthesis of the site as a whole.

Although the tendency to publish in catalogue form is not unique to archaeology underwater, the tendency does correlate strongly with MPs' interest in artefacts rather than interpretations. This correlation is particularly strong in respect of certain specific categories of artefacts. Mr. Sproat, for example, typified the contents of wrecks as 'antique brass cannons or cargo, and personal possessions of the passengers and crew, such as coins and jewellery...' (HC 855: 1666). The Earl of Cork and Orrery gave a slightly wider definition: '"contents" ... may mean anything from an anchor or an astrolabe to a set of dentures or a gold moidore [a Portuguese coin]' (HL 342: 918). The common references to cannon, coins and jewellery in the 1973 debates is matched by the frequent occurrence of equivalent classifications in the published 'catalogues'. The preoccupation with cannon and armament is particularly striking; the fascination runs right up to the present (e.g. McBride 1973; McBride 1976; Hildred 1988; Tomalin, Cross and Motkin 1988; Owen 1988: 290–291; Owen 1991: 329–330; Preece and Burton 1993: 261–264; Roth 1996). Of course, a 'practical' reason can be

offered for the preoccupation; many of the designated wrecks were spotted due to the presence of cannon, which are relatively visible. Moreover, cannon are fairly straightforward to record, they often have distinctive forms, decorations and inscriptions, and they are often associated with documentary material. Consequently, cannon are useful for dating and identifying wrecks and offer a number of avenues for subsequent investigation. However, publications relating to designated sites rarely pursue the interpretation of cannon beyond age, source and construction. This weakness is in marked contrast to interpretations on sites not designated, for example, on the shipboard operation of ordnance (e.g. Guilmartin 1988) or on the economy/technology of supplying armaments (Martin, C. 1975: ch. 7; Wignall 1973; Wignall 1975 b).

In Polanyi's terms, the MPs were dwelling in certain methodologies – principally excavation and recovery – as they approached artefacts as a distal term. They seemed barely able to conceive of a situation in which they could dwell in the ancient material in order to approach 'the past' as a distal term. Moreover, it appears that archaeology underwater in the UK has been arrested at this stage – preoccupied with the presence and character of material, rather than with new ideas about the past. Furthermore, the inclination to attribute relevance to the distal term – i.e. the material – seems to have encouraged the view that acquisition of identified, recovered and conserved material is adequate justification for the entire endeavour.

Although, in the course of the 1973 debates, there was plenty of interest in the characteristics of artefacts associated with wrecks, only two references were made about the knowledge that might be gleaned about the past from wrecks protected by the 1973 Bill. On Second Reading, Mr. Sproat suggested that wrecks can generate 'valuable information about early ship design and construction and the life of the period' (HC 851: 1849). His thoughts were reflected almost exactly be the Earl of Cork and Orrery in the House of Lords: '... valuable information on ship design and the life of the period may be lost for ever. Knowledge of the construction of ancient ships is still scanty, and the remains of a vessel lying on the seabed may tell us much' (HL 342: 915). These comments mirror Marsden's contemporary reference to 'very many details of construction and life on board these ships which are not known' (Marsden 1972: 88). However, the potential for increasing understanding of life of the period/life on board expressed in the debates seems to have had no correlate in the publication of investigations directed to wrecks designated under the 1973 Act. There are few published example of an interpretation of 'life' based upon ancient material from a designated site, though some articles point towards the interpretative potential (e.g. Redknap 1984: 93; Redknap 1985: 46; Gawronski 1990: 58–61; Wittop Koning 1986: 88–91). Most accounts are limited either to catalogues – which occasionally list 'personal possessions' but make no attempt to build lives around them – or to document-based descriptions of the events leading up to and subsequent to wrecking (e.g. Forster and Higgs 1973; Marsden 1972; Marsden and Lyon, D. 1977). In these cases, ancient material serves as little more than confirmation or illustration.

In contrast to the lack of concern for 'life', ship construction derived from investigations of designated sites has received appreciable attention, though again the accounts are descriptive rather than interpretative (e.g. Hutchinson 1991; Owen 1991; Redknap 1984; Redknap 1985; Marsden 1972; Martin, C. 1978; though see Adams 1986). The close association of the significance of wrecks designated under the 1973 Act with ship construction has been expressed unambiguously by McGrail: 'the indisputable importance of the remains of the R. Hamble ship to the history of European shipbuilding more than justifies its designation as an Historic Wreck' (McGrail 1993: 49). It is worth noting, however, the disjunction between the detailed technical description of the *construction* of the vessel arrived at archaeologically (McGrail 1993: 45–49) and the more humanistic account of *constructing* the vessel derived from historical materials (Friel 1993). The articles are juxtaposed in a single volume of the *International Journal of Nautical Archaeology*, so it might be claimed that they complement each other rather than indicating omissions. To me, however, the juxtaposition amplifies an apparent unwillingness of archaeologists working with designated sites to move from assiduous recording of ancient material to an interpretation of the rôle of such material in previous ages. Such unwillingness is at least partly attributable to the expectations current at the time that 1973 regime was introduced.

A further example of the preoccupation with construction is presented by the contrast between the accounts of the Pwll Fanog wreck – a cargo mound of slates pinning a section of hull structure to the seabed – by Jones and by Roberts (Jones, D. 1978; Roberts 1979). Jones' article concentrates on the slate cargo whereas Roberts' article consists largely of a detailed account of the construction of the vessel. Roberts gives the impression that the slate mound is simply an encumbrance to finding out about construction: 'A cross-sectional trench was regarded as the one most likely to prove quickly the existence of ship remains. Early digging was slow, uneventful, hard work' (Roberts 1979: 249). The notion of encumbrance or irrelevance is encouraged by the 'figurative' illustration of slates in the article's diagrams (notably figures 1 and 2), which are in contrast to the relatively detailed drawings of ship structure. Most tellingly, Figure 1 includes a label 'Slate cargo mound *about* 6 layers deep' (my emphasis), whereas Jones bases his estimate of a

cargo of 23,000 slates on their being 'at least two layers and probably three' (Jones, D. 1978: 154). Roberts makes no reference to any revision of Jones' estimate of the size of the cargo or of the relevance of its loss, even though the excavation presented evidence that may have doubled or trebled Jones' figures. Although Roberts' account is subtitled 'An interim report on the ship's remains...', the excavation need not have been limited to gathering information about construction. If the excavation did give rise to more information about the mound and its interpretation, it is a pity that the results were not published.

Jones' interest in cargo indicates an area of research that was not discussed in the 1973 debates, but which has received some prominence since them. Other examples of research into cargo include: Marsden's comparative work on the treasure (a cargo of specie) of the *Amsterdam* and the *Hollandia* (Marsden 1978); Muckelroy's discussion of the Moor Sand and Langdon Bay sites (Muckelroy 1980; Muckelroy 1981); and work on the *Kennemerland* – notably the ingots (Price, Muckelroy and Willies 1980). However, these investigations seem to have arisen either from a barely directed hunger for data – hence the first objective of the *Kennemerland* investigation was 'to make the material yield up *as much information as possible* about the type of goods which a Dutch East Indiaman of this period would be carrying as equipment, stores or cargo' (Price and Muckelroy 1974: 258, my emphasis) – or from the immediate proclivities of the material – as if it is the coins, ingots or slates themselves that demand to be counted, compared and classified. In short, while the few studies into the cargoes found on designated sites do indicate a willingness to go beyond life on board and ship construction, such interpretations are material-led nonetheless and, as such, do not mark a major departure from the terms in which the 1973 Act was debated.

It might be argued that the lack of interpretative enterprise is a characteristic of 'field' archaeology as a whole, not maritime archaeology alone. Insofar as terrestrial fieldwork has, to a large extent, remained empirically oriented – notwithstanding the development of processual and post-processual archaeologies in the 1970s and 1980s (see Champion 1991) – it is perhaps unsurprising that many reports of investigations of wrecks protected under the 1973 Act are little more than accounts of the presence, the extent and the age of material. However, at least some attempts were made to generate ideas of the past on the basis of designated sites. Muckelroy's discussion of bronze age trade following investigation of the sites at Moor Sands and Langdon Bay (Muckelroy 1980; Muckelroy 1981) stands out from all other published material on designated sites because it offers an interpretation extending beyond the sites themselves and the immediate circumstances of their wrecking. To a certain extent the same can also be said of Marsden's discussion of the treasure of the *Amsterdam* and of the *Hollandia*, though his references to the *Amsterdam* are based on documentary rather than material evidence, and work on the *Hollandia* was not subject to the 1973 regime (see Marsden 1978). The potential for drawing upon both archaeology and history in developing interpretations of post-medieval wrecks has been pointed out repeatedly (e.g.

Muckelroy 1976; Gawronski 1991; Parthesius 1987), but again, the only sites in which such techniques have been are ones that were not protected under the 1973 Act, notably the Armada wrecks investigated by Martin and Wignall (e.g. Martin, C. 1975; Wignall 1975 b). While the archaeologists working on designated sites were certainly exposed to more interpretative enterprises, they do not appear to have taken them to heart.

In sum, interests expressed in the early 1970s characterised the investigation of wrecks protected under the 1973 Act from its inception to the present day. It is difficult to say whether the presumed relevance of wreck sites was transmitted by the archaeological community or by the administration of the 1973 Act. Nonetheless, there is sufficient coincidence between the views of the MPs and the products of 30 years of archaeology underwater to infer that the expectations of 1973 constrained the aspirations of people who worked under the regime established at that time. It may not be too great an exaggeration to state that under the 1973 regime, archaeology underwater has become a discipline resigned to – and characterised publicly by – the use of ancient material as a repetitious proof of method. Notwithstanding the tremendous allure of shipwrecks, the (in)significance of designated wrecks in UK society suggests a past that offers little excitement and few challenges.

The attribution of specific categories of significance to protected wrecks at a systemic level is structured by negotiation of meanings in the course of communication in unfamiliar circumstances and between dissimilar groups. In Section 2.2.1 I showed that communication between archaeologists and non-archaeologists was problematised by dissimilar structuring of their respective environments, resulting in frustration on the part of archaeologists and disillusion on the part of non-archaeologists. It was also noted, however, that certain points of commonality could – with care – be used to establish meaning. In the case of archaeology underwater in the UK in the early 1970s, as examined in Section 2.2.2, meaning coalesced around a common conception of evident problems in terms of salvage law. This conception appeared to constrain archaeologists' and MPs' ability to envision alternative modes of management, resulting in an administrative regime that enshrined some of the least desirable characteristics of salvage law.

The struggle to establish meaning is attributable to the inherent distinctiveness of each individual's conception of any particular sign. The constitution of signs was explored with reference to direct perception, dwelling and the relationship between practical and discursive consciousness, showing that people's engagement with the world takes place through a succession of interpretative leaps that are incorporated subliminally as a lived-in 'environment'. Identification of this process was used to illuminate problems that can occur as each archaeologist extends from method to material to knowledge in apprehending the past.

In the following Chapter, I examine the same set of relationships – between individual, group and system – in respect of domination.

3. DOMINATION: STRUCTURES OF POWER IN ARCHAEOLOGY UNDERWATER

I turn now to the second structuring principle – domination – in order to demonstrate how resources are generated and how they are mobilised in unequal relationships. I also consider how such mobilisation in unequal relationships can constrain (and enable) people's capacity to engage with ancient material.

3.1 Resources

Agency (see Section 1.4) supposes the existence of resources, that is to say things that are manipulated by individuals in the course of intervening in events in the world. Resources, as a component of structure, only exist in their instantiation, i.e. only insofar as they are applied. Consequently, the conception of resources advocated here is quite different to that commonly found in references to cultural resource management (e.g. Schiffer and Gumerman 1977) and archaeological resource management (e.g. Hunter and Ralston 1993; Knudson 1982). Such accounts conceive of 'the resource' as having some kind of independent existence, at least up until the present, when 'it' *requires* management. The presumed independence of the resource does not preclude an acceptance that ancient material is multifaceted (see Carver 1996; Darvill 1993; Darvill 1995; Schiffer and Gumerman 1987: 241-247). However, the variety of interests that people have in ancient material as researchers, conservationists, treasure hunters, collectors, religious groups, descendants and so on are seen to be exactly that – multiple facets of a unitary gem waiting to be unearthed. In contrast, the approach adopted here considers the facets to lie in the eye of the beholder, not in the ground. Hence, 'value' or 'significance' arise only from engaging with ancient material in the course of agency.

Three forms of engagement with ancient material are particularly recurrent among the countries considered (cf. Brieur and Mathers 1996):

a) Material: the physical attributes of ancient material such as age, survival and the skill embodied in shape and decoration, are investigated.

b) Interpretative: ancient material is used to prompt interpretations about past lives, based on the residual impression of past agency upon the material.

c) Public: ancient material is handled according to its public character, although it may be owned privately.

3.1.1 Material

Concern for the material qualities of ancient material was expressed most strongly among the archaeologists I interviewed in references to the quality of preservation and associated phenomena such as the survival of organic material (see Section 2.1.4). The interviewees also referred repeatedly to the range of material preserved off a country's coast, in terms of age, function or form. Particular items were specified, as were certain sites that presented good preservation or especially dense and complex remains.

Ancient material is conceived of 'materially' irrespective of its use in gaining knowledge about the past, i.e. it generates a certain awe simply for having survived, distinct from the meanings that may be generated from such survival. However, although the physical qualities of ancient material – shape, colour, texture, smell and so on – may generate an immediate response, the response does not arise from those qualities alone, but from the archaeologist's engagement with them. The archaeologist brings to the artefact all kinds of preconceptions that are confronted or confirmed by the engagement; it is the agency of this confrontation or confirmation that instantiates the ancient material as a resource. Equally, the physical qualities of ancient material imply a commitment to their future survival, hence an archaeologist's awe at the moment of uncovering a well-preserved object may give way immediately to a sense of obligation for conserving the artefact and its relationships with the rest of the site. Again, the constitution of ancient material as a resource turns not upon its physical qualities as such, but on what a person brings to those qualities in respect of their being an archaeologist.

3.1.2 Interpretative

Ancient material is also constituted as a resource through interpretation (see Section 2.1.4). Both comparatively and historically, ship construction and details of life aboard have featured strongly in the 'resource' of ancient material situated underwater. The interviewees generally referred to specific sites or site types in relating the extent of the resource within their jurisdiction. For example, Rieth listed the following specific sites, together with their importance (in parentheses): Bon Porte (stitched planking, sixth century BC); Point Lequin (Greek ceramics); Madraque de Giens (hull structure and cargo, first century BC); St Gervais II (oldest example in France of skeleton-first construction, seventh century AD); Villefranche (late-medieval construction, sixteenth century); Aber Wrac'h (clinker construction, fifteenth century); Ploumenac (lead ingots); Baie de la Hougue (seventeenth century warships) (Rieth pers. com.). Similarly, Westenberg listed the most valuable elements of the submerged heritage as the *Vasa*, the *Kronan*, the *Jutholmen* and another merchant ship, and the Eastindiaman *Gothenburg*, though he placed more emphasis on their survival and quality as closed finds than upon their potential contribution to general interpretations (Westenberg pers. com.). Larsen used one find – a wreck of 1346 – to raise the different ways in which ancient material could be valued – citing local and national history, ship construction and trade – indicating how the same material can be engaged as a multiplicity of resources simultaneously (Larsen pers. com.). Rather than cite specific sites, Reinders and Rieck referred to the resource within their jurisdiction in terms of a series of site-types, such as medieval vessels and small trading ships of the Fifteenth Century to Seventeenth Century (Reinders pers. com.; Rieck pers. com.). Rieck also referred to harbours and ship blockages and – as did Naevestad – to submerged prehistoric settlement sites (Rieck pers. com.; Naevestad pers. com.).

Insofar as the material is referred to in relation to a 'class' of sites, then interpretation has occurred, and in this respect the material is constituted as a resource simply by labelling it. Jasinski remarked upon the contingent character of ancient material constituted as a resource through interpretation; he resisted any general evaluation of ancient material off Norway, explaining 'sometimes one piece of pottery can be of bigger interest, bigger value than a whole shipwreck' (Jasinski pers. com.).

Maarleveld also referred to types of sites in noting current 'gaps' – early medieval vessels, prehistoric sea-going vessels – yet to be filled because although the resource exists, the sites have not been discovered. His comments about the potential for discoveries of material relating to bronze-age shipping are particularly notable:

> Unlike Salcombe beach and unlike the Dover harbour [cargoes of bronze implements without any trace of the vessel (see, e.g. Muckelroy 1981 b)], when any such finds would be [made] in the Dutch coastal zone then the ship would be there, the whole thing would be kept together ... Even for plank-built boats like the Ferriby boats [see Wright, E. 1990], they don't have the design to be used on the high seas. But with those techniques you can make boats that ply the oceans, and they should be there.

(Maarleveld pers. com.)

This comment was made in January 1992; in late September 1992 a largely intact Bronze Age sewn-plank boat capable of Channel crossings was discovered in Dover (Waterman n.d.), vindicating Maarleveld's expectation. While the Dover Boat did not come into being as a resource until September (if it had 'existed' prior to discovery it might not have had sheet-piling rammed through it), seagoing bronze age sewn-plank boats were a resource in January – as far as Maarleveld was concerned – even though none had been discovered. In effect, Maarleveld was already drawing upon a class of vessels that could only be inferred interpretatively, but such interpretations may have affected his decisions concerning, for example, development proposals as if he had already encountered physical evidence. The instantiation of undiscovered ancient material as a resource is, arguably, especially common in the management of archaeology underwater because of the patchiness of knowledge of the seabed and the general invisibility of sites.

3.1.3 Public

The constitution of ancient material as a resource by virtue of its public interest may include fascination at the material's physical survival, or interest in the insights into past lives provoked by the material. The interviewees' concern for access to ancient material implies that public interest is not reducible to preservation or to knowledge, however. It remains unclear precisely how ancient material is constituted as a public resource (see Section 2.2.1), as the interviewees noted the public's general interest but suggested that such interest could be quite superficial. In Chapter Two I attributed some of the failure of archaeologists to amplify public interest in archaeology to the differences in the way in which archaeologists and non-archaeologists come to dwell in ancient material and the past. Despite the apparent superficiality of public interest, the archaeology supported with public administration, funds and regulations is far from superficial. Moreover, the emphasis placed on publication and popular dissemination by archaeologists themselves implies that they are not proclaiming the public character of the resource simply to safeguard their own jobs. Although the public's access to ancient material may be limited by charges, statutes and injunctions, and some archaeological literature may be written in a style that precludes wide appreciation, the principle that ancient material is a public resource is often assumed in management literature. However, as Carman notes 'what is not clear is where this "public interest" derives and why it is given so much emphasis in AHM' (Carman 1993 b: 8–9).

In short, there appears to be a disjunction between archaeologists' construction of ancient material as a public resource, and the public's own construction of the same material as a resource. Notwithstanding the public support for archaeology noted by some of the interviewees, it seems that such support is not proportional to the support for archaeology given by public institutions. Mr. Onslow referred to public concern expressed about the lack of protection for shipwrecks in 1973 (HC 851: 1865, see also HC 855: 1673; Mr. Sproat, HC 855: 1665). Nonetheless, it seems that popular support for wrecks as a public resource had little influence on the introduction and implementation of the Protection of Wrecks Act 1973, even though the statute concerned was a public act.

3.1.4 Ancient material as an authoritative resource

Giddens divides resources into two types, 'allocative' – capabilities used to generate command over objects or other material phenomena – and 'authoritative' – capabilities used to generate command over persons (Giddens 1979: 100). He provides the following examples of the major forms of allocative and authoritative resources:

[Allocative]

(a) Material features of the environment (raw materials, material power sources).

(b) Means of material production/reproduction (instruments of production, technology).

(c) Produced goods (artefacts created by the interaction of (a) and (b)).

[Authoritative]

(a) Organisation of social time-space (the temporal-spatial constitution of society).

(b) Production/reproduction of the human body (organisation and relations of human beings in society).

(c) Organisation of human-life chances (constitution of chances of self-development and self-expression).

(Giddens 1981: 51–52)

The relation between resources and materiality is complex; resources 'provide the material levers of all transformations' (Giddens 1979: 104), 'but their "materiality" does not affect the fact that such phenomena become resources ... only when incorporated within processes of structuration' (Giddens 1984: 33). The contingent character of the link between material and its qualities as a resource facilitates some useful insights into the changes that occur to material when it is 'created' as something that is ancient. Archaeologists may refer to the things that they find primarily (though not exclusively) as raw materials, means of production and produced goods in their original use, but once that material is created in contemporary society it can only be regarded as an authoritative resource. Hence, ancient material is an authoritative resource because the interpretations 'command' people (other archaeologists, the public), not objects. One danger of uncritical presentation of ancient material is that outwardly allocative features may mask authoritative qualities. For example, displays of old cannon outside a maritime museum might seem to be a collection of produced goods, but they may also imply that seafaring is predominantly concerned with fighting – an assertion about society, human relations and self-development etc. It follows, therefore, that the creation of ancient material involves processes that change material from being an allocative resource to being an authoritative resource.

It should be clear that ancient material never serves as an allocative resource, i.e. as raw material, means of production or produced goods, even if the language of allocative resources is often used in its description. The authoritative character of ancient material is implied by the comments of several of the interviewees. For example, when asked to explain the grounds for prioritising one site over another, Maarleveld, Reinders and Rieck focused upon matters of timetabling, indicating the qualities of ancient material in respect of the organisation of social time-space. The material has an immediate correlate in the amount of time that it will take to deal with it, such that it may be hard to conceive of the material without anticipating its temporal requirements. Similarly, Naevestad repeatedly emphasised the length of the Norwegian coastline and the impossibility of covering it equally, hence the need to prioritise certain areas (Naevestad pers. com.) – effectively prioritising material according to its location, such that the material is conceived of in terms of place. The authoritative character of ancient material is also illustrated by the field season of the Archaeological Diving Unit. In the course of a 5-6 month field season, the Unit must visit 25 of more than 40 sites. However, these sites are spread (albeit unevenly) from Tearing Ledge to the Out Skerries, and from Lacada Point to the Goodwin Sands (see Oxley 1995: 173). It is not surprising therefore, that in daily work the 'resource' of designated sites is conceived of in terms of how long it will take to get to each one.

Several of the interviewees indicated the qualities of ancient material in respect of organisation and relations of human beings in society, which Giddens' conceives of as the production/reproduction of the human body. Reinders, for example, related prioritisation of sites to the availability of staff; in the development-driven work in which he was involved it became a problem 'just to try to find people to do the job, because you cannot wait'. He admitted that on one occasion, during a busy winter of foul working conditions, the contents of a threatened wreck site were recovered

without recording due to the pressure on staff (Reinders pers. com.). Insofar as the ancient material was diminished by the lack of contextual information, then the lower 'quality' of the material was related directly to the lack of expertise with which it was recovered. Similarly, Christiansen and Larsen's reliance upon recreational divers within their respective regions in Denmark meant that ancient material could hardly be conceived of other than in terms of organising divers, i.e. as an authoritative resource. In these cases, the relation between the availability of personnel and engagement with ancient material is such that ancient material is conceived of in terms of anticipated staff requirements. The composition of field teams is based on the anticipated characteristics of material, hence the material is conceived of and approached primarily in terms of personnel. In this respect, ancient material is a resource that reproduces the human body.

The third respect in which ancient material can be considered as an authoritative resource is in the organisation of human-life chances (the constitution of chances of self-development and self-expression). Maarleveld suggested that, at certain stages of the development of management, the importance of ancient material might reside principally in its capacity to draw new people and agencies into an engagement with archaeology underwater: 'even if this report isn't that interesting archaeologically, you will react just to involve that new authority in ... general work' (Maarleveld pers. com.). Naevestad commented that although personally he would be most interested in finding a well-preserved medieval vessel and its cargo, the discipline might benefit far more from the discoveries of submerged prehistoric sites:

> ... lets find two or three really good stone age sites and hope that development in that direction makes everybody more conscious of what we have got, so we don't ruin it at this stage because we don't have the fantasy enough to see what's there.

> (Naevestad pers. com.)

Similarly, Christiansen felt that archaeology underwater in Denmark needed a 'golden wreck' as a catalyst in galvanising public and political opinion in support of funding for a regional approach (Christiansen pers. com.). It is not the physical characteristics of the material as such, but those characteristics drawn upon in agency in the context of specific, contingent circumstances. In these cases, the use of ancient material in opening people's eyes to the management of archaeology underwater is more important than its use in developing knowledge about the past.

It will be recalled from Chapter One that Giddens associates the theory of resource authorisation with political institutions (see Table 1.3). Insofar as ancient material is an authoritative resource, then it is appropriate to consider its mobilisation – alongside other authoritative resources – in a political arena. In the following section, I examine the introduction of the Protection of Wrecks Act 1973 in terms of the transformation of authoritative resources associated with parliamentary proceedings into an authoritative resource of protected shipwrecks. In contrast to the rôle of Congress in the passage of the Abandoned Shipwreck Act of 1987 (see Giesecke 1992: 104-105), Westminster served not simply as a passive venue of conflict resolution, but as a locale in which available resources were wrought into something new, namely 'designated wrecks'.

3.2 Power

Resources cannot be divorced from power; the creation of ancient material as a resource requires prior access to resources, and the freshly created resource adds to subsequent transactions. For example, archaeologists call on their knowledge and professional status in claiming that an old thing is ancient material; acceptance of such a claim adds to their knowledge and professional status in future interaction. Power is neither a type of act nor a resource, but the capacity to instantiate a resource – which resides in interaction:

> Power ... concerns the capability of actors to secure outcomes where the realisation of these outcomes depends upon the agency of others
>
> (Giddens 1979: 93)

In this configuration, power is a ubiquitous quality rather than something that one individual wields over another. Power is, however, characteristically imbalanced, so the relationship between agents is one of autonomy and dependence (Giddens 1979: 93). Insofar as resources are the medium of power, the recognition of archaeological resources becomes linked to the exercise of power.

3.2.1   Mobilisation of resources in 1973

The constitution of shipwrecks as a resource by way of the 1973 Bill could not have taken place if the actors concerned – principally the CNA and the Government – did not have prior access to other resources that could be mobilised within the legislative process. In the following sections, I explore the exercise of power in the management of archaeology through an account of the mobilisation of 'higher authority', fortune and Government support, Members of Parliament and political parties in constituting a resource of historic wrecks.

Higher authority

Dr. Owen indicated how attention could be stimulated by appeal to higher authority while commenting about the *Mary*: 'I wrote to the Prime Minister, and I must say he responded extremely well, and went round the Navy Department in double quick time' (HC 851: 1858). Such mobilisation of higher authority may have been crucial in initiating the switch in policy that generated the 1973 Act. Up until late 1971, the DTI Committee on Wreck was principally concerned with amending the Merchant Shipping Act. At the last moment, the agenda of its second meeting, on 4 November 1971, was changed to a discussion of separate interim legislation; papers on the protection of wrecks lying *in situ* were tabled by the DTI, and the discussion subsequently led to the introduction of the 1973 Act. The reasons for this crucial change in direction are unclear. The minutes of the CNA meeting in November state that a letter sent by the CNA Secretary (Croome) to the Prime Minister had been influential in the change of attitude (CNA Minutes 09/11/71). The letter itself was tabled, and was dated 22 October 1971. The possibility of contacting the Prime Minister had been mooted at a CNA meeting in February 1971 while discussing the need to spur things on and bring 'weighty pressure' to

bear. The minutes record that 'the Prime Minister was mentioned and Prof. Grimes thought there would be no harm in obtaining the support of the "yachtsman who steers our affairs"' (CNA Minutes 24/02/71). However, according to Wignall, the cause for the change had been an intervention by Prince Philip. Prince Philip's interest in archaeology underwater – and his potential for lobbying – had been noted by CNA in September 1971 (CNA Minutes 16/09/71) and there are other references to Prince Philip's interest (CNA Minutes 05/02/69; CNA Minutes 06/02/72; CNA Minutes 20/07/72; see also McKee 1982: 86–87). Wignall was approached by Buckingham Palace on 12 October 1971 – possibly in connection with the receipt of an award for the *Santa Maria de la Rosa* expedition from the Duke of Edinburgh, which was presented on 9 November (see Martin, C. 1975: 107) – to prepare a short paper on the legal situation and 'the sort of legislation which needs to be passed at once'. Wignall replied on 20 October with three documents – an outline of proposed legislation, a more detailed proposal and additional notes – which were duly acknowledged by the Palace. According to Wignall, Prince Philip was unable to pass these to the Prime Minister and handed them to Douglas Home who then sent them to the DTI (Wignall to Croome 15/11/71). The DTI acknowledged that it had received the three documents via Prince Philip in a letter to the CNA on 18 November, asking if CNA wanted them circulated (DTI to CNA 18/11/71).

It is, however, difficult to say whether it was the Prime Minister's or Prince Philip's intervention that prompted the DTI to change direction. Wignall's letter to Prince Philip and Croome's letter to the PM were dated 20 and 22 October respectively, and by 3 November the DTI had written to CNA about the change in agenda for the meeting on the following day. This chronology leaves less than a fortnight for the change to be conceived and put into effect. Given the brief timetable and the differences between the DTI's proposals and Wignall's suggestions, I believe that DTI had already considered measures to restrict activities on sites as an alternative to extensive state ownership. The DTI's retreat from confronting salvage law may have been prompted by the difficulties over the *Mary* that commenced in summer 1971 (see Section 2.2.2) and/or fears about the implications of state ownership of wreck in relation to pollution from shipping accidents. The DTI had cited concern over oil pollution as one of the reasons for the slow progress of the DTI's deliberations in a letter to the CNA in August 1971 (DTI to CNA 02/08/71). Moreover, the deliberations of the Wreck Law Review Committee were sandwiched between Government statements expressing concern about the possible link between Crown ownership of wrecks and responsibility for oil pollution. On 6 April 1967, the Government expressed its satisfaction with the existing law relating to wreck and salvage just as questions were being put to the Prime Minister about the cost and consequences of the loss of the *Torrey Canyon* (HC 744: 71–72w). On 28 February 1978, Clinton Davis – who had considered it premature to change the law on the recommendations of the Wreck Law Review Committee (HC 906: 708–709w, 4 March 1976) – stated, in connection with oil leaking from a wrecked trawler, that there was no statutory requirement for

DOT to establish ownership of wrecks on the seabed (HC 945: 151–152w).

Fortune and Government support

It was Sproat's good fortune to have drawn sixth place in the Ballot for Private Members' Bills (Burton and Drewry 1981: Table 8.8) which guaranteed that whatever bill he presented, it would receive an extensive debate and a vote at second reading (see Marsh 1988: 39; Richards 1977: 116–117). Important though this guarantee is, it does not follow that bills from the top six places are automatically enacted. Private Members' Bill procedures are such that progress is easily stalled, hence Marsh comments that 'such bills, even if opposed by only a handful of MPs, have virtually no chance of making progress' (Marsh 1988: 3). As a result 'ballot number is by itself an imperfect predictor of whether a bill is destined to be enacted ... even a high place on the ballot is not proof against genuine unashamed opposition' (Burton and Drewry 1981: 226, 250). Marsh adds: 'the position a bill drew in the ballot [has] virtually no influence on its passage' (Marsh 1988: 40). It might be concluded, therefore, that although Sproat's luck was important in creating the opportunity, it was not sufficient alone to secure enactment.

In general, the most significant factor affecting enactment of backbench bills is government support, or at least 'benign neutrality' (see Burton and Drewry 1981: 214, 224; Marsh 1988: 49-50). This factor was also vital to the passage of the 1973 Bill, as Mr. Sproat acknowledged (HC 851: 1849). Mr. Onslow quickly confirmed the Government's endorsement (HC 851: 1864) as well as emphasising his personal commitment to the 1973 Bill. Mr. Onslow's interest in archaeology underwater was very strong, as noted in Section 1.3. Arguably, Mr. Onslow's role at DTI was very influential in, and perhaps essential to, the introduction of the 1973 Act. Although the 1973 Bill was nominally Mr. Sproat's Bill, it had been drafted by the Government, as the Earl of Cork and Orrery stated in the Lords (HL 342: 914; see also Burton and Drewry 1981: 214; Marsh 1988: 41–48). Such a situation is not unusual, as members who have been lucky in the ballot but are short on inspiration may approach the Government Whip's office for a minor item of projected legislation (Richards 1977: 119–120). Alternatively, Sproat may have been approached directly. As Burton and Drewry point out, 'it is common knowledge that some bills are officially drafted, under the auspices either of the Law Commissions or of a government department, and handed to sympathetic backbenchers (particularly those who have won a good place in the ballot) by the whips' (Burton and Drewry 1981: 214). However, Marsh suggests that this procedure is rarer than the MP making the approach to the Whip (Marsh 1988: 43).

Lucky MPs may also be approached by interest groups, and it is conceivable that a similar bill might have come about if the CNA had chased an MP who had been successful in the ballot. This is not, however, how the 1973 Bill came about, nor is it likely that a CNA initiative would have been successful as they would probably have found it difficult to draft a bill that would have satisfied the scrutiny of even supportive MPs. As Marsh comments, 'while interest groups are an important source of bills, the success rate of such bills is considerably less than that of bills which originate from the

other two sources [Government and Law Commission]' (Marsh 1988: 62). In the event, Mr. Sproat's good fortune at the end of 1972 seems to have been a surprise to the CNA. Notwithstanding their contact with DTI, the CNA learned of the introduction of the Protection of Wrecks Bill by Mr. Sproat through a newspaper report (CNA Minutes 05/12/72), and it seems that the CNA had no previous contact with Mr. Sproat.

Notwithstanding this level of Government support, the 1973 Bill could easily have failed if it had been opposed. However, opposition was unlikely to arise from the Opposition, as Labour MPs clearly welcomed the 1973 Bill and had been involved in lobbying on behalf of the CNA on other occasions. The spiky remarks that characterised Labour Members' contributions in Committee, and a thinly veiled threat to cause the 1973 Bill to fail, were directed solely to Conservative filibustering (see below). A greater danger lay, perhaps, in certain outside interests mobilising a small number of MPs – of whatever party affiliation – to cause delay. This seems to have occurred on an earlier occasion; an attempt had been made to introduce a bill, in the winter of 1971-72, with the assistance of Brian Batsford MP. However, Mr. Batsford declined to take the bill further after – it appears – he and the relevant Minister (Anthony Grant) were approached by salvage interests (CNA Minutes 15/03/72; see also *The Guardian* 18/04/72). Although, as quoted above, Marsh dismisses interest groups' ability to generate successful bills, he notes that 'interest groups can fairly easily use the procedure to prevent private members' legislation being enacted' (Marsh 1988: 63). It is, therefore, tempting to see much of the debate as an attempt to head-off opposition in parliament from interests unsympathetic to archaeology underwater (though see Section 4.2.2), hence the need to marshal parliamentary resources as carefully as possible.

Members of Parliament

In the course of the debates a succession of Members expressed their own support for the 1973 Bill, their dismay that it had been so long in arriving, and the expectation that it would receive swift and general support without contention (e.g. Mr. Mason HC 851: 1852-3; Dr. Owen HC 851: 1857; Mr. Stewart HC 851: 1861; Mr. Faulds HC 851: 1865). It seems that their support was genuine and substantive, rather than an exercise in Parliamentary courtesy. It might be recalled that archaeological matters had been relatively high on the Parliamentary agenda in the preceding year, especially in respect of the furore over the constructing of an underground car park for MPs on the New Palace Yard site. As Jones comments 'the noise of mechanical excavators was clearly audible within the House of Commons to remind members that "history's loss is the motorised MPs' gain"' (Jones, B. 1984: 61). The crossover from terrestrial to underwater archaeology was easily made. New Palace Yard grabbed the headlines in late February 1972, just as the dispute over an exclusive contract for the *Mary* was developing. The *Mary* featured in the Royal Navy debate of 10 April 1972, while the Field Monuments Bill was heading to Standing Committee. At the Third Reading of the Field Monuments Bill, in July 1972, Mr. Dalyell – starting with a reference to New Palace Yard – closed the loop by raising the matter of the *Amsterdam*: 'does what applies on land also apply on the sea?' (HC 841: 557).

Given the heightened sensitivity of Parliamentarians to archaeological matters in the early 1970s it is not surprising that while various Members raised specific concerns, only Viscount St. Davids said anything in the 1973 debates that was critical of the Protection of Wrecks Bill. Even then the criticism was only in passing: 'I do not think the Bill as it stands is adequate for carrying out its purpose' (HL 342: 926). Many of the MPs concerned had an interest in nautical archaeology, maritime history or archaeology generally, and were amenable to approaches by CNA members. The interventions by Dr. Owen, Mr. Dalyell and Mr. Hamling in the Royal Navy debates in 1972 had, for example, followed briefing notes provided by a member of the CNA (CNA Minutes 10/05/72). The same CNA Minutes noted that other MPs – namely Mr. Faulds, Mr. Judd and Mr. Deedes – were responsive to the CNA's aims, and that Mr. Hamling (a trustee of the National Maritime Museum, HC 855: 1702) had offered to introduce a bill or to help the CNA in any way. Evidently, CNA members moved in the right circles to have direct contact with MPs, and their contacts encompassed different political affiliations. There are relatively frequent references to MPs and Lords in the minutes and correspondence of the CNA indicating the relatively high degree of access that its members had to the legislature. The 1970 Bill, for example, came about because Mr. Nott offered his opportunity to introduce a Ten-Minute-Rule Bill to Basil Greenhill (then Director of the National Maritime Museum and linked to CNA via George Naish) after having chatted to him at the London Bidefordians Dinner late in 1969 (Mr. Nott to Greenhill 10/12/69).

Political parties

Support was not drawn from one Party; while both the Nott and Sproat Bills were supported principally by Conservatives, they were welcomed by Labour members, many of whom asked Parliamentary Questions and made interventions both before and after the introduction of the 1973 Act. The bi-partisan politics of the CNA are not unusual for a pressure group, as Jordan and Richardson make clear, and CNA's access to various channels accords with their observation that 'sectional groups ... have so many other means of influencing policy-making that they tend not to rely on the vagaries of party behaviour' (Jordan and Richardson 1987: 238). CNA's bi-partisan contacts maintained avenues for both criticism and co-operation, ensured support for the 1973 Bill from both sides once it was introduced to Parliament, and guaranteed a degree of continuity as the fortunes of Governments changed. It is worth remembering that there were three general elections between Mr. Nott's Bill in 1970 and the report of the DTI Committee on Wreck in 1975.

Party agendas did, however, come into the open on 4 May 1973 during the Committee Stage of the Protection of Wrecks Bill, when there were clear indications that the timing – not the content – of the debate was being used for political ends. Mr. Hamling voiced these suspicions as follows:

I began to wonder whether the hon. Gentleman had some consideration at the back of his mind other than that of getting his Bill through. I began to wonder whether, by speaking at such length, someone might want to prevent the Heating for the Elderly Bill from being discussed, but that is perhaps supposition.

(Mr. Hamling, HC 855: 1671)

Mr. Lyon's opening statement on introducing the Heating for the Elderly Bill indicates the quandary caused to Labour members such as Mr. Hamling and Mr. Maclennan, as well as demonstrating the potentially fatal costs of gaining a small measure of protection for archaeology:

... it is clear that an issue of immense importance to 8 million pensioners, at least ½ million of whom are at risk as to life and health by the absence of proper heating in their homes, is to be frustrated by the way in which the previous Bill was dealt with. That was, no doubt, a perfectly proper Bill to bring before the House. I heard what was said in the closing speeches and I accept what was said then, but to use the device of taking that Bill in Committee on the Floor of the House at such length in order to stop proper discussion of a Bill which would provide adequate heating allowances for elderly people seems to me to be a complete negation of what this House is about.

(Mr. Lyon, HC 855: 1707)

Labour members were well aware of the device – it is a common feature of debates surrounding Private Members' legislation (see Richards 1977: 116; Burton and Drewry 1981: 226-227) – and were set to respond in kind. Consequently, the passage of the Protection of Wrecks Bill was nearly upset by manipulation of the debates for political ends:

The whole of the Opposition are as anxious as is the hon. Gentleman to see that the Bill reaches the statute book. But if he seeks to open up wide-ranging discussion about the Bill, and not only about the Bill but about the matters he told us on Second Reading were under discussion by the Wreck Law Review Committee, the Opposition will likewise be bound to consider at considerable length many of the points he is raising. That raises the question whether the House would pass the Bill today. It would be most unfortunate if we did not succeed in that.

(Mr. Maclennan, HC 855: 1692)

Mr. Sproat and Mr. Onslow rejected the implied accusation, but Mr. Sproat certainly went into considerable (and time-consuming) detail on several points. The Speaker seems to have felt that some misuse of Parliamentary time was occurring, curtailing Mr. Sproat as he initiated yet further discussion at Third Reading (HC 855: 1696). One consequence of the manoeuvring, if it were such, is that the lengthy debate included a 'fairly full account of the way in which we [the Government] see the Bill working' (Mr. Onslow, HC 855: 1676). The debate also included some important statements of policy, such as the details of the 'constitution' of the advisory board. Arguably, this detail would not have been made available if the 1973 Bill had gone through 'on the nod'. Even if much of the debate in

Committee was intended to be time-wasting waffle, it has turned out to be an accurate account of subsequent implementation.

3.2.2 The constitution of 'a resource', 1973–1995

The mobilisation of resources in the introduction of the 1973 Act was not neutral in respect of the resource of shipwrecks so produced; negotiated 'accommodations' associated with passage of the 1973 Bill were impressed upon implementation of its provisions. Although the means of protection – the 1973 Act itself – was set out in abstract as a statute of general application, the protection that would be afforded in practice was developed by the interactions of a small number of people in the CNA, Whitehall and Westminster, in advance of the 1973 Act reaching the statute book.

Number of sites

It seems that the interim legislation initially proposed to the Wreck Law Review Committee in November 1971 may have been of a blanket character. The CNA Minutes record:

> A scheduling system was being proposed as a basis for declaring certain sites protected from interference ... Scheduling would cover wreck material 100 years old or older.
>
> (CNA Minutes 09/11/71)

The CNA's understanding seems to have been mistaken, as the DTI wanted to establish protection site-by-site. The DTI approached the National Maritime Museum and McGowan was asked 'to provide an initial list of sites for scheduling apparently required to complete the draft interim legislation' (CNA Minutes 15/03/72). However, some CNA members were still pursuing the notion of blanket protection, with exceptions:

> Other members suggested that the essence of the matter was the descheduling, not the scheduling – this should reassure the general diving population – and, as a corollary, a simple blanket restriction was the most appropriate system of protection.
>
> (CNA Minutes 10/05/72)

The matter must have been clarified in ensuing discussions, because by July the CNA was being asked to accept a relatively small number of designations:

> As a matter of urgency the Sec with the agreement of as many members as could readily be reached in the past week had reassured the Department that an initial scheduling (for the Bill's introduction) of 2 dozen sites would satisfy the Council, providing subsequent scheduling after enactment was open-ended. This was endorsed.
>
> (CNA Minutes 20/07/72)

This statement implies that CNA thought the Protection of Wrecks Bill would be accompanied by a schedule specifying an initial list of protected sites, as in the original Ancient Monuments Protection Act 1882, with provision for the addition of further sites to the list in future. By the time the 1973 Bill was debated it was, however, clear that there was to be no schedule as such – though certain sites were being held

in mind (see below) – and discussion focused principally on raw numbers. Although Mr. Mason referred in the debates to five million wrecks around the UK (HC 851: 1854), the number of designations envisaged was far, far lower. Dr. Owen commented 'we do not know how many sites will have to be designated. I gather there are about six or seven round the coast' (HC 851: 1861). Mr. Sproat talked about the same order: 'I do not know how many wrecks the Secretary of State might wish to designate. It has been suggested that six or seven will be designated. It might be six or seven, it might be none, or it might be a dozen; we do not know at the moment' (HC 851: 1878). Mr. Onslow went on to set the figure, within an overall view of what it was thought would be designated:

> We anticipate that the designation of historic wreck sites will be restricted to those of special importance. They should not amount to more than half a dozen at the outset ... The number of designated sites will increase as important new sites are discovered, but it is not expected to exceed 24 in all.
>
> (HC 851: 1867)

Mr. Onslow's expectation matches the initial figure that the CNA had been asked to agree the previous July. However, it should be noted that 24 was no longer the 'initial schedule' that CNA had accepted on condition that subsequent scheduling was open-ended; rather, it was to be – in effect – an upper limit. Mr. Onslow confirmed the link between numbers and other interests by commenting that 'if there is a need to extend this figure, there will be consultation with the interests involved' (HC 851: 1867-1868). Consequently, his reference to 'special importance' might be understood as a relative measure – i.e. the top 24 – rather than a more absolute standard. It is not clear whether Mr. Sproat's remark that 'it is likely that over the years the number will be fairly considerable' (HC 851: 1878) approximates Mr. Onslow's two dozen, or perhaps hundreds or thousands (if not Mr. Mason's millions). It should be recalled, however, that the debate was conducted in terms of an interim bill and 24 sites was, perhaps, not an unreasonable expectation for, perhaps, 3-5 years. However, Mr. Sproat's reference to 'over the years' implied that even when superseded by amendments to the Merchant Shipping Act, the 1973 Act would continue to be used to protect specific sites, which implied rising numbers. Lord Kennet certainly felt that the figure could expand exponentially:

> ... I hope the Government realise the extent of the commitment which they are undertaking here, and I hope they realise how thick the other end of the wedge is ... When I was reading this Bill, and was reading the Report of the debate in the House of Commons, I was constantly reminded of the 1913 Ancient Monuments Act ... I think there were something like 15 or 20 buildings on that Schedule; and every single protection order was to be subject to Negative Resolution of Parliament. In other words, it was very close to this Bill; a tiny number of specified historic objects, each one subject to an individual order and each order subject to Parliament ... It has led on now to a situation in which we have a quarter of a million buildings listed and no question of individual orders or appeals to Parliament about it at all. The listing of historic

buildings and their protection is very big Government business now ... I wonder whether we may not expect a parallel development ... I think we may.

(HL 342: 922-923)

Lord Kennet raised a further point with respect to numbers as an amendment at the Committee stage of the 1973 Bill, suggesting the removal of the provision that every designation order should be laid before Parliament for approval. Viscount Amory, who was keen to reduce the number of orders that have to be laid before Parliament, supported Lord Kennet. Earl Ferrers replied that neither delay nor extra work was anticipated, as the orders would be subject to the Negative Resolution procedure. He added: 'I do not think his analogy with historic buildings legislation is entirely apt, because there are far more historic buildings ... than ever there would be historic wrecks or wrecks of archaeological importance' (HL 343: 316). Earl Ferrers' further comment in favour of direct Parliamentary control illustrates the perception that the 1973 Bill infringed common liberties and ought to be confined and controlled wherever possible 'by making such a designation area the Secretary of State is impinging on the freedom of people to do what they would otherwise be allowed to do' (HL 343: 316).

De-designation

Although the number of restricted areas did eventually – in 1981 – exceed two dozen, the total in 1995 was still of the same order – forty-one. Moreover, it seems that efforts were made to stay within the limit of two dozen sites specified in 1973 by de-designating certain sites. In 1973 Mr. Onslow stated with respect to the 24 sites that 'there are powers in the Bill to de-designate, so I do not anticipate a need to go above that ceiling' (HC 851: 1868). Mr. Sproat explained that the 'Secretary of State is required to revoke an order designating a restricted area if there is no longer any wreck in the area requiring protection. Again, that is only common sense' (HC 851: 1851). On 4 May Mr. Sproat gave more detail, explaining that de-designation could occur where initial evidence suggested that designation was necessary but subsequent work proved this not to be so (HC 855: 1683). The other case for de-designation presented by Mr. Sproat was 'where recovery operations at a wreck have been completed' (HC 855: 1683). This affirms the interpretation that the 1973 Bill was intended to facilitate recovery, rather than ensure the long-term survival of sites (see Section 2.2.2). It also indicates a belief that archaeological values could be dealt with, and ultimately recovered, discretely. This notion corresponds to the conception of licensing as 'salvage plus conditions' referred to below (Section 4.1.2). Lord Kennet made the clearest connection between discrete relevance and de-designation, as he expressed his understanding that: '... as wrecks were explored and archaeologised (sic), and as their valuable cargoes were lifted, then they would be de-protected' (HL 342: 922). Remarks by Mr. Onslow and Earl Ferrers (HC 851: 1870; HL 342: 932) on licence conditions carry similar implications.

The impression left by the debates is that de-designation would apply to the sites which were 'finished' and that the turnover would be such that there were never more than 24 sites designated at once. Again, the idea that designation

served simply to protect a salvor for the duration of their work is overwhelming. The mode of implementation that was announced at Westminster was carried out in the following years; the *Dartmouth*, Frenchman's Rocks (Rhinns of Islay) and *Colossus* were all de-designated using the formulae 'there is no longer any wreck which requires protection ... in the area specified'. *Dartmouth* was de-designated in 1979 (SI 1979/6), *Colossus* in January 1984 (SI 1984/2) and Frenchman's Rocks in June/July 1984 (SI 1984/802). Both *Dartmouth* and *Colossus* had been subject to extensive investigations (Martin, C. 1978; Morris 1979) and may have been considered to be 'de-archaeologised', to adopt Lord Kennet's nomenclature. However, reports of the *Dartmouth* investigations show that a substantial segment of hull structure remained on the site, along with several guns (Martin, C. 1978: 32; 41). Hence, there was wreck in the area specified. De-designation must have turned, therefore, on whether such wreck as remained required protection. According to Dromgoole, the original licensee of the *Dartmouth* was not consulted about de-designation (Dromgoole 1993: 3-17), so the grounds on which it was decided that the remaining wreck did not require protection are unclear. Damage from recreational divers seems to have continued and, consequently, the *Dartmouth* was re-designated in 1992 (Archaeological Diving Unit 1994: 27). De-designation of the site at Frenchman's Rocks is even more enigmatic, as it appears that the site was never 'de-archaeologised' by investigation during the time it was designated. Arguably, designation decisions were being constrained by the 24-site limit; the designation order affecting the *Dartmouth* was revoked at the same time as the Tal-y-bont site was designated, which would have brought the total of designated sites to 20. The *Colossus* and Frenchman's Rocks designations were revoked in 1984, which would have brought the total back down to 25 if it had not been for unexpected discoveries at Yarmouth and Studland Bay. After that point, however, the only substantive revocation (i.e. not simply an amendment to the size or position of the restricted area) concerned the *Admiral Gardner*, which was designated and then found to lie beyond the three-mile limit (SI 1986/1020).

Size of restricted areas

It may be overplaying the point to suggest that staying below the magic two dozen was the principal factor in revocation policy. However, discussion of the size of restricted areas in 1973 – and subsequent implementation – suggests a conscious effort to minimise the total area restricted by the 1973 Act, at least until 1984. In the course of the 1973 debates, Mr. Sproat noted that '... the remains of a vessel wrecked possibly centuries ago ... become scattered over the sea floor following the gradual disintegration over the years of the vessel...'. He stated ' It is for that reason that it is necessary to take power to designate ... an area round the site of the wrecked vessel, as well as what might be termed the specific site itself' (HC 855: 1666; see also the Earl of Cork and Orrery, HL 342: 917-918). Earl Ferrers noted the importance of the size of restricted areas for the purposes of policing, observing: 'This is one of the reasons why it is necessary to include around the wreck an area larger than the wreck itself so as to see who is diving within the area' (HL 342: 933). Site morphology and the practicalities of

Table 3.1: **Radii of areas restricted under the PWA 1973**

radius (m)	300	250	200	150	100	75	50
restricted areas	6	3	1	4	11	7	8

enforcement might have been expected to cause restricted areas to be expansive, but this was not the case. Mr. Sproat commented 'I am informed that it is the intention that restricted areas in relation to historic wrecks will be strictly limited in number and extent' (HC 851: 1851). Mr. Onslow specified that 'in practice I do not expect that a restricted area is likely to exceed a radius of 500 yards' (HC 851: 1868). This figure may have arisen from the terms of leases concluded by the Crown Estate; all fourteen wreck sites subject to leases off Shetland were defined as 500 yards around a point (see Henderson 1985: 191). It seems that at one stage the figure was to be incorporated directly within the 1973 Bill, as the CNA Minutes of 1 November 1970 note:

> The dropping of the 500 m radius provision to protect a site was commented on and it was felt that referring this to the Minister's discretion was quite acceptable.

(CNA Minutes 01/11/72)

Designation orders over the last 20 odd years reveal that no restricted areas of 500 m radius have ever been introduced. Although there have been some 300 m radius areas, two thirds of the restricted areas are 100 m or less (Table 3.1).

It appears that, as elsewhere, the principal aim was to minimising the impact of protection on other interests, and consequently to keep the designated areas small. Mr. Onslow made this abundantly clear: 'There will be consultations with the British Sub-Aqua Club regarding the extent of each restricted area to keep the area as small as possible...' (HC 851: 1868, see also Earl Ferrers HL 342: 929). Once again, the resource was defined in relation to other interests (see Section 4.2.2), emphasising its authoritative rather than allocative character.

Selection criteria

While the notion of selection is implicit in the contrast between the potential quantity of wrecks and the number that would be designated, very little was said about the process through which such selection would take place. Only Dr. Owen made any comment of any relevance to this matter: 'if experienced archaeologists are to visit the site and if there is to be diving on the site, there will be a requirement for survey prior to designation' (HC 851: 1860). However, he was merely stating an assumption in relation to the unavoidable costs of the 1973 Bill. No other member, including Mr. Onslow and Mr. Sproat, responded to it, hence it is not clear whether they accepted this assumption or ignored it. Very few such inspections took place until the introduction of the ADU so it might be suggested that they were not anticipating such a procedure.

Unsurprisingly, one statement of the criteria on which designation would proceed minimised the interference with recreational diving interests: 'It is not intended to designate restricted areas on a mere suspicion that an historic wreck may lie somewhere within it. We shall require physical evidence of the existence of an important wreck – for example, artefacts lying on the sea bed – before designation' (Mr. Onslow HC 851: 1868, repeated by Earl Ferrers HL 342: 930). It is not easy to reconcile this with Mr. Sproat's comment that '... the evidence before him [the Minister] will no doubt be factual and sufficient to justify designation but may fall short of the visible presence of a vessel on the sea bed' (HC 855: 1667). Mr. Onslow added to the confusion on this matter by stating 'Nor can I say whether the *Mary* would necessarily be one of the immediate sites for designation...' (HC 851: 1867). Onslow's comment suggests that even a site that played such a vital role in prompting the 1973 Bill may not satisfy the unspoken criteria that would apply. This is intriguing as on 4 May he stated 'I think something like the *Mary Rose* is a fairly obvious example of a candidate for designation' (HC 855: 1675), though once again the criteria are unspoken. It would appear that to a certain extent the Department wanted to distance itself from the selection procedure, possibly to reassure the 'other interests' that the Government was not about to dictate the designation of large amounts of sea bed, and to demonstrate that the advisory body was notionally independent. This interpretation is supported by Mr. Onslow's reluctance to say that the *Mary* should be designated, and by his comment:

> In case hon. Gentlemen feel we have had time to consider the matter and so should be able to say what would be the top priority for a designation order, I think that on reflection they may agree that we must depend on the advice of the committee ... Although we would have recommendations to put to it ultimately, what we do will depend upon what it advises that we should do...

(HC 855: 1675)

The lack of discussion of criteria by which the resource might be characterised is in marked contrast to the detail on numbers and extent and generates uncertainty and potential tension. The lack of criteria compounded the indeterminacy of the advisory board's constitution (see Section 4.3.2), resulting in an archaeological decision-making process that was opaque and which has not been clarified.

Some indication of how sites were selected for designation can, however, be gained from a number of documents in the CNA archive. The DTI's proposals in 1971 had favoured, in line with terrestrial antiquities legislation, a schedule attached to the interim bill listing the sites to be protected – including, possibly, whole 'classes' of sites, such as 'any Spanish Armada vessel' – together with the power to add further sites to the schedule (Department of Trade and Industry 1971 a; Department of Trade and Industry 1971 b). As the limit of two dozen sites was accepted in July 1972, the 'class' approach to protection had clearly been shelved, though it does seem that the proposed sites were still to be included in a schedule attached to the Protection of Wrecks Bill itself. It is not clear when the schedule was dropped in favour of

Table 3.2: **Sites considered for designation, 1973**

Site	Age	Function‡	Location	Hand-written list (CNA 1973 a)	Typed list (CNA 1973 b)	Table (CNA 1973 c)	HWR Annex* (DTI 1973 e)	Designated
Grace Lieu	14..	W	Tidal Hamble	X	X	X		05/02/74
Amsterdam	1749	M	Hastings beach	X	X	X	A	05/02/74
Mary Rose	1545	W	Spithead	X	X	X	A	05/02/74
Mary	1675	W	Anglesey	X	X	X	B	05/02/74
El Gran Grifon	1588	W	Fair Isle	X	X		B	
Adelaar	1728	M	Shetland	X	X		B	
Romney	1707	W	Scilly	X	X		C	13/03/75
Gun Rocks site	16c ?	U	Farne Is	X	X			
Kennemerlandt	1664	M	Shetland	X	X		B	01/06/78
Penlee cannon site	1691	W	Plymouth	X	X		C	31/03/78 03/01/89
Holland Fa	1743	M	Scilly	X	X		B	
Assurance	1753	W	Needles	X	X	X	D	11/04/74
More Ferriby boats	Bronze	U	Humber	X	X			
Pudding Pan wreck	Roman	M	Kent	X	X			
Resolution		W	Sussex	X	X			
Colossus	1798	W	Scilly	X	X		F	12/05/75
Anna Duchessa		U		X	X			
HMS *Ramillies*	1760	W	Bolt Tail, Devon	X	X			
HMS *Weazle*	1799	W		X	X		C	
Santa Catarina	1590	W	Aberdeen-shire	X	X		D	
Western Trader	c 1840	M	St Davids	X	X		C	
Port Isaacs spaniard	1588?	W			X			
Royal Oak	1939	W	Shetland			X		

‡ Key: W = Warship; M = Merchant; U = Uncertain

* Key: A = Strong candidates for designation; B = Possible candidates for designation; C = Doubtful cases; D = Sites unlikely to merit designation; E = Wreck sites believed to have been cleared of artefacts; F = Wrecks yet to be located.

discretionary designation, as even without a specific list it seems that the sponsors of the 1973 Bill wanted to have particular sites in mind as the Bill passed through Parliament. The 'middle road' between a schedule and broad ministerial discretion is indicated by the following comment from CNA meeting of 17 January 1973:

> Since DTI had not prepared a list of sites for scheduling and had expressed an interest in argued cases, it was agreed that a small working party should develop such a list together with priorities and documentation ... A list of sites was immediately drawn up – total about 12 – for circulating and comment.
>
> (CNA Minutes 17/01/73)

No detailed criteria for designation have been published (cf. the Secretary of State's criteria for scheduling ancient monuments (Department of the Environment 1990 b: Annex 4)), so this list and subsequent lists gives the best idea of what the CNA and the Government had in mind (Table 3.2). It seems probable that the six sites identified in 'List of Sites Recommended for Immediate Designation' were the 'six or seven' referred to by Dr. Owen and Mr. Sproat (HC 851: 1861; HC 851: 1878) as discussed above. It is notable that the first four wrecks on the hand-written sheet were the ones announced for designation on 9 August 1973 (Department of Trade and Industry 1973 b). However, the first wreck to be protected was actually the Cattewater Wreck, by the

emergency procedure, on 5 September 1973 (Department of Trade and Industry 1973 c). The Cattewater wreck was noted as a category B wreck on the DTI list. It is unclear why the same list referred to the *Assurance* as category D – 'unlikely to merit designation' – given that it was one of the six prioritised by CNA, and was eventually protected only three months after the 'top four'. An initial reluctance to designate the site may have been attributable to the lack of a prospective licensee (see Section 4.1.2). It is worth noting the *Grace Dieu* was not included on the DTI list at all; this may simply have been because no material had been reported to them, though such an answer is not wholly satisfactory. Many of the sites on the original CNA list did not make it to the DTI list, and the DTI list included many sites that the CNA did not refer to. Only 9 of the 23 CNA sites have ever been designated. However, the close correspondence between the CNA's lists and the eventual pattern of designation can be seen from Tables 3.3 and 3.4. Although the numbers and some of the specific sites are different, the general pattern is the same, with the bulk of sites lying in the sixteenth to eighteenth centuries. Of the 23 sites on the original CNA lists, fourteen were warships (W), six were merchant vessels (M) and three uncertain (U) – and five of the sites on the list of six recommended for immediate designation were warships (Table 3.5). The predominance of warships has grown in the course of implementation, resulting in the pattern apparent in Table 3.6.

Table 3.3:   **Age of sites considered for designation, 1973**

							Weazle		
							Ramillies		
							Colossus		
					Port Isaacs		*Assurance*		
					S' Catarina		*Hollandia*		
					Gun Rocks?	Penlee Can'	*Romney*		
					Gran	*K'merland*	*Adelaar*		
					Grifon				
Ferriby		P'ding Pan	*Grace Dieu*	*Mary Rose*		*Mary*	*Amsterdam*	W' Trader	*Royal Oak*
Bronze	**Iron**	**Roman**	**Med**	**C16th**		**C17th**	**C18th**	**C19th**	**C20th**
1	0	1	1	5		3	8	1	1

NB: excludes *Resolution* and the *Anna Duchessa* – not dated

Table 3.4:   **Age of sites designated 1973-1995**

					Dunwich		
					Duart P't	*Royal Anne*	
				Girona	Wrangles P'	*Hazardous*	
				Gull Rock	*Schiedam*	*Restoration*	
				Studland B'	Tal y Bont	*Northumb'd*	
				Yarmouth R	*K'merland*	*Invincible*	
				Brighton M'	*Coronation*	*Stirling Ca'*	
				St Anthony	Rill Cove	S Ed Ch'nel	
				Ba' Ledges	*Anne*	*Colossus*	
				Ch' Rocks	*Assurance*	T' Ledge	
Langdon B'y			Smalls	*Mary Rose*	Dartmouth	*Pomone*	*Iona II*
Moor Sand			*Grace Dieu*	Cattewater	*Mary*	*Amsterdam*	*Ad Gardner*
Bronze	**Iron**	**Roman**	**Med**	**C16th**	**C17th**	**C18th**	**C19th**	**C20th**
2	0	0	2	10	12	11	2	0

NB: The Erme Estuary site and the Frenchman's Rocks site include material from a number of periods, and the Pwyll Fanog site has not been dated – it appears to be medieval but may be later. Similarly, there is no date for the Erme Ingot site.

Table 3.5:   **Original function of sites considered for designation, 1973**

	Bronze	Iron	Roman	Med		C16th		C17th		C18th		C19th	C20th
							W		W		W		
							W			M	W		
							W	W		M	W		
	M		M		W	U	W	M	W	M	W	M	W
Bronze	**Iron**	**Roman**	**Med**		**C16th**		**C17th**		**C18th**		**C19th**	**C20th**	
1	0	1	0	1	1	4	1	2	3	5	1	1	

Table 3.6:   **Original function of sites designated 1973-1995**

	Bronze	Iron	Roman	Med		C16th			C17th			C18th		C19th	C20th
									W			W			
									W			W			
									W			W			
									W			W			
									W			W			
						M	U		W			W			
	M					M	U	W	W			W			
	M			U	W	M	U	W	M		W	W	M		
Bronze	**Iron**	**Roman**	**Med**		**C16th**			**C17th**			**C18th**		**C19th**	**C20th**	
2	0	0	1	1	4	4	3	2	1	9	2	9	2	0	

It will also be noted that the broad geographical spread of sites on the CNA lists is the same as that of the designated sites (see Oxley 1995: 173) – basically, Scilly - Devon - Solent - Sussex - Kent - Northern Isles - Anglesey. The exceptions are the Ferriby boats and the Gun Rocks site on the Farne Islands, both on the east coast of England. Until the Dunwich bank site was protected in 1994 there were no designated sites between the Thames and the Shetlands, notwithstanding the number of founderings on the east coast in historical periods (see Dean et al. 1992: 24–25).

In all these respects the list of sites scribbled by CNA members as they sat around a table in January 1973 is remarkably close to 'the resource' of designated sites in 1995. The 1995 tally comprises 41 sites – generally of warships – dating to the sixteenth, seventeenth and eighteenth centuries, unevenly distributed around the coast of the UK protected by restricted areas that are predominantly of 100 m radius or less. The unevenness of the resource is marked by the fact that of the 41 designated sites, 23 wrecks (including 18 warships) fall within just 158 years between the losses at Duart Point in 1653 and the *Pomone* hitting the Needles in 1811. There is, of course, no suggestion that the predominance of warships, particularly in the seventeenth and eighteenth centuries reflects either the volume of shipping or the number of founderings in those centuries. Even if there was a relationship it would be largely incidental, as there has been no explicit attempt to make designations 'representative'. Consequently, the character of the resource in 1995 is best seen as a physical expression of power relations in 1971-73.

Conventionally, the explanation for the similarity between the resource anticipated in 1973 and the resource of 1995 would be that the factors affecting discovery – the visibility of cannon, the availability of documentary sources, the pattern of recreational diving activity – were the same in the early 1970s as in the ensuing years, hence the CNA's lists are the product of an external environment that has not changed. However, this argument ignores the constructedness of the CNA's environment, which was created in the context of its discussions with DTI about numbers, lists and so on. This particular environment was abstracted in the course of negotiation into a general environment that has been re-produced ever since. The structuring of expectations has been amplified because attention has focused upon factors that prompted designation in the past, so that the ADU's field season is based around known sites even though the unit has a mandate to search for new sites. Visits and contacts relating to existing sites lead to further designations, generating a self-reinforcing 'resource'. If relations within CNA and with DTI had been different in 1973, then other factors might have prevailed. An entirely different 'resource' might have arisen if the initial designations had been based upon an analysis of historic shipping patterns, geophysical investigation or collaboration with marine developers, rather than a quick list of recent cannon finds and well-documented losses.

3.2.3 Production, reproduction and transformation

The transformation of political resources into an archaeological resource in the course of 1973 can be placed in a broader account of the creation of ancient material, which consists of three modes – namely production, reproduction and transformation (see Section 1.4). First, archaeologists who are *outside* the system of managing archaeology but who want to gain access may seek recognition of a new class of ancient material. Insofar as the archaeologists cannot draw on resources within the management system, they must draw upon external resources, i.e. resources other than ancient material. Once the ancient material is recognised within the system then it will constitute a resource in itself; hence, the ancient material has been *produced*.

Second, the recognition of a new class of ancient material *from within* the management system may *reproduce* asymmetry as archaeologists attempt to maintain their position. The act of recognition draws upon existing authoritative resources – such as expertise, reputation, achievement – but it also creates new resources by adding to ancient material. Hence archaeologists may maintain their position through continuous expansion of the classes of ancient material that are recognised, either by accommodating erstwhile unrecognised classes or by discerning sub-classes within existing classes (cf. Carman 1993 b: 133).

Third, the reclassification of previously recognised classes of ancient material indicates *transformation*, where archaeologists within the system of management seek to change an existing asymmetry in favour of their own interests. In this case, the archaeologists draw upon existing ancient material in order to recast it as a resource that they can draw upon more readily.

These three modes can be illustrated by reference to attempts to promote shipwrecks as 'heritage' in the UK from the late 1960s to the present. Thirty years ago, shipwrecks *were not* ancient material; they were beyond the concern of archaeologists and the management of archaeology. A small group of people – some archaeologists, others not – believed that shipwrecks *should* receive attention, especially as treasure hunters constituted them as a commercial resource at the time. As the people concerned and the material were largely 'outside' archaeology, then recourse was had to external resources such as newspapers, contacts and – in particular – legislation. Consequently, the account of the 1973 Act set out above emphasises the mobilisation of resources external to archaeology in order to produce a resource within archaeology.

Once constituted as a resource, shipwrecks could be drawn upon in subsequent rounds of campaigning. In this respect, the lobbying by the CNA in the late 1960s and early 1970s that culminated in the Protection of Wrecks Act 1973 can be contrasted with lobbying associated with the Joint Nautical Archaeology Policy Committee in the late 1980s. Whereas the CNA's lobbying was characteristic of the first mode – production – the JNAPC aimed at the third – transformation. In the late 1980s, shipwrecks *were* ancient material but the treatment they received was not equivalent to the treatment afforded to ancient material on land. As shipwrecks were, however, a resource, they could be used more immediately in lobbying in the 1980s than in the 1970s; established archaeologists (and civil servants) are, it would seem, more sensitive to claims about inconsistent treatment of recognised material than to claims that unrecognised material should be recognised. In this respect, the use of specific sites by the lobbying groups in the early 1970s and the late 1980s can be contrasted. Whereas in 1970 the case of the *Amsterdam* was paraded in the press, in 1991 JNAPC used case studies in a direct dialogue with the Departments concerned (Joint Nautical Archaeology Policy Committee (June 1991) 'The Merchant Shipping Act 1894: its detrimental effects on material underwater and the sites where it is found', reprinted in Dromgoole 1993: Appendix 12). In a further contrast, lobbying in the 1960s and 1970s was aimed at salvors and divers whereas in the late 1980s and early 1990s attention turned towards established archaeologists and civil servants.

Returning to the second mode – reproduction – attention might be directed to the key rôle played by a number of established archaeologists – particularly in the late 1980s – encouraging first, the election of shipwrecks to the status of an archaeological resource and second, the integration of shipwrecks within terrestrial management. The efforts of Tomalin on the Isle of Wight and Aberg at the Royal Commission on the Historical Monuments of England (RCHME) (see Croome 1988: 115–116) seem, for example, to have been crucial to advances in the management of archaeology underwater in the UK in recent years. In the course of reproduction, archaeologists draw upon existing resources – represented in this case by the Isle of Wight Sites and Monuments Record and the National Archaeological Record – and re-cast them. Although such reproduction may enhance the position of the archaeologists involved, such a strategy is not without risk to the reputations of the archaeologists concerned if their efforts fail.

So far, I have concentrated on how ancient material is constituted by negotiations concerning implementation of management policies. In such cases, implementation is relatively open to renegotiation; in the case of the 1973 Act, for example, the number of designations, the extent of restricted areas, de-designation policy and designation criteria could be changed quite easily if the appropriate resources could be mobilised. Other aspects of the 1973 regime cannot be changed so readily. For example, it is not possible to use the 1973 Act to protect ancient material other than wreck sites without further recourse to the legislative process – because the term 'site of a vessel lying wrecked' is set out in the statute. The comparative inflexibility of statutory terms means that their structural effects can be more persistent than implementation policies. Statutory terms are no less prone to negotiation than implementation policies, so they also tend to reproduce the power relations at the time legislation was enacted. The imbalanced shaping of the resource that results, can be seen by comparing the legislative terms used to define ancient material in different countries, to which I now turn.

3.3 Dominance: defining the object of archaeology underwater

In Section 3.2, I focused on relations between the CNA, DTI, parliamentarians and so on, and upon the contingent mobilisation of resources within those relations as a manifestation of power as a property of interaction. The capacity of the CNA to mobilise MPs and newspapers was linked to the position of CNA members within society, their education, affiliations, contacts and so on. Insofar as the power infusing relations between CNA and DTI related to broader fluxes of power, then it is appropriate to talk of domination: 'domination refers to structured asymmetries of resources drawn upon and reconstituted in power relations' (Giddens 1981: 28; 50). Importantly, as the relationship between the CNA and DTI gave rise to a new class of ancient material – shipwrecks – then it produced resources, and the new resources reflected the power relations through which they were produced. In short, the pattern of designated sites is a manifestation of domination in relations between CNA and DTI. The pattern of domination that inheres in designated sites continues to structure relations between archaeologists and Government, to the extent that JNAPC had to struggle against the existing administration of the 1973 Act in trying to make its case for better protection. As far as the Government was concerned, the 'resource' of 1990 confirmed the adequacy of the accommodation reached in the early 1970s: 'The Government considers that the existing provisions of the Protection of Wrecks Act 1973 have served quite well ... [the Government] is not convinced that serious damage is done to archaeological material ... simply as a result of the requirements of salvage law' (Department of the Environment 1990 c).

The abstraction of specific power relations into institutionalised patterns of domination also occurs elsewhere in Europe. It is not, however, necessary to examine the particular legislative history of each country's management regime in order to demonstrate that vestigial power relations are deeply embedded within current management. Comparative analysis shows that definitions applied to ancient material are far from functional tools that can be judged solely in terms of inclusiveness or effectiveness. Rather, such definitions convey past patterns of domination to the future by way of the resources constituted within their terms, exerting a strong structuring effect upon both collective and individual experience of ancient material.

3.3.1 Characterisation

One of the most common divisions forced upon ancient material by legislation is that between objects and features (such as assemblages or monuments). Of the seven countries considered, only France asserts a notion of ancient material that transcends such a division:

> Maritime cultural property shall comprise deposits, wrecks, artefacts or in general all property of prehistoric, archaeological or historical interest...
>
> (ACMCP 1989: 1)

The provisions of the Monuments and Historic Buildings Act (MHBA 1988) in the Netherlands also go some way towards avoiding a dichotomy because the definition of 'monument' covers objects as well. The term 'monument' includes 'all objects constructed at least fifty years ago which are of public interest because of their beauty, scientific significance or cultural and historic value' together with 'sites which are of public interest because of the presence of [such] objects...' (MHBA 1988 s. 1(a)). However, further provisions

Table 3.7:   Division between features and objects in legislation

	Features	Objects
Denmark	ancient monuments, shipwrecks (PNA 1992 ss. 12, 14)	objects, including shipwrecks (AM 1984 [1989] s. 28)
Sweden	ancient monuments (ACAMF 1988 ch. 2 s. 1)	archaeological finds (ACAMF 1988 ch. 2 s. 3)
Ireland	monument (NMA 1930 [1987] s. 2), historic wrecks (NMA 1987 s. 3)	archaeological object (NMA 1930 [1994] s. 2)
UK	designated site (PWA 1973 s. 1(1))	wreck (MSA 1995 s. 255(1))

Table 3.8:   Division between features and objects in administration

	Features	Objects
Denmark	ancient monuments, shipwrecks National Forest and Nature Agency	objects, including shipwrecks State Antiquary
Ireland	monument, historic wrecks Office of Public Works	archaeological object National Museum
UK	designated sites Department of National Heritage/Scottish Office/Welsh Office/HMBB	wreck Department of Transport

distinguish movable monuments from protected (immovable) monuments (e.g. MHBA 1988 s. 1(d)). Similarly, in Norway, the term 'cultural heritage' comprises all ancient and medieval monuments, antiquities and ship's finds (CHA 1979 s. 2), but all further protective provisions are divided between monuments (ch. II), antiquities (ch. III) and ship's finds (ch. IV). A division between features and objects is fundamental to protection in the countries listed in Table 3.7. Such divisions are also pivotal to organisational arrangements, as shown in Table 3.8.

The common division of features from objects suggests that the distinction is central to perceptions of ancient material. Insofar as the division structures both archaeologists' and non-archaeologists' approaches to the past it may be pertinent to question both its source and its effect in confirming a division between objects and features throughout society. Certainly, the apparent proclivity of ancient material to fall into one or other category might suggest that the division is essential and, therefore, unquestionable.

The flaws of the division become apparent at the point at which an object 'becomes' a feature, and *vice versa*. In Denmark 'shipwrecks' are treated as monuments, yet the provisions on objects apply equally to objects that are wreck. Hence, an apparently isolated bit of wreckage might be notified to the State Antiquary under the provisions of the Act on Museums (AM 1984 [1989] s. 28(3)), when the bulk of the wreck has already been reported to the National Forest and Nature Agency under the Protection of Nature Act (PNA 1992 s. 14(2)). Consolidating the information is, presumably, a burden that would not occur if monuments and objects were managed through the same regime. The French example suggests that there is no inherent reason why features and objects should be distinguished form each other. Fresh

legislation in France was introduced in 1989 to remove the iniquities of a preceding division that favoured the finders of objects over the finders of features, leading to the dismantling of entire wrecks into their component objects (Beix 1989: 11, 27; Firth 1992 b: 60–61). This unfortunate situation may have been attributable to the particular characteristics of the material most often encountered – amphorae can be recovered and sold discretely – though it is conceivable that other forms of erstwhile coherent (but detachable and saleable) ancient material might also suffer from dichotomous identification that affords differential appreciation. However, the practical benefits of removing the division should not draw attention from a more fundamental effect, which is that ancient material in France can now be addressed in terms of its own particularities, without first forcing it into one category or the other.

In certain respects, features and objects *do* require a generalised form of differential appreciation. For example, discovery of an apparently isolated object underwater presents the finder with a dilemma (see Section 4.1.1); if they leave the item *in situ* they may never relocate it, whereas if they remove the item it may be destabilised catastrophically. The dilemma is much less marked should a feature be discovered as, arguably, the chances of relocating it are greater and any immediate removal may destabilise the feature as a whole rather a single item. The qualitative difference in the dilemmas may be sufficient to generate separate treatment, whereby objects are exempt from non-disturbance provisions that apply to features, hence the 1994 Amendment to Ireland's National Monuments Acts allows the removal of archaeological objects that appear to be in danger (NMA 1930 [1994] s. 23).

I have used the term 'feature' to highlight the rôle of terms such as 'wreck' and 'monument' in constituting ancient material as a discrete entity. Discreteness is imposed in two ways. First, the material is separated from its physical matrix of soil, sediments and so on. This separation is mitigated by use of terms such as 'site' (Netherlands, MHBA 1988 s. 1(2); UK, PWA 1973 s. 1) or 'place' (Ireland, NMA 1987 s. 11) to implicate the entire contents of a monument, or by 'fringing' the monument or wreck, as in Norway:

> Each ancient monument includes a zone surrounding its visible or known edge as far as is necessary to protect the monument. The zone is delimited by the appropriate authority, but until the zone is delimited it comprises a 5m wide area from the visible edge.
>
> (CHA 1979 s. 6)

A similar effect is achieved in Sweden through the following provision, which avoids drawing a hard line between inclusion and exclusion. However, the provision remains focused upon the character of material as a discrete site, in this case 'ancient monument':

> An ancient monument includes a large enough area of ground or seabed to preserve the remains and to afford them adequate scope with regard to their nature and significance
>
> (ACAMF 1988 ch. 2 s. 2)

Second, the material is fenced off from the social interactions from which it emerged; 'sites' are viewed as islands of past activity surrounded by blank, irrelevant space. Wheatley has drawn attention to the capacity of Geographic Information Systems (GIS) to overcome this structuring effect of 'sites' by encourage archaeologists to perceive ancient material (and the activities presumed to have structured it in the past) not as a series of discrete entities but as a 'spatially discontinuous variable' (Wheatley 1995). In archaeology underwater the fencing-off of ancient material is sometimes expressed as the notion that the location of wrecks is 'accidental', obscuring the network of social relations that cause a vessel to be in a particular place when the mishap of wrecking occurs.

The isolation of ancient material from social interaction may be remedied by protecting abstract areas rather than self-encompassing terms such as site, object, monument or wreck. An area defined by co-ordinates and distances does not pretend to any connection with ancient material other than spatial coincidence. Consequently, an abstract area need not impose any meaning on the material, indicating only that a different form of behaviour is appropriate within its limits. Insofar as protection of an area will impinge upon activities that pose no threat to the material, then there will be pressure to limit such areas and to justify their boundaries, as occurred in negotiation of the extent of restricted areas in 1973 (see Section 3.2.2). However, if the area approximates to the physical extent of the material, or if the area itself is given archaeological meaning – as, for example, a 'historic landscape' – then the distance achieved between protection and meaning will break down.

The principal benefit of area-based definitions is that *a priori* interpretation and enforced discontinuity are circumvented, but such definitions also have certain practical advantages that should not be ignored. For instance, areas avoid the problem of distinguishing a small feature from a large object. Moreover, ancient material underwater is rarely visible to water-users, nor is position-fixing precise enough for them to skirt specific points; designation of a broad avoidance area reduces the risk of inadvertent damage. Furthermore, policing is easier if activities within an area are prohibited rather than damage to the ancient material itself (cf. Mr. Onslow, HC 851: 1868).

The UK makes the most extensive use of abstract areas: over 40 have been designated under the Protection of Wrecks Act, 1973. However, the 1973 Act is currently the sole form of statutory protection being applied to archaeological sites underwater in the UK; the more limited use of abstract areas in the other countries arises because such areas are just one layer within a tiered protective framework (Table 3.9).

Although abstract areas are used quite extensively, they are – with the exception of the UK – only supplementary to systems that are based preponderantly on a division between features and objects. Moreover, the use of abstract areas seems attributable principally to their practical advantages rather than a desire to avoid *a priori* interpretation and division of ancient material. Such structuring effects could be

Table 3.9: Examples of abstract areas

Ireland	areas may be delineated around wrecks and archaeological objects through an 'underwater heritage order' (NMA 1987: 3(1))	*Lusitania* (OPW 1995), *Aude* and the *Leinster* under consideration (Kelly pers. com.)
France	specific sites may be protected by local acts	the site of the Battle of Saint Vaast-la Hougue is subject to an *Interdiction de plongée par arrête prefectoral du Prefet maritime de Manche Atlantique* (Brest) (Division des Recherches Archeologiques Sous-Marines 1991)
Denmark	the Minister may make regulations prohibiting certain activities within 100 metres of a specified ancient monument or wreck (PNA 1992 s. 14(4))	*St George, Crescent* and *Danneborg* subject to regulations that prohibit sports diving (Rieck pers. com.)
Sweden	the State County Administration may issue regulations for the protection of an ancient monument or a place where archaeological finds have been discovered (ACAMF 1988 ch. 2 s. 9)	s. 9 regulations have been applied to the *Svanen* and to the blockage at Birka, among other sites (Forsberg pers. com)
Norway	the Ministry may make a resolution to protect a zone around an ancient monument or ship's find (CHA 1979 s. 21).	

alleviated if abstract areas were less closely linked to size and to specific concentrations of material.

3.3.2 Exemplary lists

A concern for discrete items is especially striking in the legislation of Norway, Sweden and Denmark where monuments are defined by reference to a list of feature types (CHA 1979 s. 4; ACAMF 1988 ch. 2 s. 1; PNA 1992 s.12 (2), Annex (parts 1 and 2)). The lists are paradoxical because on one hand they focus upon physical attributes abstracted from their relict social relationship, while on the other they impose an interpretation upon the physical attribute. For example, in Norway one category of monuments is as follows:

> d. Roads and all other tracks ... dams and weirs, bridges, fords, harbour works ... landing places ... landmarks for use on land and at sea.

> (CHA 1979 s. 4(d))

To some extent this clause can be read as a series of physical attributes – features that cross land and rivers, enclose water, afford access to water and so on – with the emphasis on protecting the attributes rather than the information such attributes might yield about past activities. However, many of the terms used to describe the attributes in each of the three statutes imply specific activities. Such terms impose an *a priori* interpretation upon the physical attributes, based on contemporary notions about the use of certain features. The imposition of an interpretation is particularly striking in the following example from Sweden:

> 4. places of assembly for the administration of justice, cult activities, trade and other common purposes

> (ACAMF 1988 ch. 2 s. 1(4))

The ambiguity of many features may impede either protection, or reinterpretation. For example, a row of stones projecting into the water could prove problematic. Would it be necessary to prove that the stones were a harbour work in order that protection might apply? Would protection on that basis preclude any reinterpretation of the stones as a place of cult activity? What would be the position if the stones showed signs of having been both a harbour work and a cult

site? Arguably, there will be no difficulty so long as the lists are sufficiently comprehensive to meet all possible attributes and activities, but this argument presumes an extraordinary capacity to anticipate everything that might be discovered. The Norwegian law provides an escape clause, allowing the Ministry to make a decision as to what constitutes an ancient monument in cases of doubt (CHA 1979 s. 4). Moreover, in respect of antiquities, the Norwegian list is exemplary rather than definitive:

> Objects from Antiquity and from the Middle Ages ... *such as* weapons, tools, cult objects and stones, pieces of wood or objects of other materials with pictures or inscriptions, remains of buildings found apart from the buildings or remnants of these, furniture, church inventory, jewellery, archive material, skeletons and parts of skeletons and the like.

> (CHA 1979 s. 12, my emphasis)

The examples suggest not only that these types of material are commonly found or anticipated, but also that they are admitted as ancient material automatically; the lists of types provided are summarised thematically in Table 3.10. It might be argued that not only is *a priori* interpretation inherent in the lists of monument types, but that the interpretations imposed are predicated upon a functionalist paradigm. Functionalism, or even *a priori* interpretation, does not cover all of the types listed, however. Sub-section six of the Swedish provision cited above indicates a particular interest in highly visible architectural 'gems':

> 6. ruins of fortresses, castles, monasteries, church buildings and defence works, and also of other remarkable buildings and structures;

> (ACAMF 1988 ch. 2 s. 1(6))

This example, and some of the other types, might also be read in terms of the interests of certain predominant groups, notably the church and the army, in the identification of monuments associated with their particular past and/or activities.

Table 3.10: **Types of sites specified in legislation**

	Norway	Sweden	Denmark
	CHA 1979: 4	ACAMF 1988: ch. 2 s. 1	PNA 1992: Annex
burial	j	1	1(1), 1(2)
settlement	a	5	2(9)
worship	a, f, h	3, 6	1(6); 2(6)
defence	e	6	1(4), 1(5)
transport	d	7	2(3); 2(7)
food production	c		2(1)
industry	b	5	
art (notably rock art)	g	2	1(8), 1(9)

Lists of site types are also used in Ireland and the UK, where monuments are defined as:

a. any artificial or partly artificial building, structure or erection or groups of such buildings, structures or erections;

b. any cave, stone or other natural product whether or not forming part of the ground, that has been artificially carved, sculptured or worked upon, or which ... appears to have been purposely put or arranged in position;

c. any, or any part of any, prehistoric or ancient tomb, grave or burial deposit, or ritual, industrial or habitation site;

d. any place comprising the remains or traces of any such building, structure or erection, any such cave, stone or natural product or any such tomb, grave, burial deposit or ritual, industrial or habitation site,

(NMA 1987 s. 11)

a. any building, structure or work ... and any cave or excavation;

b. any site comprising the remains of such building, structure or work or of any cave or excavation;

c. any site comprising ... the remains of any vehicle, vessel, aircraft or other movable structure or part thereof ...

(AMAA 1979 s. 61(7))

Although both definitions do involve some *a priori* interpretation (ritual, habitation or industrial site, and – arguably – vehicle, vessel, aircraft), the definitions are far more abstract than the Scandinavian examples, focusing principally upon the physical attributes of the material. The definitions concentrate upon the feature rather than social relations, but they do not preclude interpretation and reinterpretation. One drawback is that the emphasis on features in the UK legislation and also the Netherlands – monuments are 'all objects *constructed* at least 50 years ago ... (MHBA 1988 s. 1(b)(1), my emphasis) – militates against protection of ancient material pertaining to populations that did not 'build', e.g. Palaeolithic people (Wenban-Smith 1995). In this respect the interpretative categories that are concerned with past activities offer certain advantages; the interpretative references to activity in the Norwegian and

Swedish legislation, and the Irish example cited above, would overcome the problem.

3.3.3 Generic terms

Although abstract terms for ancient material such as building, structure or work (AMAA 1979 s. 61(7)) avoid excessive *a priori* interpretation they are, as the Palaeolithic example demonstrates, selective evaluations nonetheless. The term 'coin' is a further example, emphasised in the Norwegian case by an age differential that constitutes coins as antiquities if earlier than 1650 AD, as compared to the bulk of antiquities which must date prior to 1537 AD (CHA 1979 s. 12). The paradox of interpretative labels referred to above also applies to 'coins'; the term restricts the object to a certain use and simultaneously obscures the variety of meanings that might be placed upon such use. A 'coin' is not a 'token', but what does that reveal about exchange, inflation, payment, hoarding, banking, extortion, tribute and so on? Why then should coins be singled out? I consider the effect of generic definition with reference to 'wreck' and related terms, not least because of the close association between wreck and archaeology underwater. Of the seven countries considered, all but the Netherlands make specific reference to wreck or similar (Table 3.11).

Wreck broadly covers the remains of vessels, their fixtures and fittings, cargo and other former contents. However, the precise wording of the reference to wreck may generate inconsistencies in some instances. For example, a disparity in the time periods applicable to ship's finds and to antiquities/ancient monuments in Norway caused a problem in protecting the *DS Edith*, a wreck in Oslo Fjord containing Staffordshire pottery. Although the vessel was built more than 100 years ago, its cargo is less than 100 years old. Consequently, the Ministry of Environment gave its opinion that even though the vessel itself was protected, the cargo was not (Naevestad pers. com.). Similarly, doubts are sometimes voiced over designation of sites at Langdon Bay and Salcombe where Bronze Age metalwork has been found but no 'wreck' (Burr pers. com.). Although the cargo and contents of a vessel may contribute to the interest of a site designated under the 1973 Act (PWA 1973 s. 1(1)(b)), it is the suspicion that the area contains a wrecked vessel that warrants designation (PWA 1973 s. 1(1)(a)). A lost cargo alone could not be protected.

Table 3.11:   References to wreck, etc.

Sweden	wrecked ships ... (ACAMF 1988 ch. 2 s. 1(8))
Ireland	'Wreck' means a vessel, or part of a vessel, lying wrecked on, in or under the sea bed or on or in land covered by water, and any objects contained in or on the vessel and any objects that were formerly contained in or on a vessel and are lying on, in or under the sea bed or on or in land covered by water. (NMA 1987 s. 1(1))
Denmark	Wrecks of ships ... as well as cargoes and parts of such wrecks ... (PNA 1992 s. 49(2))
	Objects, including shipwrecks ... (AM 1984 [1989] s. 28(1))
Norway	Ship's finds ... boats ... hulls, gear, cargo and all else that has been on board, or parts of such objects ... CHA 1979 s. 14
UK	any site comprising ... the remains of any ... vessel ... or part thereof (AMAA 1979 s. 61(7))
	'wreck' includes jetsam, flotsam, lagan and derelict (MSA 1995 s. 255(1))
	any site ... that ... is, or may prove to be, the site of a vessel lying wrecked on or in the sea bed (PWA 1973 s. 1(1))
	any objects contained or formerly contained in it which may be lying on the sea bed in or near the wreck (PWA 1973 s. 1(1))
France	Maritime cultural property shall comprise deposits, wrecks, artefacts or in general all property of prehistoric, archaeological or historic interest ...(ACMCP 1989 s. 1)

Such problems are avoided in the Netherlands as wreck is held to fall within the existing terms of the legislation. The problems that arose in the mid-1980s were concerned with the jurisdictional extent of that legislation, not with its subject. Consequently, the interpretation of the statute was simply clarified such that ancient material in the sea was covered – there was felt to be no need to refer specifically to wreck (MMA/Mo-1497).

In France, wreck is referred to specifically but in such a way that there is no difference in the measures that apply; wreck is an integral element of maritime cultural property. Similarly, the Ancient Monuments and Archaeological Areas Act 1979 in the UK equates vessels with other types of monument. In Denmark and Sweden, wrecks are given treatment that is largely equivalent to any other monument, except in that different age limits (100 years) apply. However, in Sweden wrecks and non-wrecks are subject to contrasting presumptions concerning permits to displace, alter or remove ancient monuments (ACAMF 1988 ch. 2 s.12), though the purpose of the contrast is not clear. The Swedish legislation makes specific reference to shipwrecks in subsections to a number of general provisions (e.g. ACAMF 1988 ch. 2 s. 8). In contrast, Norwegian provisions on shipwrecks have been largely kept together (see CHA 1979 s. 14), though the provisions are roughly equivalent to those on monuments (with the exception of an age differential). In Ireland, the provisions on wreck are largely distinct from those that apply to monuments and archaeological objects (see NMA 1987 s. 3). In the UK entirely separate legislation applies, namely the 1973 Act and the Merchant Shipping Acts, though insofar as the 1979 Act makes provisions for vessels and for the territorial sea then wrecks and non-wrecks could be integrated within the same regime (see AMAA 1979 s. 61(7)).

Why should wreck be singled out? Insofar as no effective distinction is made in the Netherlands or in France, why is a distinction necessary in the other countries? Three possibilities can be suggested. First, the physical character of wrecks might be sufficiently different to other forms of material to warrant distinct provision. However, the many examples of successful investigation of wrecks and other maritime structures by terrestrial archaeologists within terrestrial regimes undermines any argument for separate provision for wreck on such grounds. Second, material discovered in the sea is subject to different legal regimes to material found on land, especially in relation to ownership and salvage. Nonetheless, several of the countries considered have successfully included provision for ancient material at sea within terrestrial antiquities legislation. Third, insofar as submergence is a defining characteristic of archaeology underwater because of its effect on working practices, certain matters such as safety, visibility and position fixing have legal implications. These matters do not respect a wreck/non-wreck distinction and, moreover, there are strong parallels with the management problems facing material under alluvium or in wetlands (see van de Noort and Davies 1993: 93; 131–135). In sum, each of the possible reasons for distinguishing wreck from non-wreck within antiquities legislation has been overcome by at least one of the countries considered. The legal distinctions that remain can generate

contradictory administrative repercussions that respect neither the environment of the find nor its maritime/non-maritime character. In Norway, for example, 'bars [blockages] made of sunken vessels' subject to provisions on ancient monuments (CHA 1979 s. 2(d)) – to be dealt with by archaeological museums – are separated from other sunken vessels, which are dealt with as ship's finds (CHA 1979 s. 14) that fall under the remit of maritime museums (see 4319 C-080.22/91 HKH/HS; see also Section 5.1.2). Overall, reference to wreck as a generic type of material seems to carry several disadvantages and no advantages, prompting the conclusion that distinctions between wreck and other ancient material are an anachronism attributable to the vagaries of legislative histories and the power relations imbued within them.

3.3.4   Specific sites or objects

There is some provision in each of the countries considered for protection of specified examples of ancient material. In the UK protection of named sites is the principal basis of statutory protection; a 'scheduled monument' is ancient material that is protected because it is listed on the Schedule, and the Protection of Wrecks Act 1973 provides for protection of ancient material only in specified locations. In the Netherlands, 'protected monuments' are only those monuments that are recorded in a register maintained by the Minister (MHBA 1988 s. 1). However, registration is complemented by broader measures requiring reporting of monuments (MHBA 1988 s. 47) and prohibiting unlicensed excavations (MHBA 1988 s. 39). In addition, the Netherlands' Cultural Heritage Protection Act 1984 (CHPA 1984) provides for registration of objects and collections of objects. Although the terms of the Act encompass archaeological material, its principal purpose is to protect 'works of art' and it has not been invoked in relation to ancient material from underwater (Maarleveld pers. com.). In Ireland, France, Denmark and Sweden provisions for specific sites are supplementary to the principal forms of protection, and are largely concerned with protecting zones around ancient material, as discussed above. In Norway the Minister may make a binding decision concerning what constitutes an ancient monument or an antiquity in cases of doubt, and may decide that specific monuments or objects shall be protected even if they do not satisfy age criteria (CHA 1979 ss. 5, 12).

The attribution of importance is inherent in the practice of specifying sites for protection. Selection does not arise automatically whatever criteria are used; a further act of designation, registration or listing is required. The optional character of this act – the Minister *may* designate/include (MHBA 1988 s. 3(1); PWA 1973 s. 1(1); AMAA 1979 s. 1(3)) – introduces a second level of selection that adds to the material that is selected but detracts from that which is not, even if it meets the first tier of criteria. All monuments are equal, but some monuments are more equal than others.

Insofar as designation etc. rests on the Minister's volition, it may be difficult to identify the criteria that are drawn upon. In the case of the 1979 Act, the Department of the Environment has published the Secretary of State's criteria for scheduling monuments. There are no published criteria for the 1973 Act but, as discussed in Section 3.2.2, lists of designated sites do indicate some common characteristics, implying that implicit criteria are in use.

3.3.5 Qualifiers referring to age or value

A number of terms are also used to qualify the significance of material. Scientific interest is posited in Norway (CHA 1979 ss. 5, 21) and the Netherlands (MHBA 1988 s. 1(b)(1)). Arguably, the references to prehistoric, archaeological and – possibly – historical interest mentioned above also carry a scientific connotation. References are also made to beauty (MHBA 1988 s. 1(b)(1)) and artistic interest (PWA 1973 s. 1(1)(b); AMAA 1979 s. 61(12)(b)). Aesthetic values may also prevail in use of the term 'culture' (CHA 1979 s. 2; MHBA 1988 s. 1(b)(1)). References to architectural interest (AMAA 1979 s. 61(12)(b); CHA 1979 s. 2) may arise from the application of general acts to standing buildings, though the qualification might be relevant to megalithic structures and, as naval architecture, to ship structures. Only the Norwegian legislation makes reference to the value of ancient material as a feature of day-to-day life, permitting protection of a zone: '... in so far as this is necessary to preserve the effect of the Monument etc. in the landscape or in the environment...' (CHA 1979 s. 21). The same statute expresses an interest in 'memory', as it permits the protection of official monuments and other locations with important historical associations (CHA 1979 s. 5). Moreover, 'monuments' comprise places with which tradition, belief, legends or customs are associated (CHA 1979 s. 4(f)). Similarly, Swedish legislation makes provision for places associated with ancient customs, legends and cults (ACAMF 1988 ch. 2 s. 1) and the reference to traditional interest in AMAA 1979 s. 61(12)(b) imply that contemporary memories may acquire value through protection.

Many of the countries considered use age as a qualifier, and references have already been made to it above (Table 3.12).

As a qualifier, age is generally underspecified, so the purpose of the qualification is unclear. However, several reasons can be postulated that appear to be supported by the wording used. First, age may imply abandonment, i.e. that no one is likely to put in an ownership claim that has to be contested or compensated by the state. A concern for subsisting rights of original owners is apparent in most of the statutes considered, for land and sea, with clear statements to the effect that claims of state ownership are subservient to the claims of genuine owners. In Sweden, for example, abandonment is an integral part of the definition of ancient monuments:

> Permanent ancient monuments are the following traces of human activity in past ages, having resulted from use in previous times and been permanently abandoned.
>
> (ACAMF 1988: 2, 1)

Consequently, age limits may serve as quarantine period after which it is relatively safe to assume that abandonment has occurred. A quarantine period marked by a date may also sever the past from the present, so that definition brings to an end the type of behaviour that was associated with the thing in its earlier use, demanding 'archaeological' behaviour henceforth. Such a change in behaviour will be difficult to identify in respect of living traditions, so an arbitrary date might remove ambiguity. Clearly, the imposition of a date by one set of people upon another will be an exercise of dominance. The different ages at which Saami (100 years) and non-Saami materials (1537 AD) qualify as monuments and antiquities in Norway (CHA 1979 ss. 5, 12) might be investigated from this point of view. The process involved in terminating one set of behaviours and insisting upon another are best illustrated in reverse, i.e. when preferred archaeological behaviour is rejected, hence western horror at the 'destruction' of material upon its return to participants in living traditions (see Ucko 1990 [1994]: xvii).

Table 3.12:   Age as a qualifying term

Denmark	... which are considered to have been wrecked more than 100 years ago (PNA 1992 s. 14(2))
UK	For the purposes of the Merchant Shipping Act, historic wreck is defined as items which are over 100 years old. (Coastguard Agency 1994 a) [NB: this is an administrative rather than statutory definition]
Ireland	1700 AD or such later date as the Minister may appoint (historic monument)
	... wreck (being a wreck which is more than 100 years old) (NMA 1987: 3(4)). There is no limit for Underwater Heritage Orders
Netherlands	50 years (MHBA 1988 s. 1(b)(1))
France	prehistoric, archaeological or historic interest (ACMCP 1989 s. 1)
Sweden	shipwrecks –if at least one hundred years have presumably elapsed since the ship was wrecked (ACAMF 1988 ch. 2 s. 1(8)). The other categories of monument are not defined by age.
	Archaeological finds ... found in other circumstances and are presumably at least one hundred years old (ACAMF 1988 ch. 2 s. 3(2))
Norway	a. Objects from Antiquity and the Middle Ages (up to 1537).
	b. Coins from before AD 1650
	c. Saami antiquities which are more than 100 years old.
	and it may be decided that an object shall be considered an antiquity irrespective of date. (CHA 1979 s. 12)
	... boats more than 100 years old (CHA 1979 s. 14)
	Monuments from Antiquity and the Middle Ages (up to 1537 AD). Sites in the ten categories may be protected as ancient monuments irrespective of age if scientific or cultural-historical reasons dictate, if they are official monuments or they are locations with important historical associations. (CHA 1979 s. 5)
	Buildings from more recent times (post-1537) may be protected. The protection resolution may apply also to ... bridges ... quays and other industrial monuments. (CHA 1979 s. 15)

An age limit may be used to imply, simply, old-ness. General references to 'prehistoric' (ACMCP 1989 s. 1) and to 'archaeological' (ACMCP 1989 s. 1; PWA 1973 s. 1(1)(b); AMAA 1979 s. 61(12)(b)) may also serve to imply age. Such a qualification allows non-archaeologists, insofar as they are equipped with an intuitive grasp of what is old and what is young, to recognise that the material that they are faced with is subject to controls. A hard definition of what is the past, i.e. a cut-off date or a rolling period, may create a discontinuity in otherwise seamless pasts. Intuitive consideration of the instant at which something passes from the past into the present may also generate the impression that ancient material is valued principally according to its age. In turn, this impression may give rise to the assumption that material becomes more significant with age, and that recent material is less important.

Finally, age limits may refer to dates of historic significance to contemporary society. For example, legislation in Ireland refers to 1700 AD and in Norway to 1537 AD. Whereas the first seems relatively arbitrary – about 300 years but without the drawback of a rolling period – the latter corresponds to the Reformation in Norway. Ucko has cited South African use of a cut-off date (1652) as an example of disenfranchising groups and societies of their own pasts (Ucko 1989 a: xi). More general use of the term 'history' within qualifying criteria may have a similar effect, especially if 'whose' history is not specified. 'History' or 'historical' is found in many of the statutes considered (Table 3.13). Unsurprisingly, the meanings of 'historic' and 'historical' are not specified in the statutes. The ambiguity might be read pragmatically as a means of facilitating flexible implementation, but this begs the question as to whose interests are served by such flexibility.

I have shown that the terms used in legislation serve to constitute ancient material in terms of dominant interpretations, in that certain types of material are identified rather than others and particular ideas about past relevance are impressed upon the material selected. Preferential preservation of legally constituted ancient material serves to embed such dominant interpretations within people's environments where, as locale, they can structure perspectives and practice at a subliminal level. Some forms of terminology – such as abstract areas and exemplary lists – are less exclusive than other forms, and inconsistency in the use of legal terms suggests that the effect is not intentional. However, in the context of some forms of definition – those dealing with 'national' importance, for example, as I shall show in Chapter Five – the effect may constrain people's capacity to conceive of alternative pasts, and futures.

The way in which dominance comes about can be addressed through an analysis of power, as I have shown in respect of the introduction of the Protection of Wrecks Act 1973. In this example, 'political' resources such as Government support, access to MPs and party politics were transformed into a new archaeological resource, in the form of a very particular collection of sites that has endured well beyond the moment of its origin in 1973.

The potential for a persistent archaeological resource to arise from transient political resources is explicable in terms of a distinction between allocative and authoritative resources. Although ancient material has an outwardly allocative character – as the relics of raw materials, technology and produced goods, for example – it is more properly regarded as an authoritative resource as ancient material commands people – through the constitution of social time-space, human relations and life-chances – rather than objects. As an authoritative resource, ancient material is quite readily mobilised in conjunction with other authoritative resources, such as the political assets referred to above.

Referring back to the matrix set out in Chapter One, however, the management of archaeology underwater is characterised solely by the interplay of resources, power and dominance no more than it is by the interplay of signs, meaning and significance. In the next chapter, I continue my analysis of the management of archaeology underwater through an exploration of the structuring of rules, trust and legitimacy.

Table 3.13:   Use of 'historic' and 'historical' etc.

UK	historical (PWA 1973: 1(1)(b))
	historic ... (AMAA 1979 s. 61(12)(b))
Norway	from the point of view of the history (CHA 1979 s. 2)
Ireland	... associated with the commercial, cultural, economic, industrial, military, religious or social history of the place where it is situated or of the country ... (NMA 1987 s. 1(1))
Netherlands	historic value (MHBA 1988 s. 1(b)(1))
France	historic interest ... (ACMCP 1989 s. 1)

4. LEGITIMATION: ACHIEVING TRUST

In this chapter, I explore why people act 'archaeologically' without being coerced, bribed, duped or deceived. In other words, I want to examine the dimension of social behaviour that constitutes legitimation – structured rule-following that is not reducible to a response to resources or to signs. Voluntary compliance is not readily comprehended by analyses that rest wholly upon the study of meaning (e.g. Chapter Two) or of power (e.g. Chapter Three), especially in respect of managing archaeology in relatively transparent societies where policing and enforcement are difficult, notably at sea. In the following sections, I demonstrate why people meet expectations about behaviour even when they are aware that disobedience is unlikely to be punished, and when there is no apparent incentive to the behaviour desired – i.e. there is neither carrot nor stick, nor deception. I consider behaviour on three levels of integration, corresponding to the matrix set out in Section 1.4. First, the incidence of rules that individuals follow by their own volition, beyond the immediate influence of other people. Second, the development of trust between people in the course of face-to-face interaction. Third, the formation of legitimacy, i.e. of behaviour that is expected throughout society, irrespective of the particularities of time and place.

4.1 Rules

In Section 2.2.1 I discussed differences between archaeologists and non-archaeologists in terms of their perceptions of ancient material; here I want to examine such differences in terms of behaviour. I contend that 'archaeologists' are not identified solely because of their interest in ancient material, but also by virtue of rules of behaviour – personal or otherwise – that distinguish their activities from the activities of non-archaeologists. The close link between the rules constituted by archaeologists' behaviour and the definition of 'an archaeologist' is especially clear in efforts by archaeological organisations to establish membership conditions. The rules of archaeology promulgated by organisations such as the Institute of Field Archaeologists (IFA), the Society of Professional Archaeologists (SOPA) and the World Archaeological Congress (WAC) are linked directly to the agency of the people concerned. For example, the IFA does not assert what archaeology *is*, rather it focuses upon what archaeologists *do*; all IFA members are required to abide by a Code of Conduct that is based upon principles of personal behaviour:

Principle 1: The archaeologist shall adhere to the highest standards of ethical and responsible behaviour in the conduct of archaeological affairs.

Principle 2: The archaeologist has a responsibility for the conservation of the archaeological heritage.

Principle 3: The archaeologist shall conduct his or her work in such a way that reliable information about the past may be acquired, and shall ensure that the results be properly recorded.

Principle 4: The archaeologist has responsibility for making available the results of archaeological work with reasonable dispatch.

(Institute of Field Archaeologists 1988; cf. WAC 1991: 22–23; Davis 1982: 161–163 [SOPA])

Although it may be possible for the members of an organisation such as the IFA to agree upon what they consider the norms of archaeology, such norms cannot be generalised beyond the context of the organisation's purposes. Moreover, it is not possible to establish definitively the norms of any one person, whether they are an archaeologist or not, because the norm will be constituted by rules that, as structure, may be transformed through successive instantiations. Hence, archaeologists' norms are contingent even where they are institutionalised, though certain consistencies might be noted. In examining the management of archaeology underwater across a number of countries I have noted three particularly recurrent norms, which correspond to the common conception of the qualities of ancient material as a resource (see Section 3.1), i.e.

preservation: a belief in promoting physical persistence of ancient material

interpretation: a belief in the capacity of ancient material to prompt ideas about the past

presentation: a belief in making ancient material and interpretations available to a wide public

Doubtless, these recurrent norms could be refined and, perhaps, other archaeological norms might be discerned (see, e.g., Carman 1993 b: 2–3; King 1983). Although there is a degree of crossover between the four IFA principles and the three norms outlined above, little purpose would be served by attempting a merger. My interest lies principally in using the norms heuristically as 'roughs' in discussing the behaviour of archaeologists and others in respect of ancient material situated underwater.

One of the aims of managing archaeology underwater is to encourage non-archaeologists to behave according to archaeological norms when they encounter ancient material in their daily lives. In some respects, the institutions of management attempt to instil specific behaviour in society in the same way that the IFA Code of Practice applies to its members. Nominally, both provide for enforcement, through the courts and disciplinary procedures respectively. However, there are important differences in the relationship between society and antiquity laws and between IFA members and the Code of Practice. First, whereas archaeologists sign up to the IFA's Code of Practice individually, the majority of a population become subject to any new law on antiquities by default – irrespective of the democracy of the society concerned – by virtue of citizenship, residence or presence. Second, although archaeologists may be involved in drafting legislation, they are not legislators; the conversion of archaeologists' norms into society's laws will involve the incorporation of many non-archaeological considerations as a consequence of a society's form of government. Third, the 'reasonableness' of an archaeologist's behaviour in respect of archaeological norms will be achieved self-reflexively in the presence of their peers, but the 'reasonableness' of non-archaeologists' behaviour in respect of archaeological norms will require monitoring that is external to them or their peers – by state archaeologists, civil servants and police, for example.

These points of difference have corresponding consequences for efforts to encourage non-archaeologists to behave archaeologically through management. First, simply because a procedure has been established by law or with public money does not mean that the public will regard it as valid (cf. Section 2.2.1, Section 3.1.3). Second, the archaeological norms that gave rise to a management provision may have been buried in among many other – not necessarily compatible – norms in the course of its implementation. Third, in the absence of extensive monitoring, management depends on non-archaeologists accepting archaeologists' norms as their own.

Additional complications arise insofar as the three norms referred to above are often incompatible with each other in concrete situations. Whereas archaeologists are (or should be) practised at achieving a 'reasonable' resolution of such contradictions, non-archaeologists may be neither familiar with the norms, with the balances that might be achieved, nor with what may constitute 'reasonableness' to archaeologists. Consequently, as well as impinging upon non-archaeologists' own norms, management provisions may be designed to offer (or impose) a resolution of contradictions that has general relevance and can be applied by non-archaeologists in the absence of archaeological assistance. However, there are two drawbacks with offering an 'ideal' resolution. First, it may impinge upon the non-archaeologists' uptake of archaeological norms; presented with a solution they have no need to develop the reasoning. Second, a set solution may inhibit individuals' abilities to recognise and cope with

wholly original circumstances, such as the discovery of an unforeseen type of ancient material.

In addressing the attempt to inculcate rule following among unsupervised non-archaeologists, two points stand out: first, non-archaeologists are expected to behave differently from usual; second, non-archaeologists' interests are not furthered by their effort to comply. I focus, therefore, on how norms within management provisions might be deciphered – and upon their 'validity' to non-archaeologists – rather than on the capacity of archaeologists to sanction non-compliance. I take two examples: first, legal provisions that are supposed to encourage individuals to report their discoveries to archaeological authorities; second, the effort to get non-archaeologists to carry out work on sites designated under the 1973 Act to the satisfaction of archaeologists.

4.1.1   Discovery

The dilemmas facing the discoverers of ancient material underwater are particularly acute. The persistence of ancient material may be severely compromised by any form of disturbance, and especially by removal from (salt) water into air. Damage will occur not only to the material that is removed, but also any material that remains *in situ*, as the disturbance could trigger general degradation of a considerable area surrounding the discovery. If a discovery is left undisturbed then its persistence is not compromised, and it may yet be interpreted or acquired by an archaeologist who can call upon resources to minimise any subsequent damage. However, it may prove impossible to relocate the ancient material, or it may be discovered and removed by the next, less scrupulous, passer-by. If the material is 'lost' in either of these ways then all that will remain is the finder's report, which may yield little that can be interpreted. To avoid such losses it may be considered appropriate to have the item recovered, even though the stability of the area may be jeopardised, the integrity of the item itself placed in the balance, and interpretable information about the find's surroundings lost by injudicious extraction, along with the location itself.

Table 4.1:   **Provisions on reporting**

Netherlands	Any person who finds, other than during an excavation, a thing which he may reasonably expect to be a monument is bound to report the find within three days. (MHBA 1988 s. 47(1))
Sweden	Any person discovering an archaeological find which accrues or must be offered for redemption to the State is to report the archaeological find without delay ... (ACAMF 1988 ch. 2 s. 5)
France	Any person discovering maritime cultural property shall leave it in situ and shall not cause damage to it. Such person shall, within 48 hours of the discovery or of arrival at the first port, report the property to the Administrative Authority. (ACMCP 1989 s. 3)
Ireland	Where a person finds an archaeological object shall report the finding of the object to the Director or a designated person within a reasonable period but not longer than 96 hours from the time of the finding. (NMA 1930 [1994] s. 23(3))
Denmark	The discovery of ... ancient monuments and wrecks, etc. shall be reported to the Minister immediately. (PNA 1992 s. 14(3))
Norway	Persons finding [antiquities/ship's finds] are under obligation to notify the relevant local police authority or the appropriate authority under this act as soon as possible. (CHA 1979 ss. 13, 14)
UK	If any person finds or takes possession of any wreck in United Kingdom waters or finds or takes possession of any wreck outside United Kingdom waters and brings it within those waters he shall ... if he is not the owner of it, give notice to the receiver that he has found or taken possession of it ... (MSA 1995 s. 236(1))

Reporting mechanisms have to inject some kind of resolution of such dilemmas into the experience of non-archaeologists. Of the countries considered, most appear to favour leaving the material *in situ* notwithstanding the possible loss of location and, potentially, of the find itself to the next passer-by. Leaving the material is thus a pattern of behaviour that is expected of individuals; the dilemma is resolved for them. Such resolution is structured within legislation through the use of the term 'reporting'; statutes in the Netherlands, Sweden, France (marine), Ireland and Denmark use the term 'report' in prescribing the activities of individuals when they come across ancient material; in Norway and UK the term 'notify' is used (Table 4.1).

The obligation to report does, nevertheless, permit the finder to exercise judgement as to how the material might best be treated, insofar as the term 'report' does not, in itself, preclude recovery. In Ireland, however, any remaining ambiguity over treatment of discoveries was removed in 1994 by the addition of provisions that all but forbid recovery:

Where a person finds an archaeological recovery he shall not remove or otherwise interfere with it...

(NMA 1930 [1994] s. 23(1))

Similarly, French and Danish laws state, respectively, that:

Any person discovering maritime cultural property shall leave it in situ and shall not cause damage to it.

(ACMCP 1989 s. 3)

It is prohibited to alter or remove shipwrecks that may at any time be assumed to have been wrecked more than 100 years earlier and cargoes and parts of such shipwrecks...

(PNA 1992 s. 14(2))

In Denmark, the 1992 law on shipwrecks contrasts with the 1984 law on objects (including shipwrecks), that states:

Any person who gathers up an object belonging to the state pursuant to subsection (1) [i.e. objects, including shipwrecks, which at any time must be assumed lost more than 100 years ago], and any person who gains possession of such an object, shall immediately deliver it to the State Antiquarian.

(AM 1984 [1989]: 28(3))

Aside from the confusion between 'shipwrecks' and 'objects (including shipwrecks)', it can be seen that contrasting presumptions apply in Denmark. Whereas shipwrecks must be reported without any alteration or removal, the only obligation to inform the authorities about objects under the Act on Museums arises from gathering up or gaining possession, i.e. through the kind of disturbance prohibited in the Protection of Nature Act. Moreover, the Act on Museums specifies what actions must follow gathering/gaining possession, that is, delivery to the State Antiquarian. Such specificity precludes the discoverer from using their own judgement in deciding, for example, that further movement will endanger the object. Furthermore, obligatory delivery militates against forms of possession in which the environment of the object can be stabilised (e.g. attempts to assert possession while the material is still *in situ*, or possession within conservation facilities). A similar constriction on the exercise of judgement by finders was apparent in the UK until 1993, as the Merchant Shipping Act 1894 required individuals that found wreck to 'deliver' it to an official:

Where any person finds or takes possession of any wreck within the limits of the United Kingdom he shall ... if he is not the owner thereof, as soon as possible deliver the same to the receiver of the district.

(MSA 1894 s. 518)

The finder's dilemma was resolved by prescribing a course of action – delivery to the receiver – even if the finder felt that 'delivery' was against their better judgement. The obligation to deliver was criticised by the archaeological community in the late 1960s because it was interrupting their attempts to ensure the conservation of material that had been raised. For example, in January 1968 Davies complained to the CNA that a local Receiver had insisted that a cannon recovered off Anglesey remain in the Receiver's possession even though arrangements had been made for conservation at Liverpool Museum (Davies to CNA 04/01/68). Such complaints resulted in the introduction of an administrative practice whereby material would not have to be delivered. McKee, searching for the *Mary Rose* at that time, claims responsibility for achieving the change in policy – which seems to have taken place in October 1968 – so that although the Receiver would retain 'legal custody' the conservation laboratory would have physical control (McKee 1982: 67; McKee 1968). This administrative arrangement later seems to have formed a model that facilitated the removal of the obligation to deliver in 1993 (MSA 1993 sch. 4, s. 22(b)), which applied to all wreck, not simply such wreck as required conservation.

Behaviour is generated by the structure of the management regime as a whole rather than by one or two provisions. For example, reporting provisions are closely tied to disposal and ownership; France, Denmark and Ireland claim state ownership of all ancient material, which might suggest the persistence of an acquisitive norm (cf. Darvill 1983: 5). However, the non-disturbance policies pursued by these countries suggest that interest in acquisition is principally a mechanism for bolstering preservation, not least because such provisions also inhibit interpretative investigation. In contrast, provisions in several countries indicate that while reporting does not require recovery, recovery will take place nevertheless. For example, rights of private ownership in isolated finds will tend to militate against *in situ* preservation of ancient material as the finder will be encouraged to take into possession what is now theirs. Both Sweden and the Netherlands provide for private ownership of fortuitous or isolated finds. In Sweden, 'archaeological finds as referred to in s. 3(1) [i.e. not discovered in or near an ancient monument] accrue to the finder' (ACAMF 1988 ch. 2 s. 4). In the Netherlands, the state or municipality owns only those movable monuments that are found during excavations (MHBA 1988 ss. 43(1), 43(2)). Equally, systems in which possession provides a strong presumption in favour of ownership eventually vesting in the possessor may encourage the prospective owner to recover material that they find underwater. The practice of giving historic wreck to salvors *in lieu* of a 100% salvage award in the UK is an example of the kind of administrative arrangement which might undermine policies that favour preservation *in situ*.

Provisions concerning behaviour subsequent to discovery may have a similar effect. For example, the following provision applies in Sweden: 'it is the duty of the finder, when requested to do so, to surrender the archaeological find...' (ACAMF 1988: 2, 5). Clearly, a finder cannot be asked to surrender the material unless they have recovered it. Similarly, in the Netherlands 'the rightful claimants of a movable monument ... are bound to keep the monument available or to make it available for scientific research for six months...' (MHBA 1988 s. 48). As in Sweden, the provision requiring claimants to make a movable monument available for study suggests that the monument is already in the possession of the claimant, i.e. the monument has been recovered. Consequently, in these countries the overall expected behaviour seems to be structured in favour of recovery even though the provisions on reporting do not require it.

In Ireland the legislation used to include the following provision:

A person who finds an archaeological object ... shall permit–

a) any member of the Garda Síochána or the said director or a servant or agent of his to inspect, examine or photograph the object, and

b) the said Director or a servant or agent of his to take possession of the object.

(NMA 1930 [1987] ss. 23(1))

As in Sweden and the Netherlands, these provisions indicate that reporting is presupposed by recovery. The provisions had their origins in a system that favoured private ownership, but since the Derrynaflan judgement in 1987 (*Webb v. Ireland* [1988] IR 353), all archaeological objects belong to the state. The findings of the court were confirmed in statute in 1994 (NMA 1994 s. 2(1)), and in amendments to s. 23 of the National Monuments Act 1930, which now reads as follows:

... in reporting the find he [a person who finds an archaeological object] shall state ... a description of the location of the place where the object was found ... and specify where the object may be inspected by the Director or a designated person.

(NMA 1930 [1994] ss. 23(4))

Whereas the 1987 provision presumed that finders had it in their power to permit inspection and possession, the 1994 provision only expects the finder to be able to say where the object is located. Arguably, even though the assertion of state ownership may have reduced recoveries by prospective owners, the structuring of expectations would not have changed if recovery was implied by provisions on subsequent behaviour.

Although ambiguity is removed by the enshrinement in law of the norm of preservation over norms of interpretation and/or acquisition, the forced resolution of the dilemma may overly constrain individuals when they approach particular

circumstances. Consequently, some provision may be made for 'exceptional circumstances' that remove the straitjacket. Two such exceptions are 'accidental recovery' and 'apparent danger'. As an example of the first, in France the recovery of 'maritime cultural property' is prohibited, unless it occurs accidentally as a result of works or any other public or private activity:

Any person accidentally removing maritime cultural property from the maritime public domain as a result of works or any other public or private activity shall not let the property out of his possession. The property shall be reported to the Administrative Authority within the time-limit specified in article 3; it shall be deposited with the said authority within the same time-limit, or shall be kept at its disposal.

(ACMCP 1989 s. 4)

Without such a provision, it is possible that fishing crews and engineers, for example, having committed the crime of recovery unwittingly, will dump the evidence. Dumping would preclude the opportunity for interpretation and/or acquisition, even though delivery to the authorities may have disastrous consequences for the integrity of the material. The provision suggests, therefore, that the balance of norms is reversed, or that only preservation within a primary context is valued; once the primary context is lost then 'secondary' norms concerning interpretation and/or acquisition take effect.

The 'exceptional circumstance' in the Irish system is unusual because it makes an explicit call on the finder's judgement:

A person who finds an archaeological object and *who has reasonable cause to believe* that it is necessary to remove it so as to preserve it or to keep it safe shall remove it to a designated place or any safe place if there is no designated place within 30 miles of its place of discovery.

(NMA 1930 [1994] s. 23(1), my emphasis)

In effect, the finder is called upon to make a decision of a type generally reserved for archaeologists. There is a risk that the public may be over-zealous in ensuring that discoveries are removed from any conceivable danger, but the approach offers certain advantages. Insofar as judgement is allowed within the law, then the finder can act according to the particularities of a discovery without causing an offence that might discourage them from reporting or may make subsequent discussion with the authorities difficult. The provision gives finders a voice in explaining their behaviour when they have found something. Insofar as this voice has legal support, then archaeologists may find that their privilege in prescribing the treatment of ancient material is eroded.

4.1.2 Licences

The management of archaeology underwater in the UK has largely revolved around work upon a small number of sites designated under the Protection of Wrecks Act 1973. In many cases this work has been carried out without direct archaeological supervision, so one of the chief concerns of management has been to encourage the non-archaeologists involved to adopt standards that are 'reasonable' in the eyes of archaeologists.

Archaeologists did not really get the opportunity to examine the standard of work beyond archaeological supervision until 1986, when the Archaeological Diving Unit (ADU) was contracted by the Government to provide technical services in support of the 1973 Act. Although the standard of work on designated sites must have been discussed in earlier years, it is not until after 1986 that the suggestion that standards were poor made it into print. Hence Croome reports on a paper by Dean – the Director of the ADU – as follows: 'For the most part, the standard of archaeological work on the designated sites so far visited was "atrocious"' (Croome 1988: 114). The evidently poor standard of work led to the publication of *Guidelines on Acceptable Standards in Underwater Archaeology* (Dean 1988) which included a Foreword by Greenhill, Chair of the Government's Advisory Committee on Historic Wreck Sites (ACHWS), stating that:

> In the course of the ADU's activities it became apparent that it would be useful to define the standards the Advisory Committee would consider acceptable for the licensed work on designated wreck sites
>
> (Greenhill 1988)

Similarly, McGrail – a member of ACHWS – referred in 1989 to 'a poor excavation record and an even worse record of publication...'(McGrail 1989: 18). The lack of publication, loss of archives and dispersal of antiquities has prompted Marsden to ask 'what has been the value of protecting wreck-sites' (Marsden 1994: 156).

Such evident dissatisfaction suggests the failure, over 12 years, of the measures that had been taken to inculcate archaeological norms in the practice of unsupervised non-archaeologists. The development of such a situation has its origins in the introduction of the 1973 Act. It will be recalled that Mr. Onslow stated that the 1973 Bill 'may, incidentally, lead to a more orderly exploitation of wrecks, but that is not the prime aim...' (HC 855: 1705). Even if 'orderly exploitation' is read generously as 'work meeting archaeological standards', it seems that the standard of work was of little concern to the Government. Saunders has confirmed this impression:

> In the first years of the Act expectations were low. Those in the Government who were concerned did not fully appreciate that the protection of historic wrecks required a greater degree of archaeological involvement, with the development of agreed criteria and the application of professional standards, than simply raising objects from the seabed and disposing of them efficiently
>
> (Saunders 1994: 317)

Moreover, it was made abundantly clear that the opportunity to work on designated sites would not be restricted to archaeologists. Some recreational divers had made representations to Mr. Sproat, which he was keen to appease:

> They put it to me that the club might be the first to discover a wreck. When they applied for a licences they could be told 'Certainly you discovered the wreck, but you are a small, amateur body. You do not have the

sophisticated equipment, the money, the persons with necessary experience. You know nothing about marine archaeology. We will not give you a licence further to exploit the wreck.' I want to say as firmly as possible that this is not our intention ... No one should feel that there is any reason why the Secretary of State will not grant a licence provided they are properly competent and the sort of people to whom we feel a licence should be given

> (HC 855: 1698)

Furthermore, the licensing of non-archaeologists to work upon designated sites was to be an important element in enforcing the 1973 Bill. To repeat a quotation from Section 2.2.2:

> Probably our greatest aid in enforcing the provisions of the Bill is that if there is an authorised salvor on the spot looking after his own interests, and the site has been designated and licensed by the Secretary of State...
>
> (Mr. Sproat, HC 851: 1877-1878)

Although the three elements – minimal Governmental concern for archaeological standards, licensing of non-archaeologists, and the use of licensing as an enforcement measure – contributed to the disappointing standards of later years, it was not enunciation in Parliament that caused the damage, but implementation. It seems that Mr. Sproat's conception of enforcement was that each licensee would police 'his own interests', i.e. the site and would report any infringements. Hence Dromgoole notes 'it has been the policy of the Advisory Committee to, as far as possible, have a licensed salvor working each site, believing that this is the best and possibly only way to protect sites' (Dromgoole 1989 a: 44). Saunders – a member of ACHWS – makes a similar comment, adding 'there was a reluctance to designate sites which did not have a prospective licensee' (Saunders 1994: 317; cf. Section 3.2.2). Saunders goes on to state that the need for licensees 'was no problem since sites were almost always reported by diving groups who wanted to keep a wreck to themselves and designation was valuable to them as a means of keeping rivals away' (Saunders 1994: 317). This comment supports the view expressed in Section 2.2.2 that the 1973 regime served as a statutory form of 'salvor in possession', and raises the question of the prospective licensees' intentions; who would ensure that the licensee's own activities would protect the archaeological values of a site? As Saunders puts it:

> ... the cynic might have said that those sites most at risk from archaeological damage were some of the designated sites where excavation licences had been granted.
>
> (Saunders 1994: 318)

The main controls upon the licensee were to be the licence conditions. However, in his reference to conditions, Mr. Onslow gives a clear impression that these were to be 'bolted on' to what was – in effect – a salvage licence, as if the 'archaeological values' of a site could be put to one side, discretely (see also Section 3.2.2). Early in the debate, Mr. Stewart stated: 'The danger with a wreck in which there is likely to be bullion or valuable objects is that the historical part of the wrecked vessel may be damaged before the museum authorities and archaeologists can get to work' (HC 851: 1862). Mr. Stewart may simply have meant that commercial enterprises will compromise archaeological qualities, but the expression is close to Mr. Onslow's statement that 'Some sites may be regarded as suitable for salvage operations without any serious loss of their archaeological value ... provided the requisite conditions are met' (HC 851: 1870). Onslow's statement was repeated almost word for word by Earl Ferrers (HL 342: 932). The perception that archaeological values are discrete carries over into Mr. Onslow's references to licence conditions, which were made in the context of the presumption in favour of salvors, hence:

> ... the owner or the salvor has the prior claim to salvage the wreck provided he can meet the conditions required for a licence necessary for the protection of the archaeological value of the site
>
> (HC 851: 1869–1870)

Mr. Onslow repeated the conception of licensing as 'salvage plus conditions' – as I shall term the notion – in discussing the proposed advisory body. He refered to: 'the licences to be granted for salvage operations and the conditions to be attached to those licences' (HC 851: 1868); and 'the person likely to carry out salvage operations ... and the conditions to be attached to the licence for the protection of the archaeological value of the site' (HL 342: 931). Mr. Onslow's idea of licensing was confirmed in Government statements about the implementation of the 1973 Act; conditions and restrictions '... will be kept to the minimum necessary to secure their object' (Department of Trade and Industry 1973 a: 2; Department of Trade 1975). In later guidance, however, references to 'minimum necessary' conditions were replaced with details of the general conditions:

a limit diving on the designated site to named individuals *and in accordance with the plans submitted*;

b require operations to be carried out under the overall direction of an archaeologist experienced in the particular field, *for an excavation licence a diving archaeologist is invariably essential*;

c require the expert conservation of artefacts recovered from the designated site *with a restriction on lifting if adequate facilities for preservation are not available*; and

d require the submission of periodical reports *(normally annually)* to the Department of Trade, for consideration by the Advisory Committee on Historic Wreck Sites.

'Licensees are also encouraged to publish reports on their excavations in the appropriate field journals.'

(Department of Trade 1979: 2; amendments in Italics added by Department of Transport 1986)

Of particular note is the insistence that only named individuals could dive on a designated site, which should have underlined the divers' personal responsibility for their

behaviour. The requirement, from 1986, of direct archaeological supervision in the case of excavations, and the restriction on lifting, may indicate growing dissatisfaction with standards of unsupervised work. However, the implied linkage of standards to the excavation/removal of artefacts reflects the preoccupation with recovery that characterised the 1973 debates (see Chapter Two). Finally, it should be noted that the conditions included a means of enforcement – the periodic report to the Department and ACHWS.

The information required in reports to ACHWS has been set out in *Reports on Licensed Work on Protected Wreck Sites: reports required by the Advisory Committee on Historic Wreck Sites (ACHWS)*, which states:

3. Reports should be concise and factual and should contain the following information–

    a) a short narrative (not more than 2 sides of A4) on the season's work, brief details of knowledge gained, and references to any relevant publications;

    b) brief details of artefacts recovered including the date of recovery, current whereabouts and arrangements made for conservation;

    c) a sketch plan of the site showing the location of the season's finds and other salient features;

    d) the names of the members of the diving team, dates when diving took place and the total number of hours actually spent diving;

    e) a statement of intent for the forthcoming season and, if appropriate, a formal request for licence renewal together with confirmation about the availability of the archaeological advisor/director, sponsorship and conservation facilities. Additionally, a completed Form C will be required if an application is made for the first time to excavate the site.

(Department of National Heritage n.d. e)

This list, which was still in use in 1995, is virtually the same as one that was set out in a document prepared by the Department of Trade dating back to at least April 1980 (Department of Trade 1980). Reports in the prescribed format have, it would seem, been crucial to monitoring licence conditions for at least 15 of the 22 years the Act has been in force. In view of the failure to inculcate archaeological norms referred to at the start of Section 4.1.2, it is important to consider why the periodic reports have not ensured a reasonable standard of work. An explanation can be derived by contrasting the *reports* on licensed work to the *applications* for the licences.

In 1975, the information required from applicants for licences was published in the *International Journal of Nautical Archaeology* (Department of Trade 1975). This information served as a basis for two application forms – Form B for survey licences, Form C for excavation licences – used from the late 1970s to the early 1990s (Department of Trade n.d. b; Department of Trade n.d. c), since rewritten (Department of National Heritage n.d. b; Department of National Heritage n.d. c). The application forms ask for far more information than the suggested format of reports. For example, the forms have required such things as written confirmation of conservation facilities from conservator concerned, a statement on deposition of the site archive, a statement regarding publication and a statement on ultimate disposal of recovered material. Moreover, the information requested has been quite consistent – if anything, the recent application forms are less demanding than the earlier ones – so there has been quite a rigorous scheme in place from the early years of implementation. Finally, the information demanded often relates directly to the maintenance of standards. In view of questions on the application form of 1975 about arrangements for the storage of records, for eventual publication and for the ultimate destination of objects recovered, it seems remarkable that Marsden should make the following comments, nearly 20 years later: 'judging from the cited publications many of the sites have resulted in little or no significant publication...' and 'under the Department of Transport little track of the site archives was kept; ... much has simply been lost' (Marsden 1994: 156). The following question is especially telling:

> One wonders why ... licences to excavate have been granted when the permanent safety of the antiquities and the paper archive has not been assured before excavation?

> (Marsden 1994: 156)

According to the application forms, information about the safety of antiquities and of the archive should have been provided to the Government and ACHWS before licences were granted. It should have been clear in advance that archaeological norms would not be met, and yet licences seem to have been issued anyway.

It is necessary to look at three, inter-related, characteristics of the licensing regime in order to understand why licences were granted to licensees whose work could prove unsatisfactory, despite the use of detailed application forms. First, there was a presumption in favour of licensing whosoever made an application, of whatever form. This presumption is evinced by the statements by Mr. Onslow and Mr. Sproat, that there was no intention to prevent salvors, owners and divers from 'working' designated sites, and by the policy of using licensing as the principle method of enforcement.

Second, although an application form may have been completed in detail to obtain an initial licence, it seems that subsequent licences were issued on submission of a far less demanding report. Consequently, undertakings made in an original application would have become increasingly distant as licence followed report, followed licence. My contention that licences were issued not in response to a completed application form but on the basis of a report is supported by the final paragraph of *Reports on Licensed Work on Protected Wreck Sites*. This paragraph states that if a fresh application form were to be submitted, there would be no need for the report to include 'a statement of intent for the forthcoming season and, if appropriate, a formal request for licence *renewal*' (my emphasis). Nor would the following reminder be necessary: 'additionally, a completed Form C will be required if an application is made for the first time to

excavate the site' (Department of Trade 1980; Department of National Heritage n.d. e).

Third, drawing upon the first two points and the term 'renewal' in particular, it appears that the licensing procedure was pervaded by an expectation of repeat licensing that reversed the relationship that 'application' implies. It seems that licences were not issued on the merits of an application, but on the grounds that the current licensee wanted to carry on. Clearly, repeat licensing facilitated planning of substantial, multi-year projects and solved the enforcement problem, but it impeded the monitoring of standards. Arguably, it is easier for a licensee to provide a smooth retrospective account in the form of a brief report than a considered appraisal of the aims, objectives and execution of an anticipated season. Such repeat licensing (in addition to the 'Permanent Licences' issued for three designated sites, see Flinder and McGrail 1990: Table 2) forged an association of specific individuals with particular sites: *Licensees*, as opposed to *licensees*. This association harks back to the concept of 'salvor in possession' discussed above (Section 2.2.2), and contributed to the expectation that Licensees would continue to work sites for as long as they wished, so long as they kept submitting reports to the Department.

The interpretation above is borne out by the pattern of licensing of designated sites up until 1986 when the ADU became operational (see Flinder and McGrail 1990: Table 2; Archaeological Diving Unit 1994). In 1986, 21 of the 29 designated sites were subject to licences. Of those that were not licensed, five had been subject to comprehensive investigations by teams led by archaeologists (Cattewater, *Grace Dieu*, HMS *Anne*, Moor Sands and *Kennemerland*) and one had never been licensed (South Edinburgh Channel). At the remaining unlicensed site (Church Rocks), interest ceased after a year of survey and 4 years' excavation (see Preece and Burton 1993: 257). Similarly, licensing seems to have been interrupted on other sites in earlier years only where a phase of work was considered complete and, again, these were principally investigations with archaeological direction, namely *Amsterdam*, *Dartmouth*, Pwyll Fanog, *Northumberland* and *Restoration*. The exceptions are Frenchman's Rocks (never licensed, de-designated 1984), *Colossus* (salvage completed in 1978, de-designated 1984), Bartholomew Ledge and HMS *Coronation*. Without access to the Advisory Committee's minutes it is difficult to say whether the interruption of licensing in these last two cases was due to dissatisfaction with the quality of a report (or of the work reported), or due to the licensee choosing to discontinue work. In the remaining cases (*Mary Rose*, *Mary*, HMS *Assurance*, HMS *Romney*, Rill Cove, Langdon Bay, Tal-y-bont, *Stirling Castle*, HMS *Invincible*, St. Anthony, *Schiedam*, Brighton Marina, Yarmouth Roads, Studland Bay) there was either a Permanent Licence, or licensing continued without interruption. Only in two of these cases were excavation licences succeeded by survey licences, namely *Assurance* in 1977-78 and *Invincible* in 1981-82. It is difficult to say whether this 'demotion' reflected the wishes of the licensee or the insistence of ACHWS. Before 1986, these are the only two cases that might fit Dromgoole's observation that 'in one or two cases where there has been inadequate recording, excavation licences have been ...

"reduced back" to a licence to survey' (Dromgoole 1989 a: 47). Altogether, the pattern of licensing reveals only four cases where licences may have been withheld or varied due to concern about standards; moreover, other explanations (lack of resources or enthusiasm, for example) could be offered for these interruptions in a regime characterised by repeat licensing. In sum, although licensing of work on sites designated on the Protection of Wrecks Act might have been expected to inculcate rule-following by unsupervised non-archaeologists, the concept of licensing advanced in Parliament and implementation of the regime militated against acceptable standards.

4.2 Trust

In this section, I examine the circumstances in which archaeologists and non-archaeologists encounter each other to demonstrate the effect of such circumstances on the promulgation of archaeological behaviour.

4.2.1 Reporting

There is considerable variation in the institutional arrangements through which non-archaeologists meet archaeologists when reports are made (Table 4.2).

Table 4.2: Administrative arrangements for reporting ancient material (paraphrased)

Denmark	ancient monuments and wrecks	National Agency for the Protection of Nature, Monuments and Sites (PNA 1992: 14(3))
	objects (including shipwrecks)	State Antiquarian (AM 1984 [1989] s. 28(3)), generally via the Institute of Maritime Archaeology
Netherlands	monuments within a municipality	the Burgomaster (MHBA 1988 s. 47(2))
	outside a municipality	the Minister (MHBA 1988 s. 47(2))
		AAO acts as the agent of the Minister for all finds made underwater
Sweden	archaeological finds that accrue to or may be redeemed by the state	Central Board of National Antiquities (RAA), the State County Administration, the County Museum or a police authority
	archaeological finds belonging to shipwrecks	as above, plus the Coastguard Service (ACAMF 1988 s. 2, 5)
		The Sjohistoriska Museet in Stockholm deals with reports of discoveries underwater on behalf of RAA
France	maritime cultural property	Administrative Authority (ACMCP 1989: 2) meaning the administrator of *affaires maritimes* (Decret 91–1226: 1) at the closest of about 40 offices arranged in 'quartiers' around France
Ireland	archaeological objects found underwater	Director of the National Museum or a designated person (NMA 1987 [1994] s. 3(6)(b))
	wrecks more than 100 years old	Office of Public Works or to the Garda Síochána (NMA 1987 [1994] s. 3(6)(a))
Norway	antiquities	local police authority or to the appropriate authority (CHA 1979 ss. 13, 14)
	ancient monuments, irrespective of whether they are found on land or underwater	regional archaeological museums (4319 C-080.22/91 HKH/HS)
	ship finds made on land	regional archaeological museums (4319 C-080.22/91 HKH/HS)
	ship finds made underwater	one of five 'maritime' museums (4319 C-080.22/91 HKH/HS), depending upon the region in which the discovery occurs (see Norges Dykkeforbund n.d.)
		As the University of Trondeim Museum and Tromsø Museum are also 'archaeological' museums, the division between ancient monuments and ship finds in their regions is immaterial.
UK	wreck	Receiver of Wreck (MSA 1995 s.248(2), based at the Coastguard Agency (Coastguard Agency 1994 a).

Table 4.3: Summary of reporting arrangements, by reference to three axes

	local	central	arch.	admin.	marine	terrestrial
Denmark (IMA)		X	X		X	
Netherlands (AAO)		X	X		X	
Sweden (SM)		X	X		X	
France (Aff. Mar.)	X			X	X	
Ireland (NM/OPW)		X	X			X
Norway (Mus.)	X		X		X	
UK (Receiver)		X		X	X	

The various points to which reports must be made can be summarised by reference to three axes. First, the reporting point may be centralised as a single office for the whole country, or there may be a series of offices that can be contacted locally. Second, the reporting point may be staffed by archaeologists or by administrators with other responsibilities. Third, the reporting point may be concerned principally with either terrestrial or with maritime affairs, hence the matrix set out in Table 4.3.

In the case of fortuitous finds, reporting may be an irregular and unanticipated burden on the 'lucky' person. Arrangements that reduce any burden and substitute a positive experience are, perhaps, more likely to encourage reporting. The implications of the different arrangements noted above on an individual's experience of reporting can be drawn out by postulating a series of attributes or 'desiderata' that may make the official more readily approachable. For example, a successful regime for reporting might ensure that the person to whom reports are made is: a) familiar with the area or circumstances of the discovery; b) able to answer the finder's questions regarding age, purpose and significance; c) able to offer advice or assistance with recording, conservation and further study; and d) authorised to make decisions regarding matters such as possession and ownership.

The categorisation offered in Table 4.3 is, of course, an over-simplification. The advantages of localness, for example, may be undermined if the number of offices does not match the geography of the country. Whereas France has around 40 offices for a coastline of 3,427 km (Couper 1989: Appendix II), Norway has only five offices for a mainland coastline of 21,347 km (Royal Ministry of Foreign Affairs 1990: 3). Given the character of the Norwegian coast, a centrally located official in the Netherlands (coastline 451 km, Couper 1989: Appendix II) may be more familiar with the area in which a discovery was made than a 'local' official in Norway.

Local reporting may ensure that the official receiving the report is familiar with the locality of the find, but the capacity to take a decision may decrease with distance from authority. This situation might frustrate finders in countries that operate an award system or allow private ownership of isolated discoveries. Moreover, the availability of specialist knowledge may decrease. Similarly, conservation and storage facilities for recovered waterlogged material are unlikely to be available locally, as demand for such facilities will be small and irregular. It may be necessary, therefore, to aggregate local reporting up to a level where appropriate expertise or facilities can be provided and sustained, and in these respect Norway's five 'centres' may have the advantage. In Denmark, the Norwegian approach to dividing competence regionally was drawn upon in developing a scheme to involve more museums – both maritime and archaeological – in the reception of finds and in investigation. A report on the scheme concluded that it would not be realistic to decentralise to a county level, but that a system of regional working groups was desirable in the longer term. The Institute of Maritime Archaeology divided Danish waters into sectors that could be used in determining which museum should receive finds (Crumlin-Pedersen 1990: 19–20).

In France, there are 40 points at which reports can be made because the officials are administrators of *affaires maritimes* rather than archaeologists. Similarly, Sweden and Ireland provide for reports to be made locally, but to members of the police or of the coastguard. There are two drawbacks with administrative reporting: first, the administrator may be unfamiliar with ancient material and so unable to answer the finder's questions about age and significance, for example; second, they are unlikely to be able to provide advice or assistance with conservation. Furthermore, an administrator is unlikely to provide comprehensive recording of the information held by the finder; additional work will be required by an archaeologist at a later stage. Finally, reporting may form such an insignificant proportion of the administrator's workload that it receives little priority or attention.

Lack of expertise and possible indifference is unlikely to encourage finders to report their discoveries on a regular basis. However, coastguards and maritime affairs officers do present a form of specialised knowledge in their own right. Insofar as coastguards and maritime affairs officers carry out work in respect of the sea, then they may seem more sympathetic to a finder than a land-based archaeologist, notwithstanding the expertise of the latter. It is for this reason that the marine/terrestrial axis in the table above is not reduced to the archaeological/administrative axis. Arguably, the marine administrators in France and the UK may encourage more reports than terrestrial archaeologists in Ireland, though marine archaeologists in Denmark, Norway and the Netherlands may be yet more successful.

Several of the countries provide alternative routes for reports, and informal arrangements are widespread. Such links tend to be encouraged to ensure that material is brought to the attention of the authorities. Informal links may be used to overcome deficiencies in the formal system, or to gather types of information that the system would not otherwise attract. For example, in the UK, of over 40 sites designated under the 1973 Act, only two (*Royal Anne* and Dunwich Bank) can be shown to have first come to the attention of archaeologists by way of the Receiver of Wreck.

In the Netherlands, information is sought from trawler crews about gully fluctuations so that the exposure of new sites can be anticipated (Maarleveld pers. com.). Such pro-active 'networking' may generate far more useful information than the essentially passive reporting systems described above, notably where certain known individuals or groups, such as fishing crews and local divers, have a proven propensity to find things. These people may be unwilling, ordinarily, to share their knowledge, hence the archaeologist may have to invest time in building trust.

It might be argued that the importance of face-to-face arrangements is diminished by the availability of telephones and of reporting forms that can be posted. However, none of the desiderata mentioned above require direct face-to-face contact, with the exception of assistance with conservation facilities. However, they still rely on trust established one-to-one between finder and archaeologist/official, and a telephone conversation may be as heavily monitored by both parties as a face-to-face meeting. Reporting forms are a little different, as they are set out in abstract terms that belong to the discussion of legitimacy rather than trust. Nevertheless, their broad format does reveal something about the presumed relationship between finder and archaeologist that can be discussed fruitfully in terms of trust.

Recording forms display two basic approaches: either they ask for minimal, principally administrative information; or they ask for appreciable detail of a more archaeological character. Given that the quality of information that is immediately available regarding *in situ* material will depend on the ability of the finder to record archaeological details, and that adequate recording may prove difficult for a finder that has not received archaeological training (as follows from the discovery being 'fortuitous'), then some insight can be gained into the 'esteem' in which non-archaeologists are held. For example, the availability of detailed finders' report forms in Denmark and Norway seems to imply that recording by non-archaeologists is considered to be either acceptable or at least 'reasonable' in procedures that favour preservation *in situ*. In contrast, forms that demand administrative information alone, such as the WRE 5 in the UK (Department of Trade n.d. a), suggest that the finder is regarded as being incapable of recording archaeological information. A new form has been introduced in the UK (TCA/ROW 1, Coastguard Agency 1994 b), and while it is still overwhelmingly administrative it is now accompanied by an additional form (TCA/ROW 2) for historic wreck finds which includes checklists for the condition and character of the site (Coastguard Agency 1994 c). The form TCA/ROW 2 was prepared in conjunction with the RCHME on the pattern of the forms used in 'Dive Into History' – a non-statutory recording scheme aimed at recreational divers (Royal Commission on the Historical Monuments of England/Nautical Archaeology Society n.d.) – and is returned, via the Receiver of Wrecks to RCHME for inclusion in the National Monuments Record (NMR). Although the information requested on form TCA/ROW 2 is fairly basic, it does imply that archaeologists are prepared to accept information recorded by recreational divers, reinforced by a commitment to acknowledge in the NMR the contribution made by people who complete the form.

Provisions that oblige finders to hand their discoveries to archaeologists upon request may imply the notion that non-archaeologists are incapable of archaeological recording. Such provisions occur in Ireland (pre-1994) ('shall permit ... any ... servant or agent ... to inspect, examine or photograph the object', NMA 1930 [1987]: 23(1)(a)), Sweden ('it is the duty of the finder, when requested to do so, to surrender the archaeological find', ACAMF 1988 ch. 2 s. 5), and in the Netherlands ('the rightful claimants of a movable monument are bound to keep the monument available ... for scientific research', MHBA 1988 s. 48). Clearly, recording by archaeologists should be more detailed, accurate and/or insightful than recording by a non-archaeologist, but in view of the reliance upon recording by finders where material remains *in situ*, apparent disinterest in finders' remarks may

undermine the development of trust. Returning to the reporting of material *in situ*, demand for a precise position might suggest that the report has to be 'verified' by way of a visit by archaeologists in the absence of the finder (cf. Department of National Heritage n.d. a: 2.3, though see 7.1).

Finally, forms and procedures that demand little other than the finders name, address and circumstances of discovery may suggest to the finder that the only interest in their report is that they have complied with the law. This is the impression given by the UK's WRE 5 and by provisions in Sweden, for example, which require that finders must state where, when and how the material was discovered (ACAMF 1988 ch. 2 s. 5).

4.2.2 Management through negotiation

The example of reporting showed that the manner in which a management regime brings archaeologists and non-archaeologists together will, insofar as it establishes trust, encourage specific instances of rule-following. Similarly, the introduction of such a regime requires, in itself, the establishment of trust. In this respect, the debates accompanying the introduction of the 1973 Act are indicative of efforts to reconcile the dissimilar rules of a variety of interests. Notwithstanding the apparent archaeological intent of s. 1 of the Protection of Wrecks Bill, reliance upon the establishment of trust meant that archaeologists' rules would not necessarily prevail over non-archaeologists' rules once the Act was implemented. Hence the 1973 regime was, in its inception as well as its implementation, an exercise in management by negotiation, not imposition.

The need for non-archaeologists to be reconciled to the proposed regime arose partly because there were to be no new resources for policing and enforcement once the 1973 Act was implemented. Both Mr. Sproat and Mr. Onslow covered policing at some length, prompted by comments by, for example, Mr. Tilney (HC 851: 1856). The Lords, in particular, regarded the 1973 Bill as being weakened by the anticipated inadequacy of enforcement. Earl Ferrers, speaking for the Government, stated: 'I readily accept that the noble Lord ... has put his finger on what one might describe as the weakest point in this particular form of legislation' (HL 343: 312). The Earl of Cork and Orrery, who introduced the 1973 Bill in the Lords, said: 'I will not go so far as to say that the Bill as it stands, without the Amendment [Clause 3 (5A) – see below], would be worse than no Bill at all; but I am not sure that it could not turn out to be like that' (HL 343: 2175). These admissions imply that not even the Bill's supporters knew how the regime could look after itself. Mr. Onslow also anticipated problems: 'there will, of course, be difficulty in enforcing the provisions of the Bill about historic wrecks' (HC 851: 1870). Such recognition did not amount to an undertaking to pursue the problem, as the Department's commitment would be kept at a minimum: 'We do not propose additional resources for enforcement ... the police will not be asked to accept the primary enforcement responsibility' (HC 851: 1870). Mr. Sproat reinforced this point: 'Any question of special police provisions or special vessels equipped for going out to the various sites is, alas, not possible under the provisions of the Bill' (HC 851: 1877).

An alternative to the provision of new resources was a reallocation of existing ones, notably through assigning responsibility to a specific agency. Lord Kennet, dissatisfied with the 1973 Bill's provision for enforcement, introduced a probing amendment at the Committee stage of the Bill in the Lords that addressed responsibility:

3(5A) The responsibility for the enforcement of the criminal provisions of this Act shall rest with the Coastguard Service, who shall pay especial attention to it during the period between its being known that the Secretary of State is minded to make an order, and the granting of a licence.

(HL 343: 311)

The first element of the amendment was intended to clear up responsibility, which Mr. Onslow and Earl Ferrers had informally divided among various agencies; Lord Kennet stated 'there is also a certain advantage in the Bill because everybody then knows where they stand' (HL 343: 311). In response, Earl Ferrers reminded the House that no additional resources would be made available for policing, but Lord Kennet retorted that the amendment did not concern resources as 'it only specifies where responsibility lies' (HL 343: 313). Shepherd pressed the amendment on behalf of Lord Kennet when the Report of the Committee was received, prompting a categorical rejection by Earl Ferrers:

I cannot agree that the Customs Service or the coastguards will be given specific and explicit responsibilities for the protection of these areas. The coastguards and Receiver of Wrecks, the Customs Service and the police will be asked to do all that they can within the normal course of their duties to ensure that no unauthorised persons interfere with these designated sites ...

I hope that the noble Lord ... will not wish to place a specific responsibility on either the customs officers or the coastguards to undertake this protection

(HC 343: 2174–2175).

As far as Mr. Onslow and Mr. Sproat were concerned, greatest emphasis was to be placed on the goodwill of those already involved in the business of exploring and recovering material; divers, salvors and receivers would regulate the investigation of wrecks, with the assistance of interested onlookers where appropriate. Their discussion of enforcement indicates that whatever its stated intentions, the 1973 Bill was largely concerned with reconciling archaeological and non-archaeological interests through the offices of the administrators with which they were already dealing. The system of policing which Mr. Onslow outlined was as follows:

It is felt that it will be better to rely on the receivers of wreck ... the Coastguard ... and the enthusiasm of the amateur diving fraternity to report unauthorised exploiting of wrecks.

(HC 851: 1870)

A degree of self-policing was also advocated with respect to recreational divers. Mr. Sproat commented that there had 'also been offers, which I am sure we will gladly take up, by British Sub-Aqua Club personnel to police the sites' (HC 851: 1877). Mr. Mason suggested that 'the British Sub Aqua Club ... will have to advise and caution its advanced divers to play a game keeping role in both discovering and guarding wrecks' (HC 851: 1855). It is not clear how this was expected to work in practice, as it depended implicitly on distinguishing between those divers and salvors who would act sensitively to archaeological material, and the divers and salvors who, earlier in the debate, had been blamed for the losses sustained. Unfortunately, neither the 1973 Bill nor the administrative measures which were described were suited to such discrimination. All that could be hoped, perhaps, is that divers and salvors would, while looking after their own interests, accept the archaeologists' appeals and archaeological conditions on their licences. Of course, such appeals and conditions could only be enforced by the divers and salvors themselves.

Some of the ways in which divers and salvors were encouraged to police themselves have been referred to above, notably the development of a regime based strongly on the principles of 'salvor in possession' and the use of conditional licences. However, it seems that one of the principal means of encouraging appreciation was to involve divers, salvors and other non-archaeological interests in the introduction and implementation of the regime itself. In the early 1970s, the different interests were given numerous opportunities to become involved in the whole process of wreck protection. These opportunities included representation on the Wreck Law Review Committee, consultation in drafting and introducing the 1973 Bill, consultation prior to designation and, finally, objections when the intention to designate was made public. The other focus of involvement was representation on the proposed advisory board, which is discussed in Section 4.3.2. The repeated opportunities to have a point discussed, and the continuity in consideration from agenda setting, through legislation to implementation reinforces the notion that wreck protection took the form of protracted negotiation rather than proscription of damaging activities. Mr. Onslow confirmed the negotiated character of the regime, in discussing the various interests:

Their views have been taken into account so far as possible and the proposals embodied in the Bill are generally acceptable to them. Although I do not imagine that they would necessarily command support from everyone involved, the proposals are supported by archaeologists and diving interests.

(HC 851: 1866; also Earl Ferrers, HL 342: 928)

The Wreck Law Review Committee was set up in 1970 following Mr. Nott's attempts to introduce amendments to the Merchant Shipping Bill in March of that year. Its representative character was referred to by Mr. Sproat (HC 855: 1666) and by the Earl of Cork and Orrery (HL 342: 917). The Committee was convened by the Government and included representatives of many of its Departments, as well as archaeologists, and representatives of other interests. Some interests were also consulted directly in the course of drafting the 1973 Bill. Mr. Sproat's claim that the drafts had been 'widely discussed with the many interests involved' (HC 851: 1850) was confirmed by Mr. Onslow:

The Bill's provisions are the result of wide discussions with all the interests concerned ... They include the

Council for Nautical Archaeology, the British Sub-Aqua Club, commercial salvage interests and other interested parties.

(HC 851: 1866)

The debates themselves offered an opportunity for various interests to have an influence, though recreational diving and salvage interests were already dominant by this stage. In particular, the period between Second Reading and the Committee stage in the Commons presented an additional opportunity for interests to be put forward: 'Since Second Reading many people have contacted me both in correspondence and in person and have made various suggestions about how the Bill can be improved' (Mr. Sproat, HC 855: 1695).

Commitments were also made to consult various interests in the course of deciding whether a site should be protected. The proposed consultees included the British-Sub Aqua Club and commercial salvage interests (Mr. Sproat, HC 855: 1669; the Earl of Cork and Orrery, HL 342: 918-919), and Fisheries Departments (Mr. Sproat, HC 855: 1669; Mr. Onslow, HC 851: 1867; HC 855: 1706). Once the Secretary of State was minded to protect a site, there would be a further period in which the intention to designate would be advertised and objections could be received: 'It is proposed to advertise the Secretary of State's intention to designate a named site in the Department's journal ... and elsewhere ... and to allow time for consideration of objections...' (Mr. Onslow, HC 851: 1869; also Earl Ferrers, HL 342: 932). Guidance in 1973 and 1979 that supported the commitment to advertise intentions and to receive objections (Department of Trade and Industry 1973 a: 2; Department of Trade 1979: 1) was, however, omitted in corresponding paragraphs in 1986 (Department of Transport 1986). This omission suggests, perhaps, that publicity before designation was no longer regarded as necessary or desirable (cf. Lord Kennet, HL 343: 312).

Turning to the principal non-archaeological interests, it might be said that with few exceptions, recreational divers were treated so gently that there was a danger of forgetting that they were partly responsible for the damage that had prompted the 1973 Bill. Mr. Sproat, in particular, trod a delicate line between condemning divers for their excesses and alienating them, hence an effort to distance the activities of certain divers from those of the majority:

> We should make it clear that there is a big distinction between people who explore these wrecks for love of adventure and those who exploit them in the sense which the right hon. Gentleman suggested, as pirates and wreckers ... We ought to emphasise how much we owe to all the people whose sense of adventure leads them to investigate the depths of the ocean ... We are indebted to them for what, through their sense of adventure, they are discovering for the nation as a whole ... I should hate to think that any Bill which I introduced would have a bad effect on those who undertake this splendid and adventurous hobby.

(HC 851: 1873)

Such damage limitation was necessary to defuse resistance from divers to the Bill, as Mr. Sproat commented: '... they were afraid at one time that the measure would in some way limit their ability to dive and to continue with their hobby' (HC 851: 1877). It seems that diving interests were at least partly responsible for the failure to introduce a Private Members Bill on wrecks in 1972 (CNA Minutes 20/07/72). Moreover, in view of the acquiescence required (because of the lack of enforcement) and the diver's potential role in policing (HC 851: 1877), it appears that provisions or phrases which might upset divers were to be avoided, both in the 1973 Bill and in the debates. This was not, however, easy to achieve, as Mr. Sproat commented on 4 May: 'I have still had representations from people who think that the Bill is directed against sub-aqua clubs'. However, he tempered his comment by ascribing such representations to 'certain individuals and small clubs, which are not always in touch with the main bodies' (HC 855: 1697-1698), thereby assuaging any fears harboured by the 'main bodies' that Mr. Sproat's exasperation was directed at them.

Mr. Sproat was similarly gentle with the salvage interests, recognising the confusion they had faced in the past and not wishing to add to their problems:

> I think we must recognise that many of those who are involved in this business find the present Acts rather restricting ... If we accept that people feel a slight resentment about the provisions of the Merchant Shipping Act ... we must also recognise that under this measure [the 1973 Bill] there is to be imposed what might be called another layer of bureaucracy on top of the layers that already exist

(HC 851: 1867)

Some individual salvors had resisted the attempt to introduce a bill in 1972 (CNA Minutes 20/07/72) and their co-operation seems to have been considered vital to the success of the 1973 Act. In addition to the conciliatory tone of comments by Mr. Sproat and Mr. Onslow, a commitment was made – as noted in Section 2.2.2 and Section 4.1.2 – to offer licences to salvors already engaged in working upon wrecks. Moreover, the salvage interests received recognition through the adoption of 'salvor in possession' as the mould for the 1973 regime (see Section 2.2.2), in the emphasis upon recovery, and in the use of the word 'salvage' in the 1973 Act itself.

Fishing interests did not emerge strongly until the Committee stage of the 1973 Bill, when Mr. Sproat flagged the issue as being '... of considerable interest to my constituents' (HC 855: 1668). He stated that it was '... necessary to assure the fishermen that we are not out to place any impediment upon the exercise of their commercial activity...' (HC 855: 1697). Mr. Sproat certainly appeared to feel that preserving commercial fishing was as important as preserving 'our national heritage' (HC 851: 1872), at least in front of his constituents. Arguably, fishing interests might never have been considered in such detail if the DTI had ambushed some other MP who had been lucky in the ballot. It is worth noting that fishing interests did not appear as a lobby but as a constituency concern, and that their interests were to be safeguarded in representation and consultation by the relevant Departments rather than through their own organisations:

... the Secretary of State ... should consult the Fisheries Departments in England and Wales and in Scotland before any restricting order was made to ensure that it did not interfere with legitimate fishing, or so that the reasons for it could be explained and communicated to the fishing communities concerned

(Mr. Sproat, HC 855: 1697)

The interests of private owners of wreck were recognised to some extent, but they do not appear to have been organised into a lobby or represented formally. Aside from a concession on preferential licensing – mirroring the concession made to salvors and noted above – owners were not well-served in the debates or in the details of implementation set out at that time. Similarly, the interests of boat users appear to have had virtually no impact on the debates. There was an exchange about anchoring between Lord Kennet and Earl Ferrers (HC 342: 931), and Mr. Sproat stated on several occasions that there would be no prohibition on navigation, sailing or anchoring in restricted areas (e.g. HC 851: 1851; HC 851: 1877; see also Department of Trade and Industry 1973 a: 3; Department of Trade 1979: 1; Department of Transport 1986). However, it seems likely that the insistence on non-interference with boating interests – seen also in the restriction on number and extent of designated sites (see Section 3.2.2) – was prompted by a general policy of freedom of navigation rather than by more specific representations.

In summary, the multiple opportunities presented for interests other than archaeology to be heard indicate the fine balance upon which the 1973 regime rested. Although the 1973 Bill was largely motivated by archaeological interests (cf. Dromgoole's suggestion that the 1973 Bill only received Parliamentary time due to the provisions on Dangerous Wrecks, Dromgoole 1989 a: 37), other interests – notably recreational diving, commercial salvage and to some extent fishing – were well represented, to the point at which they might have overwhelmed archaeological points of view. It is tempting to see much of the debate as a 'real' debate in which the supporters of the 1973 Bill successfully anticipated arguments from MPs representing unsympathetic interests, but it might also be argued that by the time the debate started the success of the 1973 Bill was secure. In this respect, the parliamentary (rather than legislative) opportunity may not have been as marginal as it might seem. Confidence in the success of the 1973 Bill could have arisen from several quarters. First, it was certain that the 1973 Bill would receive a full debate by virtue of the position in the Ballot. Second, the 1973 Bill had strong Government support, plus the support of Opposition members. Third, it is likely that Onslow, as Minister, would have been informed in advance of any potential upsets on the floor of the House (see Searing 1995: 429). Furthermore, it might be suggested that the use of the 1973 Bill in the filibustering attempt discussed in Section 3.2.1 indicates the Government's confidence that the Bill would pass without hindrance.

What then, was the purpose of the debate – other than filibustering – and why are the undertakings made in its course so significant? Two issues stand out. First, the debates provided an opportunity to honour, by way of formal undertakings, deals struck earlier to avoid opposition (see Section 3.2.2). Second, the debates legitimated an outcome that was in many respects predetermined, confirming Drewry's observation that 'parliament's main legislative function ... lies largely in legitimation, i.e. in helping to secure public acceptance and obedience to the legislative actions of the state' (Drewry 1988: 126). Some justification for the argument that the debate was largely a mechanism for securing public trust is to be found in considering the amount of time spent debating the 1973 Bill. Burton and Drewry suggest that bills inspired or drafted by the government often receive their Commons second readings without any debate. They also observe that even though almost all bills that are enacted are subjected to some debate at second reading in the Lords, in most cases the debate lasts less than an hour (Burton and Drewry 1981: 221-223). In this respect, the 1973 Bill was unlike the majority of government bills, taking 96 minutes at second reading in the Commons and 61 minutes at second reading in the Lords. The unusual length of debates at Second Reading indicates the need to secure the legitimacy of the 1973 Bill in order to encourage compliance; although the debates took place within Parliament, the Bill's supporters were well aware that their target audience lay beyond Westminster (see Jordan and Richardson 1987: 128).

4.3 Legitimacy

I have shown that management can be assessed in terms of its success in establishing trust, thereby encouraging archaeological behaviour. Trust, however, only characterises circumstances where behaviour can be monitored more-or-less directly, hence the validity of expected behaviour is tied to specific times, places, or interactions. Beyond the purview of direct monitoring, expectations about behaviour turn upon the generalised validity of that behaviour, i.e. upon legitimacy. In this section, therefore, I look at aspects of management regimes that are distant from the actual locus of archaeological behaviour to see what such separation reveals about the legitimacy of management.

4.3.1 Sanctions

In Section 4.2.2 I recounted the introduction of the 1973 regime as a process of establishing trust between the various interests concerned to obviate, in part, the need for extensive (and expensive) policing and enforcement. Such enforcement would amount to the use of sanctions to encourage rule-following behaviour; as Giddens notes, 'the operation of sanctions is a chronic feature of all social encounters' (Giddens 1979: 87). Giddens' characterisation of legitimation as the structuring of sanctions appears to contradict Weber's characterisation of legitimacy in terms of the 'validity' of behaviour irrespective of sanctions (see Weber 1968: 31–32). The two positions are not, however, opposed; if legitimation is regarded as the structuring of trust rather than the structuring of sanctions (cf. Giddens 1984: fig. 2); legitimation *is* characterised by sanctions, but sanctions appear as the 'negative' side of trust, coming into play when trust fails.

In the following discussion, I am less concerned with the actual enforcement of legislation, than with what the sanctions included within such legislation imply about the presumed legitimacy of the regime concerned. Hence, it is not necessary to wait for offences to be punished – a rare enough occasion in archaeology underwater (for example, charges under the 1973 Act have only been brought on two occasions, see Dromgoole 1993: 3-26) – for the legitimacy of management to be assessed. In short, sanctions within each statute can be used as an index of the statute's legitimacy. In the following sections, an examination of rewards (positive sanctions) and penalties (negative sanctions) reveals the validity of general rules on reporting.

Penalties

The broad characteristics of penalties are summarised in table 4.4.

Countries such as Norway and Sweden, which draw no distinction between the circumstances for failing to make a report, can be contrasted with countries such as the Netherlands, where the offence is considered less serious if it was not 'wilful', and the UK, where a defence of 'reasonable excuse' can be offered. It might be argued that the regimes in Sweden and Norway are more 'abstract' in that they do not accept that mitigating circumstances should impinge upon penalties – it is the end result that is heinous, not the circumstances leading to that end. Consequently, the condition 'in serious cases' that may result in imprisonment in Norway might refer to the 'seriousness' of the consequence of not reporting – the resulting loss of ancient material perhaps – rather than the intentionality, ranging from oversight to overt criminality. In contrast, Danish legislation links higher penalties to the circumstances of the offence, notably intentionality, gross negligence and actual or intended financial advantage (PNA 1992 s. 89(2)). Interestingly, however, the Danish legislation includes a more general clause that provides for imprisonment if the 'interests that this Act strives to protect are harmed or endangered'

(PNA 1992 s. 89(2)(1)), shifting the emphasis back to consequences rather than causes.

It might be argued that the regimes that consider specific causes in sentencing will encourage reporting by people who have offended unintentionally, without diluting the offence itself. Clearly, the degree of flexibility will not discourage people who regard conviction as an occupational hazard – and it may give them stronger grounds to plead innocence – but such 'leniency' may serve to draw in confessions of non-wilful offences that would otherwise be scared off. In this respect, there is a parallel with the French provision (ACMCP 1989 s. 4) that exempts unintentional recovery to ensure that material is not lost as a result of the general criminalisation of disturbance (see Section 4.1.1). It is worth noting that the scope for criminal manipulation of the flexibility of a provision is reduced in Ireland by the following presumption. If a person proves to be in possession or control of an archaeological object, it is presumed that the object was found since the 1994 Act came into force, unless the contrary can be proved (NMA 1994 s. 4(3)).

In most of the countries, the penalties for reporting are the same as those for other offences under the relevant statutes. This equivalence implies that reporting is considered as important an expectation as those other offences – such as damage to a monument – even though failure to report may not result in any material damage at all. In the Netherlands, for example, any person who wilfully contravenes the provision on reporting (MHBA 1988: 47(1)) shall be penalised with a prison sentence of up to 1 year or a 'Category Five' fine (MHBA 1988 s. 56(2)). The same penalties apply to any person that wilfully excavates without a permit, damages a protected monument without a permit, or contravenes any instruction halting development work for the purposes of scientific research (MHBA 1988 s. 56). By way of contrast, in France the punishments for disturbing material *in situ* and for excavating without (or other than under the

Table 4.4:   A comparison of penalties

	Condition		Fine	Imprisonment	Further penalties
Netherlands	misdemeanour	=	Category 5	6 months	
	crime (wilfully)	=	Category 5	1 year	
Norway	wilfully or negligently		no limit specified	6 months	compensate or repair damage
Sweden	deliberately or negligently		no limit specified	6 months	forfeit all rights arising out of the find
Denmark			no limit specified		financial gain confiscated, or fine increased accordingly
	intentionally or by gross negligence			1 year	sequestration of motor vehicles used in offence
France	accidental removal exempt (Art. 4)		500 FF to 15,000 FF		
Ireland	summary	=	£1,000	12 months	
	on indictment	=	£50,000	5 years	
UK	without reasonable excuse		level 4		forfeit salvage award
					pay 2x value to owner/ person entitled

direct supervision of) a licence are more severe than penalties for failing to report or making a false declaration, i.e. 1,000 to 50,000 FF rather than 500 to 15,000 FF (ACMCP 1989: 14; 15). Denmark is the most striking exception, however. Although s. 14 of the Protection of Nature Act 1992 requires immediate reporting of discoveries of ancient monuments and wrecks to the Minister, it seems that only the subsections on damage (see PNA 1992: 14(1); 14(2)) are subject to penalties (PNA 1992 s. 89(1)(1)). Both France and Denmark, therefore, suggest differential expectations concerning behaviour, effectively ranking reporting below damage. It is, then, perhaps notable that four of the seven countries have declared, by means of a legal provision, that the failure to report is a such a serious breach of expected behaviour that it may warrant a custodial sentence.

In some instances, particular attention is directed to trafficking as a form of behaviour that is especially heinous. Hence, in Ireland it is an offence to purchase, sell or otherwise acquire or dispose of an archaeological object found in the State if the object has been found since the 1994 Act came into operation (NMA 1994 s. 4(2)), or between the coming into operation of the National Monuments Act 1930 and the 1994 Act, without reporting the purchase, sale etc. to the Director of the National Museum or a designated person within 30 days (NMA 1994 s. 5(2)). In France, the focus upon trafficking is reflected in the penalties. Provision is made for prison sentences of one month to two years, and fines from 500 F to 30,000 F for persons convicted of knowingly selling or buying maritime cultural property that has been recovered illegally from territorial waters or from the seabed of the contiguous zone. Moreover, the fine can be increased to double the price of the maritime cultural property that was sold, and the court can order that its decision be publicised in the press, at the expense of the convicted person (ACMCP 1989 s. 16).

The range of penalties suggests varying expectations about behaviour from country to country; the substantial penalties that may be imposed in Ireland stand out in this respect:

> on summary conviction ... a fine not exceeding £1,000 or, at the discretion of the court, to imprisonment for a term not exceeding 12 months or to both ...

> on conviction on indictment ... a fine not exceeding £50,000 or, at the discretion of the court, to imprisonment for a term not exceeding 5 years or to both ...
>
> (NMA 1994 s. 13; NMA 1930 [1994] s. 23(8))

While the size of the penalties may be necessary to confront the incentives to not following expected behaviour – the Derrynaflan hoard, for example, was valued at £5.5M (*Webb v. Ireland* [1988] IR 353: 372) – they also suggest an extremely strong expectation in Irish society that people should report their discoveries. Departure from such expected behaviour is intolerable.

Awards

While the penalty for intolerable behaviour in Ireland may be onerous, the reward for meeting expectations can be quite

generous. In the Derrynaflan case, for example, each of the finders was paid £25,000, notwithstanding the fact that they had no ownership rights over the material, they had committed a trespass, and they had injured a site protected under the National Monuments Act 1930. The decision to reward the Webbs turned, in particular, upon their actions following discovery; they placed the hoard in the hands of the National Museum on the day following its discovery and co-operated in identifying the find spot. In the words of McCarthy J. 'their subsequent conduct and attitude has been entirely praiseworthy' (*Webb v. Ireland* [1988] IR 353: 358–359; 398). In the course of judgement in the Supreme Court, Chief Justice Finlay outlined the factors that were of relevance in assessing a reasonable reward, which were subsequently established in statute as follows:

> The Director shall take account of all or any of the following criteria in deciding whether or not to pay a reward...
>
> (a) the intrinsic value and the general historical and archaeological importance of the object found;
>
> (b) the circumstances of the finding of the object;
>
> (c) the amount of the rewards paid in the state in respect of the finding of other comparable archaeological objects.
>
> (NMA 1994: 10(3))

Finlay also included a fourth factor:

> Lastly, and of very considerable importance, is the attitude and conduct of the finders of the objects after they have been found and the alacrity with which their finding is disclosed and their possession is surrendered to the appropriate authorities.
>
> (*Webb v. Ireland* [1988] IR 353: 386)

No equivalent reference is made to this factor in s. 10 of the 1994 Act, thus marking it as a factor that has not been 'abstracted' into statute to apply irrespective of the circumstances of the case. The reason may be that following the 1994 Act, the behaviour of the finder is prescribed to such an extent that any departure from rewardable conduct would be an offence. While such prescription may ensure that the desired end is achieved, the expulsion of choice is unlikely to develop the finder's *attitude* as Finlay might have wished, in contrast to the same Act's amendment of s. 23 of the Principal Act, which encourages finders to exercise judgement upon discovery (NMA 1994: 19; NMA 1930 [1994] s. 23(1)) (see Section 4.1.1). If anything, encouragement of the 'right attitude' is expressed negatively, as s. 10(4) provides that 'nothing in this section shall impose an obligation on the Director to pay a reward unless he is satisfied that it is in the public interest to do so'.

Awards that take account of the intrinsic value of a discovery are also found in Norway and Sweden. In Sweden, archaeological finds that are discovered away from an ancient monument and are presumably at least 100 years old accrue to the finder (ACAMF 1988 ch. 2 ss. 3(2), 4). However, the finder:

> is duty bound to invite the State to redeem such find in return for payment–

1. if the find contains objects partly or wholly of gold, silver, copper, bronze or any other copper alloy, or

2. if the find consists of two or more objects which were presumably deposited together.

(ACAMF 1988 ch. 2 s. 4)

The payment for objects of precious metal must be not less than the value of the metal by weight, 'augmented by one eighth' (ACAMF 1988 ch. 2 s. 16). In Norway, all antiquities – irrespective of intrinsic value – for which no owner is likely to come forward become the property of the state. Although no distinction is made in terms of ownership, rewards are made differentially:

If the find is of silver or gold the reward shall be at least equivalent to the value of the metal by weight, with an addition of not less than 10% of the value of the metal.

(CHA 1979 s. 13)

These provisions differ to the provisions in Ireland because the reward is linked not simply to intrinsic value, but to the intrinsic value of only such items as consist of precious metals. The focus on precious metals is most marked in Sweden where the type of metal is the first factor in deciding whether the item belongs to the state or not. Precious metals have no *a priori* value over other materials in terms of preservation and knowledge, though it might be argued that gold has a disproportionate value in terms of public display. Consequently, the focus upon precious metals in contemporary archaeological statutes seems to be a relic of ancient fiscal prerogatives intended to enrich the monarch – notably the doctrine of 'treasure trove' (see Darvill 1993: 5; Carman 1995). While a relatively unmodified doctrine of treasure trove continues to be used for archaeological purposes in England and Wales it is perhaps surprising to see evidence of its appropriation surviving in thoroughly re-worked statutes in Norway and Sweden.

The most generous reward provisions of the countries considered are found in the UK, where repeated commitments have been made (e.g. Department of Transport 1986; Department of Transport 1988) to paying 100% of the value (less expenses and – until recently – fees) of discoveries of historic wreck to the salvor. However, the Government does not pay direct cash awards to finders, and the apparent generosity masks quite a different practice, namely the award of discoveries to their finders. Although the Merchant Shipping Act 1995 provides that unclaimed wreck is sold and a payment made to the salvor, finders who salve unclaimed historic wreck are often granted ownership *in lieu* of a salvage reward. This practice has not been set out in statute or policy, but it is referred to in a recent leaflet (Coastguard Agency 1994 a). The practice seems to have grown, at least in part, from the policy of awarding 100% salvage rewards. Such rewards date back only to 1973. The policy change was made public in a press release in December, titled 'Increased Rewards for Treasure Hunters'. It announced that 'salvors of underwater treasure or any other articles legally known as "wreck"' may get the whole net proceeds of the sale of the salvaged articles'. The press release quotes Mr. Onslow, then Parliamentary Under Secretary of State for Aerospace and Shipping:

The whole purpose of this new move is to encourage people to report promptly any finds they make to the local Receiver of Wreck...

(Department of Trade and Industry 1973 d)

The intention of encouraging reporting through 100% awards, and 75% for coins, was still current in 1988:

In order to encourage the recovery and disclosure of items of historic interest, the present practice is to dispose of items in such a way as to leave a reasonable amount for salvage. In the case of all items of historic wreck, other than coinage, the award to the salvor is 100% of the net proceeds ... Coins are generally more valuable and are very much more numerous and the level of award is currently 75% of the net proceeds.

(Department of Transport 1988)

At some stage between 1973 and 1988 the policy transformed into the practice of returning items of historic wreck to finders in lieu of the salvage award (see Miller 1994: 809). The cause of the transformation may have been the practice of leaving historic wreck in the care of the salvor – to facilitate conservation – in the year that has to pass while awaiting claims (see Section 4.1.1). Subsequently the two practices of awarding 100% of the value and of arranging for the salvor to retain possession seem to have blurred into the practice of handing over the material itself as the reward. The blurring of practices may have been encouraged by the fact that by rewarding the finder with the material, the Government could avoid any cash outlay to which it would have been bound by the provision for Crown ownership of unclaimed wreck. This 'saving' may have been apparent to Mr. Onslow when he contemplated the introduction of 100% awards in 1973. The Government's financial interest in the net balance of rewards is attested to by the 25% it received of recoveries of coins, and the 7.5% commission charged by Receivers on property delivered to them up until March 1991 (Young, HC 187: 197w; Blatch, HL 526: 73w). The money that the Government was making from treasure hunting in the mid-1970s was particularly irksome to archaeologists at a time when no Government funds were being made available for investigation of designated sites. Following the *Association* auction, thought to be worth £15-30,000 to the DTI, Marsden commented '... surely it would be possible for the DTI to set aside its cut of the treasure-hunters loot to enable archaeologists and museums to help save something...' (The Times 30/11/74). Unfortunately, the synthesis of 100% awards and continued possession appeared to give rise to a perception among the diving and salving public that 'finders keepers' was the general rule. Such a rule does not encourage reporting, as if the diver believes that they own what they have found then there is no reason to inform the Receiver. Equally, the Department responsible seems to have shared the opinion; Dromgoole quotes an internal Department of Transport draft paper of 1991 as stating that, as finds are returned to the finder *in lieu* of a salvage award 'little harm [is] done if they are not reported' (Dromgoole 1993: 2-12). Certainly, it seems that some Receivers – who, as Customs Officers, were principally engaged in an altogether different business – turned away reports of historic wreck, doing little to encourage discoverers who had made an effort to 'do the right thing' (see Section 4.1.1)

By the late 1980s archaeologists were berating the Department of Transport's practice of awarding ownership of historic material in lieu of salvage, even though the roots of the practice seem to lie in measures to increase reports and to encourage the conservation of reported material. The assumption that rewards encourage reporting was still current in March 1993, when Caithness, then Minister for Aviation and Shipping, made the following statement in a letter to Dalyell: 'If finders do not believe that they will be properly rewarded, they must be less likely to report what they find'. Caithness asserted that the policy had 'resulted in several important cases coming to light over the years', but he also made the following admission:

> I acknowledge Mr Firth's view that our policy of returning historic objects to finders in lieu of salvage is not having the intended effect.

(L/PSO/6890/93; see HC 223: 71-72w)

Caithness did not specify which important cases had come to light. Of the wrecks considered to merit protection under the 1973 Act, for example, few came to attention through the Receiver system; most were a result of intentional searches or were first reported to archaeological organisations (CNA, NAS), to maritime museums, or directly to the agencies involved in designation (DTI-DNH, ADU). Moreover, Caithness' use of the term 'returning' in the above phrase suggests that 'finders keepers' is a perception deeply structured within Government, even though there is no statutory basis for salvors to become owners of wreck that they remove from the seabed.

In the Netherlands and Sweden, people who discover isolated finds become their owners unless they are found during an excavation (Netherlands) or they either contain precious metal or were deposited together (Sweden). There is no provision for rewards in such cases – the material itself is the reward. However, in the Netherlands, the 'new' owner of the find is obliged to pay half the value of the finds to the owner of the land (MHBA 1988: 43(3)). Similarly, in Norway the landowner is entitled to half the reward stipulated by the authorities, though the authority may decide not to pay the landowner any or all of the reward 'if special reasons so dictate' (CHA 1979 s. 13). Moreover, in Norway, the authority may hand part or all of the discovery back to the finder or to the landowner, once the find has been investigated (CHA 1979 ss. 13, 14). In all these cases, as with the practice of awarding material *in lieu* of salvage, the structure of rewards is such that the finder, believing that they will receive the material in any case, neglects to report their discovery. Bringing their good fortune to the attention of the authorities will only result in bureaucracy or, even worse, having to lose part of the material or its value to the landowner. In such circumstances, mandatory provisions on reporting are mere exhortations that are undermined by expectations arising from reward and/or ownership provisions.

In addition to finder's ownership and rewards in kind, ancient material may be given to the finder as a way of providing for the continued care of the material while reducing the burden on the state. In such cases, the material is deposited with the finder without them acquiring ownership. In Norway, for example, special agreements are made in relation to anchors so that divers are permitted to recover them if they are to be displayed publicly and their conservation can be underwritten. In France, finds made by individuals in inland waters result in agreement between the Service Regional d'Archéologie, a museum and the finder which allows the object to be deposited with the finder. Such arrangements may also be informal; for example, in one case in the Netherlands an individual excavating a wreck site is being allowed to possess the material on condition that it is exhibited locally. If, however, the authorities do little after depositing the material, the finder may gain the impression that they have become the owner. The net effect will be to associate finding with acquisition of material – irrespective of the precise meaning of the relevant provisions – encouraging recovery rather than reporting of material *in situ*. The effort required to clarify the difference between ownership and possession, and to ensure that the integrity of the material is maintained, might be as great a burden to the state as taking the material into storage. However, benefits could accrue from the public access that is achieved.

The negative aspects of rewarding finders 'in kind' were debated in France in the course of introducing new legislation on maritime cultural property in 1989. Under earlier legislation, isolated discoveries were often awarded to their finders, while the finder of a wreck site would be given the first option of salvaging the site (by way of a 'concession' with conditions) and could ask to be rewarded in kind. Cash rewards would be paid for isolated discoveries placed in public collections on account of their interest, and for sites for which the finder did not receive the concession or which were excavated by the state. Such cash rewards were generally of about one third of the value of the object or site. The emphasis on rewards in kind and on 'concessions' characterised a regime that 'relied on the logic of salvage and recovery' that was no longer appropriate to the requirements of modern archaeology (Beix 1989: 27). Moreover, the differential of rewards for isolated finds and for sites was encouraging a 'treasure hunt' and divers were recovering sites piece-by-piece so that they could report them as isolated finds and have the material 'returned'.

It seems that the committee for which Beix reported would have preferred that rewards would be paid only in cash, not in kind, to break any perceived link with previous salvage regimes. The report includes a discussion of the level of cash award that might be paid, and emphasised that the reward be related to the importance of the discovery, not its value (Beix 1989: 28). However, it was finally accepted that to insist on cash awards alone would be unnecessarily restrictive, and so the relevant provision (ACMCP 1989 s. 6) was amended to allow the authority to set the nature as well as the amount of awards (Beix 1989: 28). This, in turn, created a problem in respect of discoveries in the contiguous zone – over which the State does not assert ownership – as there was no possibility of making an award in kind. The final provision

(ACMCP 1989: 13) only states that the authority can set the amount of the award. The differential between objects and sites that encouraged piecemeal recovery was overcome by using the overarching term 'maritime cultural property' to apply to both, and by the general prohibition upon disturbance (ACMCP 1989 s. 3).

One way of decoupling monetary values from the material is to make 'special' awards to people who report, which is to say the action of reporting is rewarded, not the material as such. The de-coupling is emphasised by statements to the effect that the finder has no right to a reward, and/or that the finder has no rights in the material. Hence in Denmark, s. 28 of the Act on Museums provides that finders may be rewarded by the State Antiquarian – and will normally be so – but they have no *right* to a reward (AM 1984 [1989] s. 28(3)). In Ireland, s. 10 of the 1994 Act, discussed above, states that payment of a reward 'shall not confer rights in respect of the archaeological object' (NMA 1994 s.10). A degree of de-coupling is achieved in Sweden because the a provision stating that the amount of an award must be 'reasonable' having regard to the nature of the find is accompanied by a provision for special rewards that 'may also be paid' (ACAMF 1988 ch. 2 s. 16).

Special awards can also serve pragmatic functions. In the Netherlands, for example, a one-off reward was given to the discoverer of two vessels to dissuade them from pursuing a salvage claim at a time when the implementation of the law was ambiguous. Similarly, in Denmark in 1984 some sport divers reported a rare bronze mortar that they had recovered from a wreck dating to 1658. The Royal Arsenal Museum valued the mortar at one million Danish kroner, but the interference with the site had been illegal. The dilemma posed by a wish to reward the report but penalise the recovery was resolved by awarding the divers twice the value of the metal (Rieck pers. com.).

Indirect awards that concern some other aspect of discovery and consequent activity may also have a decoupling effect. In the Netherlands, for example, the authorities offer no rewards to the finder but the archaeologists usually hire the reporter's boat (if they are involved in fishing or diving) when they go out to evaluate the discovery. When fishers retrieve archaeological material in their nets, the Netherlands authorities will also pay for the transport costs involved in bringing the material in. These can be considerable. For example, a shrimp trawler reported a mast step weighing 2 tonnes that had little intrinsic value but considerable archaeological significance (Maarleveld pers. com; see also Maarleveld and Stassen 1993: 283).

4.3.2   The Advisory Committee

Although it is an offence under the 1973 Act to do anything contrary to the conditions of a licence (PWA 1973 s. 1(5)(c)), no charges have been brought under this provision. Arguably, the principal form of negative sanction in respect of licences is the ability to refuse or withdraw a licence, or to 'reduce' it from an excavation to a survey licence. However, it has already been noted (see Section 4.1.2) that licensing has acquired a perpetual character, and that there seems to have been very few occasions when licensing has been used as

punishment. In the absence of information about individual cases, the gross pattern of licensing reveals little about the general legitimacy of the 1973 regime. An impression of such legitimacy can be gained, however, by looking at ACHWS as a principal institution of the 1973 regime from inception to the present day.

The impression that the 1973 regime is unsatisfactory to those whose behaviour it is intended to regulate, and that such dissatisfaction is related to the rôle of the Advisory Committee, is encouraged by the following exchange, reported by Croome in an account of a meeting held at the Royal Armouries, London, in January 1988:

> A speaker from the CBA suggested that licensees should lose their licences if they did not produce reports. At present, apparently, all they had to do was to outline their publication plans. A licensee present asked that the Advisory Committee should guarantee publication of reports; to date it has consumed reams of paper but nothing came out. A Committee member retorted that most reports were 'unpublishable'.
>
> (Croome 1988: 114)

The conflict evinced in the reported exchange does not appear to have arisen as a result of a 'personality clash' or anger at some aspect of that particular meeting, i.e. because of individual or group circumstances. Rather, the exchange indicates general concern about the validity of expectations about reporting and publishing in general; hence, the criticisms are directed to the legitimacy of the regime that has given rise to such expectations rather than to specific instances of rule following or of trust between the parties. Importantly, as legitimacy concerns institutionalisation rather than instances of individual or group practice, criticisms are to be levelled at the constitution of ACHWS and not at its members individually, except insofar as they have contributed to – or re-produced – the faults of its constitution.

ACHWS was establish to advise the Secretary of State in order to satisfy the requirements of s. 1(4) of the 1973 Act:

> Before making an order under this section, the Secretary of State shall consult with such persons as he considers appropriate having regard to the purposes of the order; but this consultation may be dispensed with if he is satisfied that the case is one in which an order should be made as a matter of immediate urgency.
>
> (PWA 1973: 1(4))

Although the obligation to consult does not extend to the issuing of licences, this matter has been within the remit of the Committee since 1973. Mr. Onslow noted in debate that 'the committee would be asked to advise whether licences should be granted for salvage operations and what conditions should be attached to such licences...' (HC 851: 1675–1676). Equally, the original terms of reference of the Committee included the following passage:

> to approve the issue of licences for the surveillance and excavation of designated sites by named individuals, the conditions to be attached to the issue of such licences, to receive reports on progress made at individual sites and to consider any matter that may

arise supplementary to its main task – e.g. problems of conservation and disposal of artefacts etc.

(see Saunders 1994: 316)

Flinder and McGrail's account of the matters upon which the Committee gives advice refers to the following topics:

2. the archaeological and underwater capabilities of applicants for licences to survey or to excavate designated sites; on the conservation and other resources available to them; whether or not licences should be granted.

3. the standards of work on designated wreck sites, including compliance with any conditions imposed on the licensee.

4. the periodic reports produced by licensees.

(Flinder and McGrail 1990: 93)

In short, the functions of the Committee have been set out quite consistently from 1973 to the present and have received little criticism. In contrast, Dromgoole notes criticism of the *composition* of the Committee and suggests that there might be less room for such challenges if the Committee was governed by statute (Dromgoole 1989 a: 40). Back in 1973, the Government expressed a strong interest in an informal arrangement, and the matter was debated explicitly by Dr. Owen and Mr. Onslow. Dr. Owen asked if 'the advisory group is likely to have some form of formal status and be publicly announced so that people will know who is advising the Minister?' (HC 851: 1869; and see Mr. Maclennan, HC 855: 1700). Mr. Onslow described what he had in mind in the following terms:

... it is not spelt out specifically in the Bill who will comprise the sum total of the advisers who are to be consulted ... it is probably a mistake to try to be over-precise in cases of this kind ... I do not think that the group should have a formal, permanently constituted membership. There is a need for informality ... It would be difficult to get a thorough and comprehensive group guaranteed to include every single possible expert.

(HC 851: 1868-1869)

Mr. Onslow did set out some administrative details concerning the Advisory Committee during the later debate, and announced that Lord Runciman of Doxford would Chair of the Committee (HC 855: 1674–1675). In view of the significant decision-making role that ACHWS came to have, and the (albeit unintended) longevity of the 1973 regime, it is unfortunate that its constitution was not set out more formally. Mr. Onslow's remark about permanently constituted membership seems ironic as some members have, by default, been on the Committee for decades. As Saunders – one of the original members of the Committee – has stated 'it is remarkable that throughout its twenty years existence there has been substantial continuity of membership' (Saunders 1994: 316). It is evident that Saunders regards such permanence as a virtue, in contrast to Mr. Onslow's earlier reservations.

Recent changes suggest that 'substantial continuity of membership' is not the asset it once was. Following the retirement of Basil Greenhill as Chair and in line with general

Government policy on appointments, ACHWS has undergone an extensive 'reshuffle' coupled with the introduction of fixed term appointments (Department of National Heritage 1996). Only four of the previous members have been reappointed – including three whose positions on ACHWS date back to 1973-76 – together with eight new appointments.

Although the changes of 1996 represent the first major break in the membership of ACHWS since 1973, there were earlier challenges. On 1 January 1982 the Committee was reduced from 17 to 12 members (HC 14: 412w). However, the reduction seems to have been achieved principally by sleight of hand, i.e. by not counting the 'Associate Members' representing Wales, Scotland and Northern Ireland. The 'Associate Members' reappeared officially a few years later (Department of Transport 1986: Annex C), but T. Wright of the Science Museum and David Blackman were permanent casualties. Mr. Blackman's contribution to ACHWS, which dated back to 1974, was not even recognised in the Department of Transport's list of past members in 1986 (Department of Transport 1986: Annex C).

The reduction in 1982 was prompted by a Parliamentary Question asking the Secretary of State – coincidentally, a certain Mr. Sproat – 'when he last carried out an overall review of the need for retaining the Advisory Committee on Historic Wreck Sites' (HC 14: 412w). Mr. Sproat stated that the need to retain the Advisory Committee was reviewed annually, and that 'it brings together people with a wide range of expertise and knowledge, connected with both privately and publicly financed bodies, including salvors, archaeologists and museum specialists'. He also stated that ACHWS was 'the best available method of obtaining objective and cost effective advice (HC 14: 412w)' on implementation of the 1973 Act.

Mr. Sproat's defence indicates the two principal justifications for the membership of ACHWS since its inception, that is, as a committee of representatives and as a committee of experts. In 1973, Dr. Owen was particularly keen that the membership of the advisory board was not restricted to archaeologists, reflecting his views about the interests that should be consulted: 'I am therefore in favour of including all the different elements in this mix on the advisory board so that the best advice is available to the Minister' (HC 851: 1860). The involvement of other interests appears to have been part of the package agreed in establishing trust (see Section 4.2.2), as Mr. Onslow and later Earl Ferrers included the British Sub-Aqua Club and 'commercial diving interests' or 'salvage interests' as advisors to be consulted alongside archaeologists and museum representatives (HC 851: 1868; HL 342: 932). The Government may have wanted a representative advisory committee in order to distance the Government from deliberation of wreck matters, thereby demonstrating that the Government was not dictating designations and licences. Such distance may have been sought to accommodate non-archaeological interests (see Section 4.2.2), which may have assumed that the Government would listen too closely to archaeologists, hence Mr. Sproat's comment with respect to licensing '... The safeguard here is the committee to be headed by Runciman' (HC 855: 1698) and Mr. Onslow's assurance that 'I was at pains to make it clear that we would depend on the advice of the consultative committee...' (HC 855: 1697).

The representative character of ACHWS is illustrated in the Guidance Note published in December 1986, which lists the names of the members of ACHWS alongside a list of organisations headed 'Representing or Associated with'. Mr. Bateson and Mr. Cowan are the only members of the Committee who are listed without an affiliation at that time (Department of Transport 1986). Consequently, the statement by Flinder and McGrail that the members of ACHWS '... are selected as individuals and *not as representatives* of groups or organizations' (Flinder and McGrail 1990: 93; my emphasis) implies a change in policy in the late 1980s. It appears that the Committee became a form of 'corporate representation', hence Flinder and McGrail state:

> ... its members have been *chosen* to collectively represent a broad spectrum of informed opinion in maritime, archaeological, historical, conservational, legal, museum and diving fields ...

> (Flinder and McGrail 1990: 93, my emphasis)

This statement may characterise the contemporary view of representation, but it is not the form of representation applicable in the early years of the 1973 regime when the majority of members were 'chosen'. Nonetheless, Saunders has confirmed the corporate conception of the Committee's membership:

> ... the balance of interests within the Committee competent to provide the range of advice sought by the Secretary of State would appear to satisfy Government.

> (Saunders 1994: 317)

Saunders introduces the above remark by noting that '... the increasing number of younger and better qualified underwater archaeologists have complained in recent years, with some justice, that they are under represented...' (Saunders 1994: 317). In raising the issue of qualifications, Saunders draws attention to the legitimacy of the Committee in terms of expertise. Notwithstanding the nominally representative role of the board, Mr. Onslow was keen to give assurances in 1973 that '... neither the House nor the Secretary of State will be acting ... without the best possible advice being made available' (HC 855: 1674). He specified the experts whose advice was to be sought as follows:

> It is our intention that the committee should consist of persons distinguished in fields of archaeology ... the Hydrographer of the Navy, the Directors of the Science and National Maritime Museums, and two experts on coins and cannon from the British Museum...

> (HC 855: 1674)

It is worth noting that specialised knowledge would focus on coins and cannon, reflecting the preoccupations of 1973 (see Section 2.3). The importance of expertise to the legitimacy of ACHWS in recent years is made abundantly clear in the press release accompanying the 1996 changes to the membership. Five of the eight new members are described principally as 'specialists' and the accompanying biographical notes emphasise the members' academic and professional eminence (Department of National Heritage 1996).

The expert and representative rôles of ACHWS are not necessarily compatible. Insofar as a person is chosen as expert or as representative, then their membership dilutes the composition of the committee in respect of the rôle that they do not serve; the more representative is a committee, the less expert it will be, and *vice versa*. It is possible that the expert and representative rôles could have been reconciled if Committee's constitution had been established formally. Moreover, the membership might have been expected to change more regularly as the committees of represented organisations changed, or – as Saunders implies – fresh expertise was acknowledged. Furthermore – and notwithstanding the recent changes – membership of the Committee appears to be restricted; Dromgoole recounts an offer by the Association of County Archaeologists to 'elect' a member to ACHWS, but the offer was turned down (Dromgoole 1993: 3-8–9). None of the new members in 1996 appear to have a background in local authority archaeology.

As time has passed it seems that any distinction that may have been drawn between rôles has been elided to produce a collective blur such that the Committee often seems to be neither expert nor representative. Insofar as all parties emphasised the importance of an advisory board that was expert and/or representative for the successful implementation of the 1973 Act, then the uncertain constitution of the Committee raises questions as to the legitimacy not only of its decisions in specific instances, but also of the 1973 regime as a whole.

Arguably, the greatest test of the legitimacy of the Advisory Committee and the 1973 regime in general was presented by the *Invincible* affair. On 8 March 1988, Mr. Channon made the following statement in response to a question put to the Secretary of State for Transport by Mr. Onslow:

> Our aim is that the disposal of items recovered from wreck sites designated under the provisions of the Protection of Wrecks Act 1973 ... should be conducted in such a way as to ensure as far as possible that they remain accessible to the general public, that collections of items are kept together and that items of particular local interest go to local museums.

> (HC 129: 155w)

This aim reflects statements made in 1979 (Department of Trade 1979), 1986 (Department of Transport 1986) and again in 1988 (Department of Transport 1988), but the consistency of the aim that Mr. Channon expressed belied an ugly situation in practice; as Dromgoole puts it:

> Two days later, 400 artefacts from the designated wreck HMS *Invincible* were auctioned at Christie's in London. The sale raised £60,000 towards the further excavation of the wreck.

> (Dromgoole 1989 a: 50)

A further question by Mr. Onslow in May 1988 to the Secretary of State for Transport – asking 'if he will place a copy of his Department's guidance to the historic wrecks advisory committee' – may have been an attempt to clarify the relationship between the Department, its Advisory Committee and licensees, in order to attribute responsibility for the failure to protect the *Invincible*. Mitchell replied as follows:

> I have placed in the Library a copy of the Department's booklet on historic wrecks, which contains a description of the committee's functions and how it fulfils them. No further guidance is supplied to the committee.
>
> (HC 134: 150w)

This answer might be seen as an attempt by the Department to distance itself from the decisions of the Advisory Committee, suggesting that ACHWS had a 'free hand' in preparing its advice. However, such distance would not absolve the Department from acting on that advice in granting licences. Mr. Onslow subsequently put questions to the Secretary of State for Defence (HC 138: 29–30w) and, once more, to the Secretary of State for Transport. Mr. Portillo's reply included the following statement:

> Disposal of artefacts recovered is subject to the provisions of the Merchant Shipping Act 1894 and cannot be the subject of conditions attached to a licence issued under the 1973 Act.
>
> (HC 138: 770w)

Mr. Portillo's answer is unsatisfactory. It suggests that the Government had no grounds for aiming to ensure that items recovered from wreck sites designated under the 1973 Act remained accessible, were kept together and went to local museums, yet such an aim had been stated repeatedly both before and after the *Invincible* sale. In addition, if the relevant Department was powerless to intervene in matters of disposal, it can have had no justification for asking prospective licensees to state their proposals for the ultimate destination of objects that may be recovered (Department of Trade 1975: 407–408; see Section 4.1.2). Moreover, even if the Department of Transport could not impose conditions, it could simply refuse to license further activity – let alone excavation – on the site. It was on these grounds that Marsden attacked the Government's administration of the 1973 Act in 1990:

> in 1989 ... the Department of Transport ... issued a licence to a salvor to excavate the 'protected' wreck of the warship *Invincible* ... in the knowledge that the salvor was financing the work by selling off the finds.
>
> (Marsden 1990 a: 3)

Marsden's attack prompted a response from Bingeman, the licensee, who noted that it was only 'surplus' artefacts that were sold to help defray the excavation and conservation costs, after the Chatham Historic Dockyard Trust had accepted custodianship of a representative collection (Bingeman 1990: 186; see also Dromgoole 1989 a: 50). Bingeman included a quote from a letter from the Ministry of Defence:

> Before granting the current salvors approval to conduct their recovery operation, the Ministry of Defence obtained confirmation that the Department of Transport's Consultative Committee on Historic Wrecks [sic] were content with the archaeological aspects of the dive. The salvor's archaeological director is Dr Margaret Rule, of *Mary Rose* fame and a full

archaeological record of the dive is held by the Chatham Historic Dockyard Trust.

> (Secretary of State for Defence to Honorary Secretary of the IFA, quoted in Bingeman 1990: 186)

The rôle of both the Advisory Committee and of archaeological directors is problematised by the references made to them by the licensee to justify the action taken. Importantly, the attempt to establish legitimacy comprises both the letter from the Secretary of State for Defence, and the licensees publication of that part of the letter. Marsden, in reply, noted that 'there is no need for excavation to continue on the *Invincible*, and any financial problems that the licensee now has are a result of pressing ahead with excavation' (Marsden 1990 b: 188), and that:

> ... two members of the Advisory Committee have recently put on public record their concern for how DOT is managing historic sites ... In view of this perhaps the DOT will allow their Advisory Committee to make statements about its position on these matters ... perhaps in annual reports, for the silence of the Committee could well be understood by some to condone such general matters as the dispersal of finds and the use of 'absentee directors' ...
>
> (Marsden 1990 b: 188)

One of the members of the Advisory Committee to which Marsden referred subsequently refuted Marsden's interpretation of his concern, and stated that it was 'presumptuous of Mr Marsden to suggest that the DOT muffles its Advisory Committee', adding 'the Committee has over a period of years vigorously expressed concern to its Minister on many matters including that of the disposal of finds' (Flinder 1990: 241). Marsden responded that his criticism was not aimed at the Advisory Committee but at the Department 'who, I am told, set the rules' (Marsden 1990 c: 242). Saunders has stated that the area in which the Committee feels most frustrated is in the disposal and dispersal of artefacts from wreck sites, suggesting that the concept of integrity of the total archaeological archive is not practically achievable for underwater sites at the present time. Saunders notes that the situation has not been helped by 'confusion' over the operation of the Merchant Shipping Act 1894, by salvage rights and 'the desire of some divers to make excavations self-financing' (Saunders 1994: 318). However, neither the Government nor its Committee has ever explained why Bingeman was licensed to continue excavations after – and presumably on the proceeds of – the Christie's sale nor, given Saunders' suggestion that the integrity of archives is not achievable, why any excavation licences are granted at all. Arguably the answer goes back to the ambiguity at the centre of the 1973 Act when it was introduced; was it intended to manage archaeology underwater, or was it intended to facilitate uninterrupted recovery? As far as some licensees are concerned, it seems that the legitimacy of the 1973 regime lies in recovery as something that is intrinsically 'worthwhile', hence Bingeman concluded his response to Marsden's call for higher standards as follows:

> New legislation to implement Marsden's proposals would further curtail the endeavours of people like myself and would be contrary to the traditions of

English amateur archaeologists. We don't claim to be perfect but at least we have achieved something worthwhile.

(Bingeman 1990: 187)

If, in the minds of people working within the 1973 regime, legitimacy inheres in recovery – as it did in the minds of the MPs who introduced the 1973 Act – then the effort to improve the quality of work on designated sites requires more than a tightening up of requirements on paper. Notwithstanding the similarity between the provisions of the 1973 Act and of terrestrial antiquities legislation, it will be necessary to re-visit the arguments used in legitimising the 1973 Act as it was introduced, and to examine the institutionalisation of these arguments through administrative practice in the course of implementation. As I have shown, the Advisory Committee is an institution whose character is intrinsic to the legitimacy of the behaviour that the 1973 Act is intended to encourage. If new behaviours are required, and are to be accepted as being legitimate, then it is not just the membership but the overall character of the institution that has to change.

This chapter addressed two areas of behaviour where the management of archaeology underwater attempts to cause non-archaeologists to behave archaeologically. Efforts to attain archaeological norms on sites regulated by the 1973 Act were examined by reference to conditions placed on individual licensees, to negotiations between interest groups during introduction of the 1973 Act, and to the constitution of the Advisory Committee on Historic Wreck Sites. Efforts to encourage the public to report new discoveries were discussed in terms of instructions to individuals contained in statutes, the circumstances in which finders meet the authorities when making reports, and the positive and negative sanctions that manifest an institutional response to normal and aberrant behaviour.

Each set of examples progressed from individual appreciation of norms in respect of ancient material, by way of the pursuit of rule-following behaviour in circumstances of face-to-face interaction, to a consideration of systemic factors that inculcate – or otherwise – an 'archaeological' relationship with the relics of the past. While constraint is evident at all three levels, minimal use of available sanctions in both sets of examples indicates that constraint is not attributable principally to an imbalance of power. Rather, there is a close relationship between the legitimacy of the system and individual rule following, where non-archaeological behaviour indicates a failure of such legitimacy. In this relationship, the circumstances in which non-archaeologists and archaeologists encounter each other have – through their structuring of trust – a marked effect on both rule following and legitimacy. It follows that, in managing archaeology underwater, attention should be directed to the circumstances in which archaeological behaviour is encouraged as much as to the content of the behaviour expected. Correspondingly, in society at large, attention can be directed to the rôle of archaeology underwater in establishing circumstances in which trust may arise between citizen and state.

I have completed an analysis of the management of archaeology underwater which gives due weight to each of the three dimensions of structure – signification, domination and legitimation – at each of the three levels of integration – individual rationalisation, social integration and system integration. In the following chapter I use insights drawn from this analysis to account for the structuring of a nationalist paradigm within archaeological institutions, and for the apparent failings of that paradigm in respect of the management of archaeology underwater.

5.   NATIONALISM AND POST-NATIONALISM

In Chapters Two, Three and Four, I explained how the management of archaeology becomes structured through the incremental actions of archaeologists, civil servants, legislators, lobbyists and members of the public. I also showed how such structuring shapes the further actions of these agents, affecting people's awareness of ancient material, the presence of such material within the environment, and patterns of behaviour in respect of ancient material. In considering structure as something that is both constraining and enabling, and that is located neither in individuals nor in institutions but in the interaction of one with the other, I have shown that peoples' relationships with ancient material are not *determined* by law and policy but arise from, and remain susceptible to, novel actions. Such novel actions could lead to the development of new relationships between people and ancient material, but first it is necessary to acknowledge the persistence of old relationships.

5.1   Archaeology and the Nation-State: substance and shape

In Section 1.8, I suggested that archaeology could be equated with surveillance insofar as information about the past is mobilised to generate a state narrative to which individuals subscribe in constructing their own identities. However, the structuring of archaeological practice is such that archaeologists' contribution to the narrative of a nation-state does not depend upon overt manipulation of interpretations, as demonstrated by archaeologists' routine but uncritical use of maps. Maps lend themselves to nation building – notwithstanding their apparent Cartesian objectivity – by smoothing the edges of a country to present an imaginable, stable identity, hence Erikson comments:

> ... the map can be a very concise and potent symbol of the nation ... Country maps, present in classrooms all over the world, depict the nation simultaneously as a bounded, observable thing and as an abstraction of something which has a physical reality.

> (Eriksen 1993: 106)

Anderson devotes a section of the second edition of *Imagined Communities* to the rôle of European-style maps in the anti-colonial nationalist imaginings of South East Asia referring, in particular, to the 'map-as-logo' (Anderson 1983 [1991]: 175). One crucial aspect of maps is the tendency – not least among archaeologists – to reproduce the coast as a permanent, impermeable and self-evident boundary, even though it is hard to imagine a more transient line than that presented by tide-pressed waves. This hard edge, though mythical, is nonetheless incorporated into the formation of identities, as Colley has demonstrated. In discussing James Gillray's 1793 cartoon *The French Invasion; or John Bull, bombarding the Bum-Boats*, Colley presents a superb example of a 'map-as logo' that identifies sea-defined territory with nation-state, royalty and England's 'Other' – France. The cartoon carries the title 'A New Map of England and Wales' and shows George III/John Bull squatting over the Channel and dumping on France, an upturned face. The

'British Declaration' is emitted from the Hampshire/Sussex border – perhaps the naval dockyard at Portsmouth – against the ships of France:

> George III is shown as ... being entirely at one with England and Wales ... They give him shape, but he gives them identity.

> (Colley 1992: 210)

The rôle of archaeology in applying a soothing balm of nationalism to modernity's rough edges is not limited to marshalling graphic information; insofar as antiquities legislation generates the differential survival of ancient material, the values of state-sponsored archaeology are manifest within the environment, hence:

> ... a general common sense acceptance of the nation ... [is] ... promulgated not only by texts ... but also by the proliferation in the external world of signs (institutions, monuments and other 'sediments') alluding to the nation and rendering its presence irrefutable.

> (Bowman 1994: 142-3)

Maritime archaeology is not exempt from such processes; Cederlund's account of salvaged regal ships – epitomised by the *Vasa* – as a 'symbol of the power of divine kingdom' in Sweden draws particular attention to the 'environmental' impact of tall ships:

> It seems that these ships were regular appearances in the environment of port cities or towns in Western societies in the same way and just as regularly as churches, castles and palaces. Were, and are, the high-rigged warships symbols which we 'need' for similar reasons as we 'need' the buildings just mentioned? The new Vasa museum has on its roof a full-scale replica of the original rig of the ship – thus making the appearance of a big, rigged warship once again part of the environment of Stockholm harbour.

> (Cederlund 1994: 78)

In Britain, an association of ships with the defence of the realm that is taught, however critically, may subside into a practical recognition of ships as a protection against invasion of the British Isles, irrespective of the pro-active rôle of ships in 'maintaining' an empire or in regaining distant islands. Hence the masts of the *Victory* and the *Warrior* over Portsmouth legitimise the presence of UK warships in the South Atlantic, the Gulf and the Adriatic. The physical presence of old warships at Portsmouth is also accompanied by an ideational presence stimulated by, for example, posters advertising the *Victory*, *Warrior* and *Mary Rose* at – it seems – every railway station in South East England. The routine presence of the posters – 'signs' that comprehend not only the icons but also the legends that accompany them – is reinforced by other publicity, such as the free magazine on the Southampton-London train:

> On board HMS Victory and HMS Warrior 1860, walk the decks once paced by the sailors whose efforts made Britain the greatest power in the world. Nelson's flagship ... putting paid to Napoleon's plan to add

England to his Empire. HMS Warrior 1860 ... the pride of Queen Victoria's fleet ... Henry VIII watched the Mary Rose sink as she set sail to do battle with the French ... The modern grey warships of today's navy are another exciting feature of your visit...

(SouthWest Trains 1995: 4)

This routine association of shipping with royalty, the defence of England (why not Britain?), and fighting 'the French' extends, therefore, beyond the sight of the masts of *Warrior* and *Victory*, establishing pre-conceptions that allow such meanings to be 'discovered' practically in street names, pub signs, black-painted anchors and cannon-shaped bollards. Clearly, the efforts of archaeologists can feed such perceptions, even though the material with which they deal may remain underwater and invisible. The information, accounts, plans and drawings that are brought ashore can – if they are not presented in a critical manner – add to the jumble of impressions from which people construct their individual and collective narratives (see Ascherson 1987 [1988]: 12). In the following subsections, I show how the institutionalised practices of managing archaeology underwater impinge upon interpretations, environments and behaviour to give substance and shape to the nation-state.

5.1.1   Nationality

The multiple meanings of 'national' are commonly discussed in two senses (see e.g. Hutchinson and Smith 1994: 4; Gellner 1983: 1). First, it is discussed in a 'cultural' sense that denotes common ancestry and ethnicity, i.e. the 'nation'. Second, it is discussed in a 'political' or 'civil' sense that carries overtones of objectivity, rationality, democracy and justice, encapsulated in the 'state'. Consequently, the term 'national' obscures the relationship between identity and administration, thereby ensuring the hegemony of that union. Ambiguity makes the term 'national' extremely valuable as a legitimising concept; Hobsbawm notes that the ambiguous criteria used to define nations are 'unusually convenient for propagandist and programmatic ... purposes' (Hobsbawm 1992: 6), and Bowman suggests that:

... the concept of the nation retains its grip on the imaginary of its population precisely by remaining unfixed.

(Bowman 1994: 144)

The difficulty in pinning down the relationship between cultural and civil senses of 'national' is compounded in that even the civil sense of nationality may be used as a cultural marker with ethnic and historic connotations. Hence, the nation referred to in a civil passport is assumed to have a cultural correlate that is satisfied by every passport-holding individual. Moreover, identification with a system of government or a political principle – such as freedom of speech – is both civil and cultural simultaneously. The notion that 'our civility is our culture' is distressingly clear in some discourses on Europe, which overlook the brutality perpetrated by inhabitants of Europe both locally and globally in favour of a myth-ridden 'inheritance' that implies a clear idea of who and where is 'outside'. Smith provides a good example in his discussion of the future of national identity:

These patterns of European culture – the heritage of Roman law, Judeo-Christian ethics, Renaissance humanism and individualism, Enlightenment rationalism and science, artistic classicism and romanticism and, above all, traditions of civil rights and democracy ... – have created a common European cultural heritage and formed a unique culture area ... This is not the planned 'unity in diversity' beloved of official Europeanism, but a rich, inchoate mélange of cultural assumption, forms and traditions, a cultural heritage that creates sentiments of affinity between the peoples of Europe. It is here ... that we must look for the basis of a cultural Pan-European nationalism that may ... take us beyond the nation.

(Smith, A. 1991: 174)

The exclusivity of such attempts to define 'Europe' have set alarm bells ringing both in the critical literature (see Neumann and Welsh 1991; Pieterse 1991; Shore 1993: 793; Webber 1991) and in European institutions (e.g. OJ 93/C 42/176: W), which are no doubt glad that Smith distances his conception from 'official Europeanism'. Moreover, Smith's conception endorses nationalism on a Pan-European scale and, thus, cannot 'take us beyond the nation' in any sense that would undermine the nation-state; it remains necessary to pick apart 'nationality' as perceived individually, communicated archaeologically and expressed abstractly in order to conceptualise its transcendence.

Interviews with archaeologists engaged in the management of archaeology underwater in Europe indicated that at an individual level, the constitution of nationality was considered a significant aspect of archaeologists' work. Naevestad, in Norway, made an emphatic link between archaeologists and nationality, almost as a rationale for archaeology:

... we provide a nationality. We provide a past to a people, and thus identity ... Nationalism has a bad ring to it these days ... but that is what we do.

(Naevestad pers. com.)

Similarly, Maarleveld attributed the importance of archaeology underwater in the Netherlands to its status as a humanity that contributes to 'the identity of man ... or of a nation' (Maarleveld pers. com.). He remarked that archaeology underwater in Northern Europe is characterised by the stress that it places on nationality; citing the strong interest in East Indiamen, navy ships in Sweden and the *Mary Rose* (Maarleveld pers. com.). Cederlund also highlighted the identification of particular ancient ships with national identities:

There is no coincidence that we have a ship from the Seventeenth Century standing in a big museum on the side of this island ... It's really a god, a kind of national symbol standing there. You have such national symbols in your country too ... you have both *Victory* and *Mary Rose*...

(Cederlund pers. com.)

The *Vasa*, *Victory* and *Mary Rose* are interesting examples because they fuse nation and state so completely, symbolising Swedishness, Britishness and Englishness through state institutions – notably the Navy – as much as through presumed descent or language. Cederlund broadened the question of national identity to royalty, as did Flemming Rieck, who drew attention to the long royal tradition of interest in archaeology in Denmark and noted the popularity of the present Queen, who is an archaeologist (Rieck pers. com.). The identification of archaeology with royalty (which has a history of its own, see e.g. Ucko *et al*. 1991: 9, 16) suggests legitimation through a narrative that personifies the state in its sovereign. Whereas personified sovereignty might have had a reified quality in the age of 'divine right', in circumstances of modernity the emphasis is more on the charisma of the particular sovereigns involved. Hence the sovereigns have become individual personalities ('Margarethe', 'Charles' – 'one of the diving team, one of the lads' (McKee 1982: 110)) who can be 'liked' and, therefore, trusted. Similarly, old ships serve to demonstrate that earlier sovereigns such as Gustav II Adolphus and Henry VIII were personalities too (cf. Wright, P. 1985: 192), as well as suggesting the continuity of succession through the loss and recovery of the ships concerned. For example, King Carl XVI Gustaf opened the new Vasa Museum, and Prince Charles is President of the Mary Rose Trust, visiting the site for the first time in 1975:

> ... the Prince declared himself 'delighted and fascinated' by what he had been able to see. It was almost exactly 430 years since Henry VIII had seen the last of the *Mary Rose*, and on just such a splendid July day as this.

> (McKee 1982: 111)

Collective identification with charismatic individuals is also encouraged by the portrayal of events surrounding recovery; the cult of personalities amplifying the anonymity of the mass. Characters such as Anders Franzén (discoverer of the *Vasa*), Alex McKee and Margaret Rule ('her name will always be synonymous with the Mary Rose' (Mary Rose Trust 1993: 3))(cf. Wright, P. 1985: 182) are made to stand out from the ten million visitors who had seen the *Vasa* by 1986 (Matz n.d.: inside front cover) and the three million people that watched one BBC programme about the *Mary Rose* (McKee 1982: 144). While the ancient material expresses the distance between mass and individual, it also presents a veneer of collective identity. The millions who visit or watch do so as equals to the famous individuals and their royal patrons – a cat can look at a king's ship – but the equality is nominal so far as decisions about the ancient material are concerned.

Although Naevestad claimed that national identity in Norway is grounded in the past (Naevestad pers. com.), other Norwegian archaeologists pointed to a more contemporary identification, based on a presumed common relationship with the sea. In conversation, Jasinski, Klosters and Cederlund seemed quite happy to generalise about a whole population that is identifiable collectively because it *is*, not *was*, a 'maritime people' in some respect or other (see Section 2.2.1). Such contemporary interest suggests that the past is being used in active negotiation of present and future, rather than as a nostalgic opiate for a society that has lost its way (cf. Hewison 1987). However, the contemporary touristic and economic benefits of national maritime

identities were also noted; Rieck commented that 'the Americans come here to see the Vikings' (Rieck pers. com.), and Naevestad remarked ironically on the commercial possibilities of that same identity:

> ... the Viking ship decoration, that's the identity, that's our selling point, and the Vikings were bold and strong people, and they sailed around the world with these beautiful ships. So that's something to be proud of, and here is our product – Viking product – look at this, great!

> (Naevestad pers. com.; see also Kristiansen 1992: 6)

Interest in the experience of earlier seafarers may constitute an identity for present day seafarers without there being any notion of continuity from one to the other, but in Denmark at least, continuity in activity is integral to current interest in archaeology underwater. Power – unequal mobilisation of resources – inheres in this relationship; Rieck commented 'I think there we have an advantage underwater because Denmark is *from old times* a seafaring nation, and ... some of the richest people in Denmark are people employed in seafaring. So raising private funds is easier dealing with ships than land' (Rieck pers. com.). Thomsen, also in Denmark, implied that the purpose of archaeology was to ensure that present populations do not turn their back on the past. He suggested that one rôle of compiling a database of shipwrecks was to remind people about how Danish society used to work, as an earlier dependence on shipping had been forgotten amid current preoccupations with bridges, motorways, roads and trains (Thomsen pers. com.). Reinders also expressed the notion of 'maritime decline' in accounting for what he regarded as negligible interest in maritime archaeology in the Netherlands. Furthermore, he implied that the interest in the East India Company in the Netherlands was a kind of false consciousness. If Netherlands society was to focus upon a ship type as a source of national identity it should not be the Eastindiamen but the small inland vessels that used to be seen on all the canals (Reinders pers. com.).

In these conversations, various interviewees indicated that the population can get their identity 'wrong' and, therefore, that one of the responsibilities of archaeologists was to 'counter those feelings' (Maarleveld pers. com.) and give interest in the maritime past 'a more serious foundation' (Klosters pers. com.). Maarleveld commented 'that's a very hazardous affair'. In this respect, the archaeologists interviewed see themselves as having a duty which echoes through a lecture by Wainwright in 1993: 'The past belongs to all of us but some have the responsibility of presenting that past to the public...' (Wainwright 1993: 12).

Wainwright was drawing attention to 'an ever-narrower nationalism which manifests itself in a form of cultural nationalism to which archaeology is particularly well suited and which is not confined to underdeveloped countries' in making the following point: 'in no sense can the use of the phrase – national identity – in PPG 16 be interpreted in this light...' (Wainwright 1993: 2). PPG 16 states that '[Archaeological remains] are part of our sense of national identity' (Department of the Environment 1990 a: para. 6) as a justification for its substantive provisions. These provisions include the statement that 'where nationally important archaeological remains ... are affected by proposed development there should be a presumption in favour of their physical preservation' (Department of the Environment 1990 a: para. 8). 'National importance' is also a principal condition of protection under relevant ancient monuments legislation (AMAA 1979 ss. 1(3)). The juxtaposition of national identity, national importance and provisions to ensure the continued survival of ancient material so identified warranted the attempt by Wainwright – Chief Archaeologist of *English Heritage* – to raise concern about the relationship between archaeology and nationalism. Moreover, the juxtaposition demonstrates that nationalist pressures are a consequence not simply of the efforts of individual archaeologists and their attempts to communicate but also of the management frameworks through which they operate. This begs the question as to whether, given such frameworks, raising awareness of archaeologists' responsibility is sufficient to counter nationalistic archaeology.

The UK is not alone in employing 'national' within its management frameworks. However, the meaning of the term is far from synonymous from country to country or from statute to statute. With one exception – the Norwegian Cultural Heritage Act 1979, which includes different age criteria for Saami monuments and antiquities (CHA 1979 ss. 12, 23) – the statutes examined do not contain any overtly cultural senses of the term 'national'. In contrast, many references invite a 'civil' reading. However, even a 'civil' reading can be understood in many different ways, indicating the mythological qualities of 'national' even within a nominally 'value-free' paradigm. Six senses in which 'national' is used within a civil paradigm can be identified, namely: collective; executive; central; evaluative; custodial; territorial.

A *collective* notion of 'national' is evident in current Swedish legislation:

> The care and preservation of our cultural environment is a matter of national concern. Responsibility for this is shared by all. Both individual persons and public authorities must show consideration and care towards the cultural environment
>
> (ACAMF 1988 ch. 1 s. 1)

In this case, responsibility falls on the populace, so 'national' refers to the collectivity. The notion that the nation is a group of people that has a collective responsibility for ancient material is also apparent in the UK. Hence in 1973, Mr. Sproat contrasted individual (ir)responsibility with collective interest:

> ... it is really a question not only of keeping people from satisfying their greed and all the other unpleasant vices which the right hon. Gentleman mentioned but of preserving *our national* heritage
>
> (HC 851: 1872, my emphasis)

An *executive* meaning of 'national' provides a similar shorthand that links the collectivity to those who work on its behalf, inviting trust through a constitutional narrative. The Danish term 'Rigsantikvaren' is translated variously as 'Keeper of National Antiquities' (Lund 1987: 149) and 'State Antiquarian' (AM 1984 [1989] s. 28); both translations

suggest that the official serves the collectivity, echoing 'representation' as the form of narrative that induces Danes to trust the Danish state (see Section 1.7.3).

A *central* sense of 'national' indicates regional alternatives. Hence in Sweden the *National* Maritime Museum might be distinguished from the *regional* maritime museums at Gothenburg and Malmö (Cederlund 1988). Similarly, PPG 16 concentrates on ancient material of national importance but notes that 'other unscheduled archaeological remains of *more local importance*, may also be identified in development plans as particularly worthy of preservation' (Department of the Environment 1990 a para. 16, my emphasis). This reference to local importance indicates that 'national' refers to 'central' conceptions of importance without implying that 'national' is ranked higher than 'local'. The Secretary of State determines what is of 'national' importance (see Department of the Environment 1990 a: Annex 4) whereas local authorities determine what is of 'local' importance, but both 'national' and 'local' remains may be preserved equally through the planning process.

In contrast to the central sense of national in PPG 16, an *evaluative* sense in which 'national' *does* mean 'high' is apparent in a phrase from the same document:

> Where *nationally important* archaeological remains, whether scheduled or not ... are affected by proposed development there should be a presumption in favour of their physical preservation. Cases involving archaeological remains of *lesser importance...*
>
> (Department of the Environment 1990 a para. 8, my emphasis)

The notion that 'national' implies a level of importance is reinforced by the scoring scheme used in deciding which monuments are of national importance (Darvill, Saunders and Startin 1987: 401–402), and is also evident in Irish legislation:

> 'National monument' means a monument or the remains of a monument the preservation of which is a matter of *national importance* by reason of historical, architectural, traditional, artistic, or archaeological interest attaching thereto.
>
> (NMA 1930 [1987]: 2, my emphasis)

A *territorial* sense can be attributed to the national appellation of English Heritage, which appears to reflect the insistence of the National Heritage Act 1983 that the organisation's functions and duties relate solely to ancient material located 'in England' (e.g. NHA 1983 ss. 33(1), 34(1)). Hence, 'English' relates to the sense that 'England' has in the Interpretation Act 1978 (IA 1978 sch. 1). A similar territorial sense of 'national' is apparent in early Swedish legislation, which stated that 'Ancient monuments which preserve the memory of the *earlier inhabitants of the realm* are placed under the protection of the law' (ACAMF 1942 s. 1, my emphasis). The territorial sense of national provides that responsibility for managing ancient material within an area falls on the state that coincidentally occupies that area in the present. Territoriality is not, however, a neutral concept.

5.1.2 Territoriality

The nationalist connotations of territory are brought to the fore by Sanger's question about maritime delimitation: 'where *does* a country begin or end?' (Sanger 1986: 56, emphasis in original). Territoriality is a principal element of definitions of the nation-state; Article 1 of the 1933 Montevideo Convention on Rights and Duties of States requires that states should possess a defined territory in order to have a legal personality in international law (see Harris 1983: 80; Akehurst 1982: 53). In his commentary to this provision Harris notes that it is not necessary for an entity to have exactly defined or undisputed boundaries (Harris 1983: 81) and quotes the following arbitration:

> In order to say that a State exists and can be recognised as such ... it is enough that ... [its] territory has a sufficient consistency, even though its boundaries have not yet been accurately delimited.
>
> *(Deutsche Continental Gas-Gesellschaft v. Polish State*
> (1929) AD 11, quoted in Harris 1983: 81)

Although a particular border may be undefined or in dispute, the notion that states *should* have a single, demarcated border is generally not contentious. Giddens, who uses territory as a defining characteristic of societies (see Section 1.7), also insists on the importance of territory to the nation-state:

> A 'nation', as I use the term here, only exists when a state has a unified administrative reach over the territory over which its sovereignty is claimed ... The territoriality of nation-states reflects a genuine internal administrative unity ... a threat to a segment of the territory of the modern state is a potential challenge to its administrative and cultural integrity, no matter how barren or 'useless' that segment of territory may be.
>
> (Giddens 1985: 119–291)

The centrality of territoriality to definitions of the nation-state raises difficulties in respect of the coast, because although the state's administrative reach and sovereignty extend to the water, they become progressively less absolute. How is the nation-state to defend its cultural integrity beyond the low water mark? This question is not only legalistic because, as Tilley points out:

> Boundaries are of major significance in structuring existential space both in and between places and regions. Boundaries are to do with creating distinctions and marking out social oppositions, mapping social and cultural differences and Otherness.
>
> (Tilley 1994: 17)

Hence, territoriality has two aspects that are challenged by archaeology underwater. First, the perception of a boundary between land and water, i.e. that the distinction between land and water is of greater relevance than, say, a distinction between different areas of land. Second, the concern for borders as limits to social activity. These two aspects are easily confused, insofar as a perceptual distinction may be taken, uncritically, to be a social border:

> The presence of boundaries, *obvious natural prototypes* being river courses, mountain chains, or rock outcrops, and *the coast*, may be of major significance in delimiting territories...
>
> (Tilley 1994: 17, my emphasis)

Mayall provides a useful corrective to such confusion:

> It is quite obvious that while some frontiers – for example mountain ranges, deserts, lakes, the sea surrounding islands and so on – may seem more plausible than others ... none is natural: they are political and cultural...
>
> (Mayall 1990: 80)

The tendency to regard land/water boundaries as borders seems to be linked historically to the increasing importance of land-based communication such as rail, road, telegraph and telephone in the modern period (cf. Giddens 1985: 173–178). Certainly, the confusion may impede ideas about how previous peoples may have regarded land and water. Moreover, the predisposition has to be rethought in order to overcome the mismanagement of water and coastal resources that has grown up through a couple of hundred years of attempting to manage the sea by dividing it according to terrestrial principles.

The importance of the coastline in particular as a hard edge is underlined insofar as the significant legal boundary is not land/water but land/sea; for example, in Ireland the National Monuments Act 1987 states that land includes land covered by water (NMA 1987: 11(c)). Similarly, the legislation affecting ancient material on land in UK and France applies equally to inland waters. In these countries, however, a strong distinction is drawn between ancient material situated under inland waters and ancient material situated under marine waters, which can lead to inconsistencies. In Ireland before 1994, for example, archaeological objects discovered in the sea had to be reported to OPW (NMA 1987: 3(6)), whereas archaeological objects discovered on land covered by water (i.e. inland waters) had to be reported to the National Museum (NMA 1987 s. 15). The inconsistency was resolved in 1994 when the interpretation of 'an object found in the State' was extended to include an object 'found in, or floating on or under any waters', including territorial waters (NMA 1994 s. 1). It is understandable that separate legal traditions for land and sea may generate distinctions in law that require specific amendment. However, the separateness of legal traditions does not warrant further institutionalisation of such distinctions into a substantial border by keeping the organisations and procedures for dealing with ancient material in the sea separate from those on land.

Management of archaeology in the Netherlands presents an interesting example of efforts to overcome the institutional separation of land and sea; until the mid 1980s the Netherlands had no distinct laws applicable to archaeology in the sea, and maritime law filled the vacuum. In 1985, the existing law for land archaeology was reinterpreted, and it was found to apply to the sea (MMA/Mo-1497). The integrated character of the law was confirmed in amendments introduced in the Monuments and Historic Buildings Act 1988. Notwithstanding this integration, a separate research unit was set up (Afdeling Archaeologie Onder water – AAO) that was only integrated within the land archaeology service in 1991. In contrast, the introduction in France of new legislation to deal with ancient material in the sea confirmed a legislative division that has just been overcome organisationally. On 4 January 1996, DRASM and CNRAS –

the organisations responsible for archaeology in marine and inland waters respectively – were merged as DRASSM (Départment des Recherches Archéologiques Subaquatiques et Sous-Marines). It is perhaps unclear, though, how the two previous organisations will merge their offices in Annecy (in the Alps) and in Marseille (on the Mediterranean) (see Arrêté du 4 janvier 1996).

In Norway, a division between land and sea in law has been overcome insofar as ancient monuments and ship's finds are subject to equivalent provisions, but responsibilities are divided in a manner that reflects neither subject-matter nor working environment. Whereas ship's finds that are found on land are to be dealt with by archaeological museums and ship's finds that are found underwater are to be dealt with by maritime museums, all ancient monuments – including those discovered underwater – are to be dealt with by archaeological museums (4319 C-080.22/91 HKH/HS; see Section 4.2.1).

Part of the reason for maintaining such borders to archaeological practice – however inconsistent – seems to be that the land/sea boundary is firmly established in the perceptions of the people involved in changing law and/or policy. This possibility is suggested by legislative developments in the UK, where a contrast can be made between Mr. Nott's Ten-Minute-Rule Bill in 1970 which might have permitted integration had it succeeded, and the Protection of Wrecks Bill 1973 which created a border that has stood firm for decades. In 1970 nothing was said about the relationship between ships and ancient material on land in terms of their compatibility, combined value and so on, whereas in 1973 references were made to ancient boats found on land and comparisons were drawn between the quality of preservation on land and underwater. Paradoxically, however, in 1970 Mr. Nott argued that archaeology underwater and on land should be treated in equivalent fashion as a matter of principle, whereas in 1973 the sponsors of the Bill professed little conviction for such a principle. Hence, Mr. Nott stated:

> All that I seek is that ships of equal archaeological and historic interest should be able to be scheduled in a similar way to buildings

(HC 797: 1366)

In contrast, Mr. Onslow made the following statement in 1973:

> I doubt whether the Ancient Monuments Act is a fit subject for which the Department of Trade and Industry should be made to answer

(HC 851: 1866; see also HC 855: 1689)

The concern about wrecks on land had been raised by Viscount St. Davids:

> ... a number of wrecks are not at sea but on land. The sea coast is by no means a rigid thing. It shifts about ... and large areas which were formerly sea are now very frequently part of our agriculture. A number of historical wrecks, particularly the oldest ... are turning up on shore among fields ... I should like to know ... whether these are preserved by the Bill. Would it not be a good thing to have a clause in the Bill to provide that

the preservation of ancient wrecks at sea includes the preservation of ancient wrecks on land?

(HL 342: 926)

Although this suggestion creates a border between wreck and non-wreck, it does imply that the border between land and sea established by the 1973 Act could have been avoided. Given the hiatus in protection in 1973 – which left wrecks discovered above high water mark outside both land and sea regimes for a further six years – it is perhaps surprising that the possibilities of an integrated approach were not pursued more fully. Although Mr. Onslow's statement indicates that the key factor in failing to overcome the land/sea boundary was the division of departmental responsibilities, such a division was more than an administrative arrangement. Both Mr. Onslow and Earl Ferrers displayed a lack of familiarity with procedures for dealing with archaeology on land, even though the provisions of the bill that they were supporting were modelled on terrestrial ancient monuments legislation (see Section 2.2.2). Their unfamiliarity suggests that the departmental division also comprised the relevant Ministers' inability to conceive of integration; it appears that the management of archaeology on land was not considered sufficiently relevant to the management of archaeology in the sea to warrant a briefing. In effect, a regime that transcended the land/sea boundary was unimaginable.

The distinction between land and sea in law and policy might seem like a simple administrative arrangement, but it easily takes on a more formative character in relation to identity. The relationship between administrative monopoly and environment-induced narrative of self can be illustrated by way of Helsinger's suggestion that Turner's painting *Coast from Folkestone Harbour to Dover* contains a subversive message:

> The round, spectral monument overlooking a confrontation of smugglers and officers in the foreground is one of Pitt's Martello towers, the expensive line of fortifications erected to protect the vulnerable English coast from invasion by French troops during the Napoleonic Wars. The radical journalist William Cobbett, at Folkestone on his rural ride of September 1823, read these towers as a telling sign of the charged relations of the state with its restive rural populations in the 1820s: 'These very *towers* are now used to keep these *loyal* Cinque Ports *themselves in order*! These towers are now used to lodge men, whose business it is to sally forth, not upon Jacobins, but *upon smugglers*!' Cobbett's emphasis). Turner's repeated scenes of transgressive activities suggest Cobbett's conviction that the limits set to the conception of the nation and its membership cannot long hold.

(Helsinger 1994: 117)

Whilst England's borders may now seem more secure, and the threat of Jacobins, restive rurals and smugglers has passed, the spectral monuments – often scheduled, and hence of 'national importance' once more – still stand to impress themselves practically upon English perceptions:

> In England ... the squat, circular buildings, sombre and forbidding, have been part of the seaside environment

for generations of holidaymakers, along with seagulls, boats and buckets and spades. They were part of my own background. I made sandcastles in their likeness beneath the Wish Tower at Eastbourne, watched flights of swallows arriving for the summer in the shelter of a Pevensey Bay Martello and ran barefoot over the sandy drawbridge to drink ginger beer in the dank gloom of the one at Seaford. Despite these experiences I had, like most people, only a cursory knowledge of their history...

(Sutcliffe 1972: 13–14)

In these terms, a defended coast seeps into collective consciousness. Beer indicates the perceptual aspect of a land/sea boundary thus:

It is a fiction, but an unwavering one among writers and other English people, that England occupies the land up to the margins of every shore. The island has seemed the perfect form in English cultural imagining...

(Beer 1990: 269)

This statement can be coupled with Colley's observation:

... in contrast to the fluctuating and uncertain borders of Continental Europe, British boundaries after 1707 seemed settled once and for all, marked out be the sea, clear, incontrovertible, apparently pre-ordained ... This conviction that Britain's physical identity, its very shape and place on the map, had been laid down by God points to the much more profound sense in which its inhabitants saw themselves, particularly in times of emergency, as a people apart.

(Colley 1992: 17-18)

As Lowenthal shows, similar conceptualisations of British insularity are still current in the higher reaches of government (Lowenthal 1994: 21–22). The presumed geography of this 'people apart' also serves to obscure 'internal' differences, along with unequal relationships in past and present that exist between inhabitants of the North East Atlantic Archipelago. Archaeologists have acquiesced, however unwittingly, in a sea-girt homogenisation that imagines a community that may, to many, seem imposed:

... it is rare to see the use of the term 'the British Isles' in a text by an Irish archaeologist whereas it is quite commonly applied by British archaeologists, very often in instances where there is very limited coverage of Irish material. There is a perception in Ireland that the use of such a phrase signifies a false and underlying assumption that the two islands can be conceived of as always having been a unit...

(Cooney 1995: 272)

In pointing out that this assumption obscures differences 'between and *within* the two islands' (Cooney 1995: 272, my emphasis) Cooney problematises 'the island of Ireland' as a homogenising frame of reference (cf. Woodman 1995: 275) but he overlooks the assumptions underlying the notion of 'island' itself. Paradoxically, Article 2 of the Constitution of Ireland 1937 – in which 'island of Ireland' is such a momentous concept – transcends a land-sea division, stating:

The national territory consists of the whole island of Ireland, its islands *and the territorial seas...*

(Constitution of Ireland 1937 art. 2, my emphasis)

The portrayal of the coast as a self-evident frame of reference on archaeological maps, unthinking acceptance of administrative arrangements that separate land from sea, and research based upon the questionable assumption that the sea causes insularity, are all cases in which archaeologists may collude in the reproduction of the nation-state through everyday practice. Nonetheless, the intimate relationship between archaeology and nationalism does not mean that archaeology is inherently nationalistic; archaeologists' interaction with ancient material need not presuppose that social organisation in the past was invariably based upon an indissoluble combination of territorial administration and homogenous identity. Moreover, neither nationality nor territoriality is essential to the practices that constitute the management of archaeology underwater; rather, presumed relations between archaeology, nationality and territoriality are becoming increasingly problematic. Leaving aside the inherent inappropriateness of a nationalist paradigm to material that was deposited long before the advent of nation-states, numerous factors are pressing upon the nation-state as a political form. Interpenetration of world and domestic economies has been accompanied by a resurgence of nationalism and racism within an international system characterised by ageing institutions introduced to cope with the aftermath of World War II and the ensuing Cold War (see, e.g. Buzan et al. 1990; Kellermann 1992; Hassner 1990; Wæver et al. 1993; Wyn-Rees 1993). The pressures upon the nation-state seem to be operating in opposing directions: disintegration is manifest in de-centralisation, 'ethnonationalist' conflicts and secession; integration is apparent in economics, communication and the increasing numbers of inter-governmental and inter-non-governmental organisations. As Mulhern comments:

Contemporary history does indeed seem to bear out the thesis that the significant unities of today are either larger or smaller than the nation state – but with the critical qualification that the nation state persists, at once too weak and too strong, as their *nearly* exclusive field and means of action.

(Mulhern 1993: 200, my emphasis)

It will be noted that Mulhern qualifies the exclusive capacity of the nation-state to service today's 'significant unities'. In the following sections I demonstrate that Mulhern's 'nearly' is warranted when discussing archaeology underwater because there is scope for fresh practices that do not respect traditional conceptions of nationality and territoriality. Under the heading 'disintegration', I outline various developments in management of archaeology underwater in the UK that raise questions about relations within, between and outwith England, Scotland, Wales and Northern Ireland. Under the heading 'integration', I consider jurisdiction over ancient material on and beyond state borders to highlight emerging opportunities to exert – and justify – control without recourse to trans-historical associations of identity and administration. I do not analyse how these developments have arisen or how they ought to be manipulated, but I do indicate the opportunities available to archaeologists if they are serious about challenging the persistence of the nation-state.

5.2 Disintegration

Although the most spectacular collapses have taken place in Eastern Europe, the nation-state is also experiencing disintegration in the West (cf. Hassner 1990; Kellermann 1992). The disintegration of the UK has been anticipated, prematurely, in previous decades (see Nairn 1977 [1981]) and separate Assemblies for Scotland and Wales may still be quite distant. However, some kind of devolution – extending perhaps to regional representation within England – is certainly conceivable. The island of Great Britain is becoming a less-than-perfect image for the identity of its inhabitants due to devolution, decentralisation and the development of new relations in Ireland. Insofar as the practices of archaeologists, articulated through ancient material, are part of the reproduction and possible transformation of the UK, then disintegration of the management of archaeology underwater is not simply an administrative matter. Consequently, UK archaeologists have to decide what contribution their practices are to make to society as traditional boundaries and identities in the North East Atlantic Archipelago become unstable.

5.2.1 Devolution

As land archaeology expanded in the 1970s and 1980s its separate administrative arrangements in the Home Countries were consolidated in the institutional forms of English Heritage, Historic Scotland, Cadw: Welsh Historic Monuments and the Historic Monuments and Buildings Branch of DoE (Northern Ireland). In contrast, archaeology underwater was managed under the unitary regime established through the introduction of the Protection of Wrecks Act 1973, within a division of the Department of Trade (later Transport) that was also responsible for administering the Receiver of Wreck system. The implicit centralism of the regime proposed was of concern to a number of MPs in 1973, indicated by their discussion of regional aspects of archaeology underwater. The interest in regionalism varied from Member to Member. For example, Mr. Stewart referred to the ill feeling of Scilly islanders towards the activities of 'outside' treasure hunters around their shores (HC 851: 1862). In contrast, Mr. Onslow – the resource-conscious Minister – appealed to 'the sense of history of a *local* community' to obviated the need for additional funding for policing (HC 851: 1870, my emphasis). Dr. Owen also played on regional identity (HC 851: 1857) and made a general plea against the centralisation of nautical archaeology in London (HC 851: 1859). Dr. Owen's contribution also included some serious lobbying for a museum in Plymouth, close to his constituency. Mr. Sproat also lobbied for a museum in Aberdeen (HC 851: 1874-5), indicating a constituency interest in the survival of fishing communities threatened by the oil industry on the east coast of Scotland. Mr. Faulds' concern for a regional perspective in relation to conservation facilities (HC 851: 1863) seems to have arisen from his general interest in the infrastructure of archaeology rather than from a constituency interest (see also HC 852: 363–364w). However, he also drew attention to the

diminution of traditions in his Scottish homeland (HC 851: 1874-5).

Concern about Scotland's rôle in administering the 1973 Act was expressed most strongly by Lord Ferrier: 'I feel that the people of Scotland would like to be satisfied, with respect to negotiations in regard to that [the Tobermory galleon] or any other wreck which is manifestly of interest to or connected with Scotland itself, that it would be dealt with by the Scottish Office' (HL 342: 925; see also HL 342: 934–935). The Scottish Office was, however, not to receive such responsibility; in setting out the membership of the Advisory Committee, Onslow made a minimal undertaking: 'the national museums of Scotland, Wales and Northern Ireland would also be consulted on sites in their areas (HC 855: 1674). Lord Ferrers response to Lord Ferrier's point was slightly different, identifying departments rather than museums: 'there will be consultations ... with the Scottish, Welsh and Northern Ireland Departments ... if sites are in their areas' (HL 342: 930).

The interest in non-UK administration of the 1973 regime expressed in the debates was largely ignored in implementation until 1990. Whereas land archaeology became firmly established on a local basis in the course of the 1970s and 1980s, the attempts by CNA and BSAC in 1973/74 to draw up a scheme for a Regional Inspectorate came to naught (Council for Nautical Archaeology 1974).

Although the Government gave undertakings in the course of the 1973 debates to consult with either the museums or the Departments of the Home Countries, it transpired that the interests of the Home Countries would be met by way of the Advisory Committee. Upon announcing the membership of the Advisory Committee, the Department of Trade and Industry stated:

> The following persons, as appropriate, will attend meetings of the Committee when sites in Wales, Scotland and Northern Ireland are under consideration:
> -
> | | |
> |---|---|
> | Dr. G.O. Jones | National Museum of Wales |
> | Mr. R.B.K. Stevenson | National Museum of Antiquities of Scotland |
> | Mr. Alan Warhurst | Ulster Museum |
>
> (Department of Trade and Industry 1973 a)

It will be noted that these appointments indicate that Onslow rather than Ferrers was correct about the direction of consultation. In later publications members representing the Home Country museums were referred to as 'associate members' of the Advisory Committee (e.g. Department of Trade 1979: Annex C; Department of Transport 1986: Annex C). The inferior status of the Home Country representatives is apparent in their 'optional' membership (one statement records only that 'the following *may* be asked to attend' (Department of Trade and Industry 1974: 165, my emphasis)) and in their restricted mandate. According to the published guidance, attendance would be limited to cases where a wreck off the shores of a Home Country was being discussed, and even in these cases the Associate Member would only be supplementing a substantially (southern) English Committee. The implication is that Home Country interests were of no relevance to discussion of wrecks off the shores of England. The notion that experiences outside England were incidental to deliberation and implementation is reinforced by Sproat's removal of the Associate Members to achieve a reduction in ACHWS membership in 1981 (HC 14: 412w; Saunders 1994: 316). The Associate Members had reappeared by 1986 (Department of Transport 1986: Annex C), but no reference has been made to them in subsequent accounts (e.g. see Flinder and McGrail 1990: Table 1).

The English bias was, to a limited extent, ameliorated in 1986 by placing the contract for the Archaeological Diving Unit at the University of St. Andrews in Fife, Scotland. The National Maritime Museum, in London, mounted an unsuccessful bid for the contract, leading to criticism when the Museum's involvement in archaeology underwater waned. Wright argued, in a letter to *The Times*, that '... the decision was mistaken and shortsighted ... the opportunity should not have been missed to strengthen the resource at what is the logical national centre for such expertise' (The Times 12/06/87). It is not clear whether it was the Museum's expertise within the Archaeological Research Centre or its location in the capital that suggested its logical centrality. After all, in the Second Reading debate Mr. Sproat had noted that 'Fife is one of those small enclaves to which one tends not to go unless one is going specifically to Fife' (HC 851: 1875). Prescott, from the University of St. Andrews, responded to Wright's criticism in a letter to *The Times*, as follows:

> It seems they [the Department of Transport] also accepted that, in these days of modern communication, a mobile unit which aims to cover Britain from Muckle Flugga to the Scillies gains no particular advantage from being based in London
>
> (Prescott, The Times 25/06/87)

According to Prescott, the location of the ADU in Scotland is irrelevant to its work as a 'national' unit, because of its mobility. This contention seems to be borne out by the pattern of designations, as the last ten years has not seen a marked change in the geographical balance of sites protected under the 1973 Act – the 'resource' has remained predominantly southern English. Moreover, it might be noted that of the eleven people who have worked for the ADU since its inception, nine have been 'English', one 'Canadian' and only one 'Scottish'.

The most significant change to the national constitution of the Protection of Wrecks regime occurred following an announcement by the Prime Minister on 15 October 1990: '... the Secretary of State for the Environment should assume responsibility for the protection of historic wrecks in English waters ... similar transfers of responsibility should take place in Scotland, Wales and Northern Ireland' (HC 177: 636w). Although this change, which took effect from April 1991, was a response to lobbying by the JNAPC – in particular its document *Heritage at Sea* (JNAPC 1989) – there had been no call for increased involvement by the Home Countries as such. Rather, the devolution of responsibility was a consequence of the transfer of responsibility from Department of Transport – a 'UK' department – to the Department of the Environment – an 'English' Department. Devolution was complicated insofar as responsibility for nautical archaeology passed to Historic Scotland, Cadw and HMBB by way of the Scottish Office, Welsh Office and the Department of the Environment (Northern Ireland), but responsibility in England remained with the Department of the Environment rather than with English Heritage. This complication seems to have arisen because English Heritage was unwilling to accept responsibility without an increase in funding, though there would also have been a legal impediment to the transfer (see below). The devolution of responsibility was accompanied by the instigation of an inventory of sites within UK territorial waters, also divided between the Home Countries by way of the Royal Commissions of England (RCHME), Wales (RCAHMW) and Scotland (RCAHMS), and Historic Monuments and Buildings Branch (HMBB) of DOE(NI). Consequently, the UK constitution of the 1973 regime, which was problematic in 1973 but was subordinated to English concerns in the course of implementation, became dynamic once more.

Although much of the movement since 1990 has been to devolve, one aspect of the regime established in 1973 has moved in the opposite direction, namely administration of 'wreck' under the Merchant Shipping Act 1894. Until 1992, receivership functions were carried out by Customs and Excise Officers located in local offices around the coast. In 1992, the responsibilities of Customs Officers were rationalised and a single Receiver, based within the Coastguard Agency in Southampton replaced the numerous local Receivers. These changes were recognised in amendments made to the Merchant Shipping Act 1894 (MSA 1993 sch. 4 paras. 21(b), 22, 31). Centralisation is mitigated in that the Coastguard Agency has a well-developed system of local and regional officers that are being used by the Receiver as local agents. Nonetheless, overall responsibility and decision-making remains centralised and UK-wide, in contrast to the other elements of management described.

Despite the changes following the announcement in 1990, some arrangements are still shared among the Home Country agencies – notably the Advisory Committee on Historic Wreck Sites and the Archaeological Diving Unit. Implementation of the 1973 Act has not diverged markedly since devolution in 1991, except in that Historic Scotland has provided rescue funds for the Duart Point wreck – a 'first' for any designated site – and has taken an innovative line in permitting public access to the same site (Oxley 1995: 178). In contrast, preparation of the inventory of sites within UK territorial waters has progressed differentially; only the Royal Commission in England and then HMBB have had extensive programmes of maritime recording, but the Welsh and Scottish Commissions have become active in this field more recently. Although there are inter-Commission links, and it seems likely that the English Commission's head start will give it a prominent rôle by default, there is no reason to expect recording and survey policies to develop in parallel.

In considering non-UK frameworks for managing archaeology underwater, it is appropriate to consider relations across the Irish Sea. The relationship between Great

Britain and Ireland is a constitutional matter that was high on the agenda in 1973; direct rule over Northern Ireland had been imposed the previous year as violence over the future of the area escalated. Such 'high politics' formed a background to debates about the Protection of Wrecks Bill in the Lords, where the following opinion was expressed:

> On the matter of co-operation, it is a pity that this Bill cannot operate round the whole of the shores of the British Isles ... This is possibly an extremely suitable matter for co-operation between Her Majesty's Government and the Government of the Republic of Ireland.

(Earl of Cork and Orrery, HL 342: 935)

The Earl's point was neither elaborated nor answered, but taken at face value it does indicate a belief that the management of archaeology underwater was a suitable arena for involvement in major affairs of state. Perhaps unsurprisingly, avenues for co-operation between Great Britain and Ireland were hardly explored until recently. No sites were designated in Northern Ireland until the *Girona* was protected in 1993, twenty years after it the site played such a significant rôle in the introduction of the 1973 Act (see Section 2.2.2). There seems to have been negligible official co-operation with the Republic, notwithstanding links between archaeologists, collaboration on projects such as *la Trinidad Valencera* and *la Surveillante*, and the introduction of amendments to Ireland's National Monuments Act modelled on the provisions of the 1973 Act (NMA 1987 ss. 3(1), 3(3), 3(4)).

However, negotiations concerning the future of Northern Ireland indicate a rearrangement that goes directly to the constitution of the UK in which the management of archaeology underwater is implicated. The outbreak of peace, however temporary it may prove to be, has involved a reworking of notions of exclusive sovereignty and national identity that have an immediate correlate in archaeology underwater. All-Ireland voluntary initiatives have received support from state archaeologists on both sides of the border (see Breen 1996: 60), and there are now opportunities for collaborative assessment of wrecks in the disputed waters that link North and South.

5.2.2 Management in England and the meaning of 'national importance'

The full implications of devolution are only likely to be felt once the inconsistency of DNH responsibility for archaeology underwater in England is resolved in favour of English Heritage. DNH has stated that its policy is to seek to transfer its responsibility to EH (HC 253: 676w, 01/02/95; Department of National Heritage/Welsh Office 1996: 48), but the timetable for the transfer is uncertain. Transfer has a number of implications that are limited – nominally – to management in England, but which may be quite far-reaching. Some rearrangement of the shared arrangements relating to the 1973 Act, namely ACHWS and the ADU, will be necessary. ACHWS seems likely to become a forum for UK-wide co-ordination (Department of National Heritage/Welsh Office 1996: 48), in which case the English bias of the Committee – reaffirmed in changes to its membership (see Department of National Heritage 1996) –

should come under scrutiny. Certainly, the desired relationship between EH, ACHWS and DNH has been set out more categorically in recent proposals than in any previous accounts of the relationship between ACHWS and the relevant Department: 'in England the Government will in future be advised by English Heritage. The Advisory Committee will give its advice to English Heritage...' (see Department of National Heritage/Welsh Office 1996: 48). If such clarity is also expressed in the relation of ACHWS to the other Home Country agencies and to the ADU, then the ambiguity that facilitated evasion of responsibility in the *Invincible* affair will be removed, and the legitimacy of the 1973 regime enhanced.

The future of the ADU is particularly hard to divine as responsibility for placing and managing the contract will pass to English Heritage (Department of National Heritage/Welsh Office 1996: 48); there may be resistance to placing the next contract in another country. Moreover, as policies with respect to the 1973 Act and to management of archaeology underwater in general change, then it is possible that the specification of the ADU contract will change also. Change to the administration of the 1973 Act, and to the management of archaeology underwater in general are likely because, upon transfer, the 1973 Act will have to be assimilated with the other mechanisms used for advancing English Heritage policies on archaeology. Insofar as EH policies differ from the policies of Historic Scotland, Cadw and HMBB then it is at this point that implementation of the 1973 Act may diverge, revealing the extent of structuring attributable to the introduction of the Act and the propensity for transformation.

The 1973 Act will have to be administered in tandem with the Ancient Monuments and Archaeological Areas Act 1979 and other protective mechanisms, remembering that the 1973 Act and the 1979 Act are essentially very similar (see Section 2.2.2). Of concern here is the way in which the Monuments Protection Programme – the focus of terrestrial protection strategy (see Darvill, Saunders and Startin 1987: Startin 1991: Startin 1995) – may be extended to marine sites, given that the maritime section of the National Monuments Record, maintained by RCHME, now provides a detailed and quantifiable context for decisions about relative significance.

One way of assimilating site protection policies would be to use the 1979 Act alone, in preference to the 1973 Act. This option is possible because the 1979 Act (and the equivalent Historic Monuments and Archaeological Objects (NI) Order 1995) includes the remains of vessels among the monuments that may be scheduled within territorial waters (AMAA 1979 ss. 53, 61(7)). However, English Heritage policy is that, in the case of wrecks, the 1973 Act will be used in preference to the 1979 Act (Council for British Archaeology 1994: 6–7, 9; cf. HC 965: 1363, 04/04/79). This is one area in which devolved administration seems likely to result in different implementation, as the preference for the 1973 Act does not appear to be shared by the other Home Countries, where it seems likely that scheduling will be used to protect at least some wrecks. Even in England, the 1979 Act has to take precedence in the case of monuments other than wrecks, as the 1973 Act is strictly limited in this respect, making it highly probable that scheduling and designation will be used alongside each other.

A further aspect of assimilation is the use of development control to protect sites, as planning procedures are regarded increasingly by English Heritage as an alternative to site designations. Assimilation of wreck protection with development control strategies raises a number of complications, not least in respect of jurisdiction, which I shall consider below. At this stage, what is important is that development control has been assimilated with scheduling through the use of common terms (notably 'national importance'), a single set of criteria (Department of the Environment 1990 a: Annex 4), and the accommodation of both scheduling and development control within the Monuments Protection Programme (see Startin 1995: 141–143).

Even though the term 'national importance' does not appear in the 1973 Act, assimilation of that Act with the other mechanisms makes it likely that the term will become central to wreck designation by EH. Hence, 'national importance' will form a common strand through use of the 1973 Act, the 1979 Act and development control. However, 'national importance' may also be a point of divergence between the Home Countries, not simply because different 'nations' are involved, but because the term is understood in different ways. In England, 'national importance' is regarded as an index of relative importance within the overall resource of known sites within the territory, based on criteria such as period, rarity, group value, fragility etc. (Department of the Environment 1990 a: Annex 4; Darvill, Saunders and Startin 1987). In Scotland, however, 'national importance' is linked more directly to its rôle in 'national consciousness' (Breeze 1993: 46). 'National importance' is also the principal criterion for preservation in the planning process. Although planning jurisdiction does not generally extend below low water mark, EH expects an equivalent degree of protection to be implemented through relevant sectoral consent schemes (see English Heritage/Royal Commission on the Historical Monuments of England 1996: 8).

It will be recalled that PPG 16 juxtaposes 'national importance' with 'national identity'; the same kind of justification is being proffered offshore. The Government has endorsed the JNAPC's *Code of Practice for Seabed Operators* (JNAPC 1995), which seems likely to become an industry-standard for archaeologically-sensitive development at sea; the preamble to the Code includes the passage from PPG 16 to the effect that archaeological remains 'are part of our national identity'. If there is any doubt as to what that identity might be, the Code is graced with engravings of big post-medieval warships, with cannon and gunfire much in evidence; the front cover centres upon Spithead, the RN anchorage, and illustrates a stoutly defended Portsmouth, its fortifications oriented to the sea.

5.2.3 The extent of the realm: statutory powers, planning and information

The reason that English Heritage has not yet taken responsibility for marine archaeology concerns precisely the extent of the realm; when the statute establishing EH was drawn up, it was drafted in such a way that EH's functions and responsibilities related solely to England. In itself, the restriction to England might not cause any difficulty. England has sovereignty over its territorial sea, which allows it to formulate and enforce legislation out to 12 nm. Hence both the Protection of Wrecks Act 1973 and the Ancient Monuments and Archaeological Areas Act 1979 can be applied to ancient material in territorial waters. However, the legal definition of England restricts the realm, ultimately, to the extent of the parishes that make up the counties (IA 1978 sch. 1). Section 72 of the Local Government Act 1972 provides that the parishes reach, at a minimum, to the low-water mark (LGA 1972 s. 72), hence England extends, generally, only to low-water mark. Consequently, EH cannot act in respect of ancient material in territorial waters, even though such material can receive statutory protection.

Over the past decade, English Heritage has encouraged local authorities to take responsibility for curatorial matters through their use of planning policies. However, recourse to development control mechanisms to overcome EH's territorial difficulties is problematic. The most authoritative guidance – PPG 16, backed by the *Hoveringham Gravels* case (*Hoveringham Gravels Ltd. v. Secretary of State for the Environment* [1975] 1 QB 754) – is limited, like English Heritage, to parish boundaries (i.e. low-water mark) because parish boundaries constitute the county boundaries that limit planning jurisdiction. Moreover, EH's encouragement to local authorities may bring it into conflict with the Government's general policy on coastal management, which favours activity-based 'sectoral' consents administered by central government (Department of the Environment/Welsh Office 1993).

Although the Government has set itself against the extension of planning jurisdiction to the 12 nm limit, preventing the application of PPG 16 to ancient material within territorial waters, a number of significant changes are occurring. The introduction of the JNAPC Code of Practice has already been referred to, and may serve to extend some of the principles of PPG 16 to the sea. Moreover, adherence to the Code is already being included as a condition to consents for coastal development, hence the Code may take on a quasi-statutory status. Furthermore, English Heritage has stated that it expects the principles of PPG 16 to be applied to sectoral consents for marine development (see English Heritage/Royal Commission on the Historical Monuments of England 1996: 8), and negotiations to establish archaeological conditions within all the principal consent schemes for marine activities appear to be underway. These initiatives are facilitated by the existence of the Maritime Section of the National Monuments Record (NMR), compiled and maintained by RCHME. This inventory also invokes complications, however, as the NMR is intended to operate in tandem with the Sites and Monuments Records (SMRs) operated by local authorities. The remit of these authorities is – as stated above – generally the low-water mark. Although some SMRs do now include marine sites, the grounds for extension are tentative – especially as SMRs generally are imperilled by their absence of statutory support (though see Department of National Heritage/Welsh Office

1996: 46) at a time when local authority spending is under extreme pressure.

Notwithstanding the use of the Code of Practice, the NMR and some SMRs to extend the management of archaeology below low water, EH's territorial remit is still a substantial problem, because regulatory provision is of little use if there is no curatorial framework to turn information into authoritative advice. Changing EH's remit is problematic because it requires primary legislation, which means that a legislative opportunity has to be acquired and manipulated successfully. The necessary change could, however, be achieved by relatively minor amendments and as the legal situation stands in the way of stated policy the Government's support is – presumably – assured.

5.2.4   Management beyond 12 nm

Any change to EH's territorial remit also raises questions about the outer limit of EH responsibility. It is not simply a case of paralleling the 12 nm limit of the 1973 Act and the 1979 Act because the emphasis on management by development control described above rests on the provision of curatorial advice in respect of sectoral consents that apply to the entire continental shelf. Hence EH has stated that 'due consideration should be given to the need for consultation on the archaeological impacts of consents and licences issued for works to be undertaken outside territorial waters' (English Heritage/Royal Commission on the Historical Monuments of England 1996: 8). The expansion envisaged is not 12 nm, but 200 nm: such an expansion requires a considerable stretch of imagination by UK archaeologists, civil servants and politicians. It is encouraging, perhaps, that the Government's proposals to extend EH powers refer to 'waters off England' rather than to 'the territorial sea' (Department of National Heritage/Welsh Office 1996: 48).

The lack of explicit concern for ancient material beyond territorial waters in the Protection of Wrecks Act 1973 does not imply a lack of concern for such material at the time the 1973 Act was introduced. The matter was raised in the House of Lords, where Lord Kennet questioned the restriction of the 1973 Bill to United Kingdom territorial waters (s. 3(1)):

> Why only three miles? Of course, there are historic wrecks outside three miles and in water shallow enough for divers to work in, and as diving technology improves so it will be possible for people to dive to greater and greater depths.

(HL 342: 923-924, see also HL 343: 314)

Presciently, Lord Kennet wanted to know why the Government could not use its rights to control exploration and exploitation of the continental shelf to protect wrecks. Earl Ferrers responded 'There is no international agreement on wrecks found on the high seas ... the provisions of this Bill have had to be restricted to our own territorial waters' (HL 342: 931). Lord Kennet pursued the matter, particularly regarding the confused state of regulation below low water:

> ... I hope it will not hold up the introduction of a major Bill to make sense of the law of the sea and of the seabed around our coasts, not only within three miles, but within twelve miles, within 50 miles, and to the

submarine frontiers which we have ... half-way across the Continental Shelf. The law is in a state of total chaos...

(HL 342: 924)

The possibility of extending jurisdiction beyond territorial waters for archaeological purposes highlights a tension in UK maritime policy between exclusion and freedom. On the one hand, the sea forms a hard edge that restricts access – the 'Channel' coast; on the other hand, the sea is a conduit that permits endless travel – the 'Atlantic' coast (see Wallace, W. 1991: 68; Beer 1990: 269–273). This schismatic relationship with the sea has been played out in UK's rôle in the development of the law of the sea. Throughout the nineteenth and twentieth centuries, the UK has been cast as 'a maritime state', favouring minimal territorial seas and discouraging seaward-creeping innovations such as straight baselines, Contiguous Zones, Exclusive Economic Zones (EEZs) and so on. During the Third UN Conference on the Law of the Sea, for example, the UK was a member of the secretive Gang of Five maritime powers (with the US, USSR, France and Japan) that met to plan tactics concerning freedom of navigation and freedom of scientific research (Sanger 1986: 32). Equally, the UK has figured in some of the most prominent anti-territorial court cases, notably the *Anglo-Norwegian Fisheries* case ([1951] ICJ Rep. 116) and the *Corfu Channel* case ([1949] ICJ Rep 1). The UK has, so far, not claimed an EEZ, or a Contiguous Zone. If these actions indicate the UK's Atlantic Coast, then its Channel coast is equally marked. The UK has pushed the limits of its own territorial interests through, for example, the *Post Office v. Estuary Radio* case ([1968] 2 QB 740) and the *Anglo-French Continental Shelf* arbitration (XVIII ILM 397 (1979)). Moreover, the UK introduced extensive exclusion zones around the Falkland Islands that have little precedent (Churchill and Lowe 1988: 308–9). The UK has also used some of the territorial innovations that it formerly opposed – such as straight baselines (see Territorial Waters (Amendment) Order in Council 1979 (1979 p. 2866)) – once they have been accepted internationally. The UK is not free, however, to switch between expansion and entrenchment at the whim of policy: 'The fixing of borders depends on the reflexive ordering of a [state system]' (Giddens 1985: 119). This position is particularly true of marine borders:

> The delimitation of sea areas has always an international aspect; it cannot be dependent merely upon the will of the coastal State as expressed in its municipal law. Although it is true that the act of delimitation is necessarily a unilateral act, because only the coastal state is competent to undertake it, the validity of the delimitation with regard to other States depends upon international law.

(*Anglo-Norwegian Fisheries* case [1951] ICJ Rep. 116: 132)

Consequently the contribution of English autonomy – in respect of managing archaeology underwater on its continental shelf – to the disintegration of the UK depends in part upon the ability of other states to agree on the limits of each other's sovereignty. In this respect, the disintegration of archaeology underwater in the UK is directly related to increasing international integration.

5.3 Integration

The twentieth century has seen a proliferation of international arrangements and agreements to address issues that nation-states cannot administer independently. International integration takes many forms, from mutual agreements between nation-states to co-ordinate policies, through co-operation between non-governmental organisations and multinational companies, to informal networks of communication between individuals physically dispersed around the globe. Archaeology underwater is implicated in many such forms of integration, including relations between researchers, international conference circuits, societies with international membership and so on. Archaeology underwater also features in a number of more formal, inter-nation-state arrangements. For example, Article 303 of the UN Convention on the Law of the Sea 1982 notes that:

> States have the duty to protect objects of an archaeological and historical nature found at sea and shall co-operate for this purpose.
>
> (LOSC 1982 art. 303(2))

Arguably, the ability of states to agree such wide-ranging provisions stems from their generality; such provisions are declaratory and might be expected to generate minimal responsibilities in practice – as Caflisch notes of LOSC 1982 art. 303(1) 'the duties of protection and co-operation imposed on all states appear far too general and vague to have any significant normative content' (Caflisch 1982: 20). However, multilateral conventions such as LOSC 1982 have also attempted to overcome issues that elude the faculties of nation-states acting unilaterally; as demonstrated in respect of the UK, the extent of state jurisdiction is a prime example.

Jurisdiction is of two forms, prescriptive and enforcement, which allows states to prescribe rules and to enforce rules respectively (see Harris 1983: 210). The grounds upon which nation-states can assert jurisdiction are commonly summarised by reference to the series of principles set out in Table 5.1 (see Harris 1983: 211).

Of the five principles, the territoriality principle is the most widely accepted, and – with the exception of 'universal' crimes such as piracy – it is central to any attempt at enforcement (see Harris 1983: 210–212; Akehurst 1982: 102–104). Insofar as territoriality is founded upon control of

land, then archaeology underwater generally falls outwith territory. Even accepting the status of inland and internal waters as 'land covered by water', ancient material located beyond the baselines places a strain on the exclusivity of the nation-state's administrative reach. This strain increases with distance, resulting in two problems. First, there is no overriding agreement about the extent and character of national control over ancient material beyond low water (though control to 12 nm is generally accepted). Second, large areas of sea are beyond any definition of state territory.

One solution to the difficulty of dividing land from sea (see Section 5.1.2) is, in effect, to keep extending the land outwards to bring more and more marine territory within the administrative monopoly. As remarked earlier, many countries have already extended jurisdiction over ancient material to the 12 nm limit. Ancient material is also found beyond 12 nm, but states are not free to keep extending control over an ever-wider strip of sea around their coasts. The exclusion of other interests – notably the 'traditional' freedoms to navigate and to fish – by the extension of sovereignty has not proved acceptable to the international community. In particular, the Third UN Conference on the Law of the Sea (UNCLOS III) marked the failure of attempts to create 200 nm territorial seas as an international standard, effectively dismissing land-like administrative monopolies in favour of a series of partial territorial limits in which other states have recognised rights. Non-exclusive territoriality also formed the basis for agreement at UNCLOS III to a degree of control over archaeology underwater out to 24 nm:

> In order to control traffic in [objects of an archaeological and historical nature], the coastal State may, in applying article 33 [which permits coastal States to exercise control to prevent and punish infringement of customs, fiscal, immigration or sanitary laws in a 'Contiguous Zone' that may not extend beyond 24 nm from the baselines], presume that their removal from the sea-bed in the zone referred to in that article without its approval would result in an infringement within its territory or territorial sea of the laws and regulations referred to in that article.
>
> (LOSC 1982 art. 303(2))

Table 5.1: Principles of jurisdiction, after Harvard Research Draft Convention 1935

Principle	jurisdiction exercised by reference to ...	Degree of acceptance internationally
Territoriality	the place where the offence is committed	primary importance and of fundamental character
Nationality	the nationality or the national character of the person committing the offence	universally accepted, though striking differences in the extent of its use
Protective	the national interest injured by the offence	claimed by most states, regarded with misgivings by a few ... generally ranked as the basis of an auxiliary competence
Universality	the custody of the person committing the offence	widely accepted as the basis of an auxiliary competence ... generally recognised as the recognised principle of jurisdiction over piracy [also war crimes, hijacking]
Passive personality	nationality or national character of the person injured by the offence	asserted by a considerable number of states and contested by others ...

Article 303 arose from an attempt by a number of states to extend control over ancient material to the continental shelf. The attempt was resisted, resulting in the above compromise (see Nordquist, Rosenne and Sohn 1989: 158–162; Oxman 1980: 23 (n. 79); Oxman 1981: 239–241; O'Keefe and Prott 1984: 98–99; United Nations 1982: 129; United Nations 1995). The provision is problematic in certain respects (see Caflisch 1982: 19–21; O'Keefe and Prott 1984: 102–105) but some states, including France and Denmark, have used the provision to exert control over ancient material beyond the territorial sea equivalent to control within the territorial sea. It is worth noting that in France provisions on ownership of ancient material still conform to the 12 nm border even though the law as a whole applies to archaeological activities out to 24 nm (ACMCP 1989 s. 12). In contrast, all the Danish provisions – including provisions on ownership – extend to 24 nm (PNA 1992 s. 14; AM 1984 [1989] s. 28(1)). Hence, there are already two 'rules' for managing ancient material to the 24 nm limit.

The attempt to extend control over ancient material on the continental shelf in the course of UNCLOS III continued in the course of negotiation of a European Convention on Underwater Cultural Heritage. Negotiation took place through the offices of the Council of Europe, following Recommendation 848 (1978) of the Parliamentary Assembly of the Council of Europe which proposed that national jurisdiction should be extended to the 200 mile limit (Recommendation 848 Annex, requirement iv; see O'Keefe and Prott 1984: 100–101). Although negotiations were hampered by a number of disagreements, it was – in particular – the failure to agree on the territorial extent of state interests that prevented completion of a draft satisfactory to all parties.

The attempt to exert control over ancient material out to 200 nm has been revived in the Draft Convention on Protection of the Underwater Cultural Heritage (DCPUCH 1994). Article 5 of DCPUCH 1994 provides that States Party may establish a cultural heritage zone up to the outer limit of its continental shelf within which the state will have jurisdiction over activities affecting the underwater cultural heritage (DCPUCH 1994 art. 5; see O'Keefe and Nafziger 1994: 409). Unsurprisingly, reservations have already been expressed about such a provision (UNESCO 1995: Annex).

UNCLOS III, the Council of Europe negotiations and discussion of DCPUCH 1994 all testify to the lack of agreement between nation-states regarding control over ancient material beyond the territorial sea. However, this lack of agreement obscures, in some respects, the amount of control that coastal states already exert (see O'Keefe and Prott 1984: 96–97, 99; O'Keefe and Nafziger 1994: 409). Controls over ancient material beyond territorial waters among the countries I examined are summarised in Table 5.2. Many of these procedures are still evolving or are not formalised, and they demonstrate the use of existing international regimes – especially in respect of continental shelf rights – rather than an explicitly 'archaeological' regime. The contrast between the extension of control in practice with the failure to agree an overall limit is emphasised by successful conclusion of the revised European Convention on the Protection of the Archaeological Heritage (ECPAH 1992), signed at Valetta in 1992. This convention, signed by the parties that failed to agree the draft European Convention on Underwater Cultural Heritage, makes provision for archaeology underwater in Article 1. This article states that the archaeological heritage includes structures etc. whether situated on land or underwater located in any area within the jurisdiction of the Parties (ECPAH 1992 art. 1(2), 1(3)). The explanatory report includes the following note:

> ... the actual area of State jurisdiction depends on the individual States and in respect of this there are many possibilities. Territorially, the area can be coextensive with the territorial sea, the contiguous zone, the continental shelf, the exclusive economic zone or a cultural protection zone ... The Revised Convention recognises these differences without indicating a preference for one or the other.

(Council of Europe 1992: 3–4)

Consequently, ECPAH 1992 offers an innovative solution to the problem of establishing a single limit to jurisdiction by opting for a formal 'agreement to differ'. In the terms of this study, such an agreement to differ is important because it recognises plurality; each state may choose the extent and the character of its control over archaeology underwater, to the extent that its choice can be sustained in international law.

Table 5.2:   Management of archaeology underwater beyond territorial waters

Denmark	Assertion of control and ownership to 24 nm (AM 1984 [1989] s. 28(1); PNA 1992 s. 14); the Raw Materials Act 1991, which covers materials on the continental shelf, states that importance shall be attached to protection of archaeological interests (RMA 1991 s. 3); cables and oil and gas production facilities are subject to agreement between archaeological authorities and the Ministry of Energy.
Netherlands	Close co-operation between AAO and the North Sea Directorate of the Ministry of Public Works – all proposals relating to work beyond the territorial sea are subject to archaeological scrutiny.
Norway	Provision in petroleum exploration legislation for reporting finds (see O'Keefe and Prott 1984: 96).
UK	Regulations affecting continental shelf activities seem likely to make increasing reference to archaeology; any person taking possession of wreck outside territorial waters and bringing it within those waters must notify the receiver (MSA 1995: 236); Protection of Military Remains Act 1986 applies to certain wrecks, UK flagged vessels and UK citizens on the high seas (PMRA 1986 ss. 1(2)(b), 3(1)).
Sweden	Little attention to continental shelf at present.
Ireland	Underwater heritage orders can be applied to protect sites on the continental shelf (NMA 1987 s. 3(1)).
France	Administrative control, but not ownership, asserted over ancient material between 12 and 24 nm (ACMCP 1989: 12, 13).

Insofar as each state party may exert differing degrees of control over archaeology underwater, then the nationalistic model of a hard boundary to control of the past is refuted. Hence, the plurality of state claims will require constant renegotiation of the grounds upon which any particular state controls any particular ancient material.

The useful uncertainty fostered by formalised plurality of control over archaeology underwater does not help, however, with the problem of ancient material located beyond any reasonable territorial claim, i.e. in the area beyond continental shelves. While it is not important to know *who* controls ancient material, it is important to know that *someone* does. An attempt has been made to exert control over ancient material beyond state territory on the grounds of a form of international territoriality, in the sense that the area beyond national jurisdiction – 'the Area' – is to be administered for the benefit of all humanity. Part XI of LOSC 1982 is concerned with the Area; Section 2 of this part is devoted to 'principles governing the area'. For example, Article 137 states that 'all rights in the resources [meaning *in situ* mineral deposits] of the Area are vested in mankind as a whole' (LOSC 1982 art. 137(1)). Article 140 states that 'activities in the Area shall ... be carried out for the benefit of mankind as a whole' (LOSC 1982 art. 140(1)). Similarly, Article 149 – the last article of Section 2 – states:

> All objects of an archaeological and historical nature found in the Area shall be preserved or disposed of for the benefit of mankind as a whole...
>
> (LOSC 1982 art. 149)

However, this territorial solution omits extensive areas of seabed on three counts. First, there are ambiguities in the delimitation of the Area by virtue of the complex definition of the outer limit of continental shelves (see Ruffmann, Townsend Gault and VanderZwaag 1988). Second, there are undesirable inconsistencies in the provisions of LOSC 1982; the Convention makes no reference at all to ancient material between 24 nm and the Area, for example. Third, there are desirable inconsistencies in the extent of individual states' jurisdiction, as discussed above. Moreover, an international territorial solution to control over ancient material beyond state jurisdiction is deficient because of the problematic justification for such control in terms of 'common heritage' (see below).

An alternative to international territoriality is to assert control over ancient material beyond national jurisdiction by reference to territory implicated in the course of, or subsequent to, fieldwork. Such a procedure forms the core of DCPUCH 1994, which is intended to protect ancient material underwater by requiring a high standard of investigation, as set out in an accompanying Charter. In outline, the core provisions of the Draft Convention are as follows:

> Article 7 prohibits the use of each States Party's territory to support activities that violate the Charter.
>
> Article 9 provides that States Party can issue licences for material recovered in accordance with the Charter to enter their territory (cf. the import ban discussed in respect of material recovered from the *Titanic*, Lindbloom 1986: 110).

> Article 10 provides that States Party can seize any material that comes within its territory that has not been recovered in accordance with the Charter.
>
> Article 11 provides that States Party must impose penal sanctions in respect of the importation to their territory of ancient material that has not been recovered in accordance with the Charter.
>
> (DCPUCH 1994 arts. 7, 9, 10, 11)

Insofar as the relevant provisions can only be implemented in respect of material that is subject to fieldwork or has been recovered, DCPUCH 1994 does not appear to provide for the management of ancient material *in situ*. However, by denying territorial bases and threatening seizure of material, States Party may be able to discourage salvage operations predicated on sub-standard methods.

As DCPUCH 1994 is focused upon the territory to which material is recovered rather than its *in situ* location, the Draft Convention applies to areas within state jurisdiction as well as areas beyond. Certain caveats are recognised in respect of the capacity of each State Party to implement DCPUCH 1994 within the territorial jurisdiction of other states (see Article 7, Article 10(2)). However, the general application of the Draft Convention removes any adverse consequences of inconsistency in the extent of state jurisdiction; material becomes liable to control upon entering a territorial limit, irrespective of the particular limit involved. Insofar as DCPUCH 1994 offers an alternative to multilateral extension of territorial jurisdiction to a common limit, it seems paradoxical that the Draft Convention also espouses such an extension in the form of a Cultural Heritage Zone (DCPUCH 1994 Article 5) as discussed above.

DCPUCH 1994 provides a further route for asserting control over ancient material beyond national jurisdiction, namely Article 8 which applies the nationality principle of jurisdiction (see Table 6.1). According to Article 8, each State party will undertake to prohibit its nationals and ships of its flag from taking part in activities that do not accord with the Charter, except where those activities take place within the territorial jurisdiction of another State Party (see O'Keefe and Nafziger 1994: 410–411). The use of the nationality principle is prefigured by the UK's Protection of Military Remains Act 1986, which prohibits British nationals from interfering with the sites of vessels or aircraft that were lost while engaged in military service (O'Keefe and Nafziger 1994: 401–402, 410–411; and see Barrowman 1987: 244).

As with recovered material, the enforcement of provisions based upon the nationality principle depends upon nationals or flagged ships returning to the territory of the relevant State. Although the use of the nationality principle is thus circumscribed, nationality is, nonetheless, a significant factor in managing archaeology underwater. However, the people whose nationality is of concern are not those who are investigating a site, but those who were originally associated with the site; there is a substantial body of provisions that promote state interest, if not jurisdiction, on the basis of the presumed origin of ancient material. Leaving aside examples of states that assert rights on the basis of demonstrated continuity of title to ownership (e.g. claims of the

Netherlands Ministry of Finance to the wrecks of Dutch Eastindiamen and UK Ministry of Defence ownership of old British warships (see Dromgoole and Gaskell 1993: 225–227)), claims advanced on the basis of a 'state of origin' are intensely problematic from an archaeological point of view.

The UN Law of the Sea Convention 1982 has served as a focus for discussion of the notion of 'states of origin' because of Article 149, which includes the following statement:

> ... particular regard being paid to the preferential rights of the State or country of origin, or the State of cultural origin, or the State of historical and archaeological origin.

(LOSC 1982 art. 149)

Criticisms of this statement (see, e.g. Caflisch 1982: 30; O'Keefe and Nafziger 1994: 398; Watters 1983: 812; Strati 1991: 879–889) have generally concerned the ambiguity of the terms, the failure to prioritise the preferential rights, and the practicalities of identifying the various states of origin of the hull, cargo, personal belongings and so on. Little criticism has been directed at the notion of 'origin' in itself, and of the implicit assumption that the material remains of ancient people can be accommodated within the framework of the nation-state. Commentators such as Strati do not envisage an absolute association of ancient material with nationality. However, her suggestion that 'preference should be given to the State to whose cultural heritage the property is *more closely* linked' (Strati 1991: 888, my emphasis) still implies a final resolution whereby an exclusive relation between the material and one nation-state is established. Hence: 'what is needed is the establishment of *criteria* on the basis of which the decision will be made as to whether a particular item "belongs" to the cultural heritage of one State or another' (Strati 1991: 887, emphasis in original). The notion of an exclusive relation between ancient material and one nation-state is not sustainable in the terms of this study because of the interruption in the existence of material between earlier use and archaeological discovery (see Section 1.9).

Insofar as material is invented anew as 'ancient', then remains and relics are constituted by their interpretation in the present, not by any intrinsic qualities of the material. While present populations may wish to embrace ancient material as part of their cultural heritage, there is unlikely to be any evidence that the architects of now-ancient material had any concern for the people that would happen upon the debris of their lives in later periods. To go beyond this by insisting that contemporary nation-states represent and protect the aspirations of such long-dead people is facetious. At best, contemporary nation-states can claim to represent and protect the aspirations of their present populations in respect of today's – and perhaps tomorrow's – interpretations of the past. Such a claim is entirely valid and warrants state involvement in the management of archaeology. However, the claim neither depends upon nor justifies a 'state of origin' doctrine, nor does it imply that all states have equal claim to every item of ancient material. Without becoming embroiled in the issue of repatriation – which is in any case utterly problematic in respect of material that was intended to move or be moved around the globe – it is consistent with my

argument to accept that some people can claim greater affinity with some ancient material than others. There is a need, therefore, for a framework upon which claims of affinity can be advanced and countered, where resolution is neither exclusive nor prejudiced by an inherent 'state of origin' doctrine.

One alternative to the 'state of origin' doctrine is to elevate management of archaeology to a supranational plane. Supranational interest in ancient material – expressed as 'common' or 'world' heritage – is problematic if such interest is held to be exclusive of other 'lesser' interests, whether these be regional, 'national' or local. In particular, the election of some ancient material to the supranational plain implies that other (i.e. most) ancient material is of inferior value. In this respect, references to 'common heritage' are reminiscent of references to 'national' importance as outlined in Section 5.1.1. The section drew attention to the unspoken ambiguity of the term 'national' (cf. inadequate discussion of the concept of 'world heritage', see Ucko 1989 a: xiii), but indicated the possibility of distinguishing 'cultural' from 'civil' senses. In this respect, discussion of 'common heritage' appears to be implicitly 'cultural' in tone. It assumes that a level can be reached at which all human culture is equal, and that at this level certain manifestations of culture can be said to have universal relevance or appeal; i.e. everyone will recognise the value of certain items and will treat them with due reverence. Hence monuments and sites on the World Heritage List are regarded as having 'outstanding universal value' (Convention concerning the Protection of the World Cultural and Natural Heritage 1972 art. 1; see Prott 1992). Clearly, the majority of the World's population is not in a position to agree on the common elements of a global culture. Consequently, some individuals and organisations find themselves in the position of telling the rest of the World which ancient material is to be regarded deferentially by everybody, and which is not. As Chapters Two, Three and Four have demonstrated, the processes involved in making such decisions are heavily structured, such that their results are prefigured by existing patterns of signification, domination and legitimation, and contribute to the reproduction of such patterns in future.

In certain respects, however, a cultural sense of common heritage should not be dismissed so readily; it might be claimed that some sites are of global relevance because of their contribution to understanding and appreciation of global events or processes. This might be particularly true of the wrecks of certain vessels that were engaged in global affairs. Wrecks of vessels such as the *Amsterdam* contain the material evidence upon which archaeologists construct their interpretations of the introduction of industrial production and administration, of the development of an international economy and of other aspects of the emergence of modernity as a global phenomenon (see Larkham 1994: 270). However, to agree that some ancient material is intimately bound up in matters of world history is not to agree that it be treated deferentially. Participation in processes of global import was not necessarily enjoyable to many of those involved, whether they were within territories subject to colonial expansion, or on the factory floors and lower decks of imperial capital. The consequences of unequal participation in the benefits of globalisation are evident throughout the world today, so it is to be expected that people around the globe will place different values on the world's relics. The management of such relics will be contested, and it is in this respect that supranational management of ancient material becomes meaningful, i.e. as a framework within which relevance can be contested, which implies a civil reading of supranationality.

If a civil rather than cultural notion of supranationality is accepted, the question arises as to who should actually administer control over ancient material on behalf of all humanity. Again, the distinctions advanced in respect of 'national' prove useful. In Section 5.1.1, I identified five civil senses of the term 'national', namely collective, executive, central, evaluative and territorial. Here, I shall consider their relevance to the discussion of supranational management, in reverse order.

Management based on supranational territoriality has been discussed in respect of the Area (see above) where it is deficient because of various inconsistencies of definition. Hence Strati argues that the powers and functions of the International Deep Seabed Authority – a global authority – in respect of the Area do not extend to ancient material or to archaeological operations because of omissions in the terms of LOSC 1992 (Strati 1991: 878–879). Even if such inconsistencies were resolved, better solutions can be offered to the problem of exerting control beyond state jurisdiction, namely control on the basis of state territory implicated in archaeological activities (as in DCPUCH 1994, see above). There is, however, scope for improving management across a series of state territories by reference to a territorial qualifier. For example, the European Cultural Convention states that:

> Each Contracting Party shall regard the objects of European cultural value placed under its control as integral parts of the common cultural heritage of Europe, shall take appropriate measures to safeguard them and shall ensure reasonable access thereto.

(ECC 1955: 5)

Leaving aside problems associated with 'common cultural heritage' (see above), the reference to objects placed under the Contracting Party's control suggests that safeguarding measures and reasonable access can be expected throughout the territories of Contracting Parties. In this respect, supranational interest in ancient material is met by each Contracting Party acting in concert; this arrangement avoids creating a 'global' authority with supranational *powers* (such as the International Deep Seabed Authority) to impose a common heritage upon the World, in favour of 'sub-global' authorities with supranational *responsibilities*. However, the formulation offered in the 1955 European Cultural Convention implies that the aggregated territory of the Contracting Parties has a common cultural heritage, and that the aggregated territory defines 'Europe'. So long as territoriality continues to be expressed in terms of exclusive borders, the territorial senses of supranationality are likely to constitute expansive 'culture areas' which replicate the model of the nation-state, but on a grander scale.

An evaluative sense of supranational interest might be held to apply where an effort is made to assess the characteristics of ancient material from around the globe comparatively. Such an evaluation might allow a grand overview of the particular needs of certain sites, such as relief from a burgeoning tourist trade. However, evaluation is likely to encourage differential deterioration of ancient material if the evaluation is used to target additional protection or funding. Although evaluation need not rank supranational importance above regional or local importance – comparisons may simply try to isolate an appropriate scale of action – identification under a supranational scheme might be taken to imply precedence. Furthermore, global comparative exercises might give the impression that some international organisation is about to impose its idea of importance upon local populations.

The threat of imposition by an international agency will be strongest when a 'central' sense of supranational is in play. In some circumstances, unilateral solutions to management problems are not possible, and a bi- or multi-lateral arrangement is required. Hence wrecks of Dutch Eastindiamen off Western Australia are administered under a scheme agreed between Netherlands and Australia, which provides for a committee to determine the disposition and ownership of material (O'Keefe and Prott 1984: 287–288). Similarly, the World Heritage Convention is serviced by a Secretariat based with UNESCO in Paris that processes applications for placing sites on the World Heritage List (Prott 1992). In neither case does centralised administration imply encroachment upon local concerns, as national authorities implement the provisions of the convention. Nonetheless, the impression that a distant committee is imposing its will – as 'cultural commissars' (Shore 1993: 794) – may emerge in some circumstances.

Such an impression might be eroded by emphasising an 'executive' sense of supranational, in that the organisation, committee or agency demonstrates that it is acting not according to an internal agenda but on behalf of people all over the globe. The success of any claim to be operating 'executively', and of any supranational scheme based upon the claim, may depend largely upon the transparency of the organisation's membership, decision-making and accountability; a supranational committee constituted on the same lines as ACHWS might have difficulties inculcating trust or compliance.

Finally, a 'collective' sense of supranational interest could emphasise the universal qualities of ancient material – its public rather than private character, for example – without implying or imposing cultural homogeneity. In this sense, 'common heritage' would be ancient material that everyone has a right to enjoy.

The possible meanings of supranationality are illustrated in the context of archaeology underwater by Mr. Onslow's statements in support of Mr. Nott's amendments to the Merchant Shipping Bill in 1970. He proposed that historic wrecks had a relevance that transcended nationality: 'These are some of the jewels of Western civilisation' (HC 797: 1372). Onslow also made the following remarks in relation to Dutch claims to the *Amsterdam*: 'How ridiculous that there should be a piece of Holland buried in the sands off Bulverhythe. You might as well say that the Italian Government own the Roman barge that was found in the Thames, or that the Spanish Government are the legal possessors of the Armada galleons wrecked around our own coast' (EC 797: 1372; N.B. such claims were made by other Governments in subsequent years). Onslow's reference to western civilisation indicates a 'cultural' interpretation – that the significance of wrecks could be ascribed to their rôle in an uninterrupted, progressive history culminating in society as 'we' know it today. Only the advantage of hindsight allowed Mr. Onslow to link the disparate remains that he refered to, and other observers might refute the claim that life on such vessels had anything to do with being civilised. In contrast, Onslow's reference to the ridiculousness of foreign claims suggests that he was trying to get at a 'civil' sense of supranational importance. Mr. Onslow was supporting Crown ownership of all historic wrecks in UK waters, but there is nothing in his speech to suggest that he considered such wrecks to 'belong' to the UK, or that they were of English or British origin. Rather, his speech appears to merge territorial, executive and collective criteria i.e. that the UK should act as 'steward' on behalf of the World's population in respect of ancient material that happens to fall within UK territory.

Mr. Onslow's position in 1970 undermines an association of contemporary nation-states with ancient material and supplants it with a form of supranational stewardship whereby ancient material is administered by the state within whose jurisdiction it lies on behalf of all. Such stewardship does not exclude other interests and claims.

Returning to the mid 1990s, DCPUCH 1994 still presupposes a 'state of origin':

> Each State Party undertakes to notify the State or States of origin, if known, of its seizure of underwater cultural heritage under this Convention
>
> (DCPUCH 1994 art. 12(1))

The Preamble recognises that responsibility for protecting underwater cultural heritage rests in part with the states most directly concerned with particular activities affecting the heritage, and with 'all States and other subjects of international law'. However, the Preamble also refers to the responsibility that lies with 'states ... having an historical or cultural link with it [underwater cultural heritage]' (DCPUCH 1994 Preamble). Nonetheless, such traces of the 'state of origin' doctrine could be removed easily to produce a regime that facilitated supranational stewardship – especially as the DCPUCH 1994 recognises that control does not impart exclusive rights – without granting precedence to claims of trans-historical association between ancient material and contemporary nation-states:

> 1. Whenever a State has expressed a patrimonial interest in particular cultural heritage to another State Party, the latter shall consider collaborating in the investigation, excavation, documentation, conservation, study and cultural promotion of the heritage.

> 2. To the extent compatible with the purposes of this Convention, each State Party undertakes to share information with other States Party...
>
> (DCPUCH 1994 art. 13)

In this configuration, the assertion of jurisdiction does not convey a right to claim a historical link between nation-state and ancient material. Rather, jurisdiction implies responsibility, where responsibility includes establishing a framework for recognising – but not necessarily acquiescing in – the claims and interests of other people.

5.4 Unimaginable Communities? archaeologists and Europe

Archaeologists can show that alternatives to the nation-state existed in the past; it should be possible to conceive of alternatives for the future, yet such a minor conceptual leap appears to be beyond many people. In the final sentences of *The Nation-State and Violence*, for example, Giddens is manifestly unable to conceive of a future in which the nation-state is superseded, falling back pessimistically to an unachievable notion of world government as super-nation-state:

> Given the distinctive dominance of the nation-state in the world system ... the possibility that this [polyarchic involvement] might lead to the formation of a democratically ordered world government seems entirely remote. If the arguments deployed in this book are valid, the increasing social integration of the globe does not betoken an incipient political unity.
>
> (Giddens 1985: 341)

Although I have highlighted the pressures of integration and disintegration upon the nation-state, neither pressure need change the underlying relationship of nation to state; secession and pan-nationalism still posit indissoluble combinations of identity and administration, though on different scales. Moreover, the existence of multiple identities and multiple administrations does not, in itself, imply the weakening of the nation-state if these identities and administrations continue to be arranged hierarchically such that one particular union outweighs all others. The nation-state is not threatened by the simultaneous existence of parishes, counties and intergovernmental organisations.

The possible decline of the nation-state lies, rather, in the existence of a multiplicity of identities and a multiplicity of states in an arrangement of fluctuating hierarchies. In such circumstances, any union of identity and state, and of the relationship between that union and other unions, would have to be actively negotiated and justified from instant to instant; legitimacy – so often assumed – would always be questionable. It is to this possibility that Tilly points when he suggests the detachment of the principle of cultural distinctness from that of statehood as a potential (though not inevitable) scenario for the future of Europe (Tilly 1992). In short, the future of the nation-state does not lie in integration or disintegration, but in both simultaneously.

Such a mix of integrative and disintegrative pressures may cause far more fluid and contestable relationships between identity and administration to supersede nation-states with their singular borders justified by reference to homogenised 'nations'. With reference to Europe, Hyde-Price characterises such a possibility as 'institutional pluralism':

> In this multi-layered structure, international functions and responsibilities will be distributed between different bodies and through different levels. Such a rich diversity of different organisations and institutions will correspond to the heterogeneity of Europe, its blurred edges, its varied historical experiences and its diverse economic and political requirements.
>
> (Hyde-Price 1993: 27)

Insofar as identity is contingently constructed in multifarious ways, varying through time and with location, then the 'new architecture' to which Hyde-Price refers may both structure and be structured by an emancipatory exploration of individual and collective identities. The dynamism that attends such diversity may break the generally unspoken connection between nation and state, unsettling the impositions of meaning and power and bringing about a far more active development of legitimacy.

Turning to the contribution that archaeologists might make to a post-nationalist future, I argue that institutional pluralism depends not only upon the identification of non-nationalist forms of social organisation in the past, but also upon archaeologists' capacity to manage ancient material by reference to shifting tiers of multiple identities and forms of administration in the course of current practice. Currently, public acquiescence in management of ancient material on a national basis – rather than on a local or regional basis, or on gender or religious grounds – implies that nationality persists as *the* governing dimension of identity. Equally, even though contemporary administrative boundaries may differ from boundaries derived from, for example, distributions of Roman pottery, the tendency to conceive of activity in terms of exclusive boundaries rather than permeable margins presupposes that territoriality is an indispensable principle of social organisation.

I have shown that the nation-state is being problematised in archaeology underwater at a 'domestic' level in and around the UK. Developments in administrative responsibility seem likely to force a debate on the meaning of 'national importance' in respect of site protection and development control, not least because of differences in use of the term among each of the Home Countries. Relationships between these countries will involve divergence and convergence alike as the curatorial agencies, including the Royal Commissions, hammer out their respective strategies in the context of common arrangements such as ACHWS and the ADU. In Ireland, bi-lateral arrangements between the north and south on some issues may outweigh relations between Northern Ireland and England, Scotland and Wales. Within England, the relationship between central and local authorities (and between different levels of local authority) remains unresolved in respect of archaeology underwater. Irresolution is evident in the contrasting emphasis on local curatorial control for land and centrally administered sectoral consents for marine areas, and in the developing relationship between local SMRs and the National Monuments Record. Finally, the territorial extent of English Heritage activities

has yet to be resolved, both in respect of the boundary of England at low-water mark and in relation to the continental shelf.

I have also shown that an international regime for managing archaeology underwater could be established on three principles. First, plurality in the territorial extent of control over ancient material. Second, control beyond territorial jurisdiction by reference to the territories to which recovered material is transported. Third, replacement of 'state of origin' doctrines with supranational communal responsibility. Although such an international regime does imply a degree of integration that may take us beyond nationalism, it must be recalled that the conventions upon which it would rest are themselves agreements *between* nation-states. In certain respects, such conventions demonstrate the capacity of the nation-state to mould itself successfully to integrative pressures while retaining its fundamental character.

In contrast, nation-states in Europe have already ceded sovereignty in many areas previously characterised by administrative autonomy. Consequently, the greatest challenge to the nation-state is, arguably, the European Union. Although the development of 'Europe' as a super-nation-state – complete with a homogenised identity and exclusive borders – might be feared, this eventuality is not inevitable. As has already been demonstrated in respect of the UK, there are many disintegrative pressures at play in Europe. Furthermore, the institutional framework of the EU is not simply that of a nation-state writ large. As a result, the debate as to what 'Europe' means in terms of identity and territory provides considerable scope for novel forms of community.

The innovative character of the EU is evident when contrasted to the Council of Europe, with which EU institutions are often confused. Notwithstanding their overlapping memberships and mutual commitments to co-operate, the integrative projects of the European Union and the Council of Europe are quite different. Whereas the European Union is a supra-national arrangement in which member states cede sovereignty to the Union's institutions, the Council of Europe is intra-national and its policies must be agreed and implemented by the member states themselves (see Firth 1988). EU legislation has direct effect upon European citizens and prevails over domestic law (see Weatherill and Beaumont 1993; Hartley 1994), but the Council of Europe drafts conventions that have to be signed and implemented by each state separately.

The difference in integrative character is apparent in the activities of the two institutions in managing archaeology underwater. The Council of Europe was the principal focus of European co-operation in relation to archaeology underwater from 1978 to 1985. The Parliamentary Assembly of the Council of Europe made Recommendation 848 on the underwater cultural heritage and sponsored the Roper Report (Roper 1978), and in the early 1980s the Council of Europe hosted the *ad hoc* Committee of Experts that prepared the Draft European Convention on Underwater Cultural Heritage. However, the Draft European Convention was shelved due to fundamental disagreement on its territorial extent (O'Keefe and Nafziger 1994: 397); the failure of the convention stalled efforts to increase collaboration through the Council of Europe's offices. The Council of Europe managed to refresh its mandate in archaeology underwater by side-stepping the territorial controversy through Article 1 of the revised European Convention on the Protection of the Archaeological Heritage in 1992 referred to above. Consequently, a new Committee of Experts was formed that met for the first time in December 1994.

The formation of the new Committee of Experts may have been a response to an EC conference on underwater cultural heritage held in Athens, April 1994, organised by the Greek Presidency and the European Commission. The mandate of the EU in the field of culture was only formalised in 1992, in the Treaty on European Union ('the Maastricht Treaty' – OJ 92/C 191). Although the European Community had policies relating to culture before the 1990s (see McMahon 1995), the only reference in the Treaty Establishing the European Economic Community (the 'Treaty of Rome') was an incidental exception to the free trade provisions. This exception permitted restrictions on imports, exports or goods in transit to protect 'national treasures possessing artistic, historic or archaeological value' (Article 36; see Oliver 1982: 143–146; *Commission of the European Communities v Italian Republic* [1968] ECR 423). From 1992, however, the Treaty on European Union amended the activities of the Community to include a contribution 'to the flowering of the cultures of the Member States' (Article 3(p)). In addition, a provision was added to permit 'aid to promote culture and heritage conservation' (Article 92(3)(d)), and an entirely new 'title' was added – Title IX Culture (Article 128):

1. The Community shall contribute to the flowering of the cultures of the Member States, while respecting their national and regional diversity and at the same time bringing the common cultural heritage to the fore.

2. Action by the Community shall be aimed at encouraging co-operation between Member States and, if necessary, supporting and supplementing their action in the following areas:

   – improvement of the knowledge and dissemination of the culture and history of the European peoples;

   – conservation and safeguarding of cultural heritage of European significance;

   – non-commercial cultural exchanges;

   – artistic and literary creation, including the audio-visual sector.

3. The Community and the Member States shall foster co-operation with third countries and the competent international organisations in the sphere of culture, in particular the Council of Europe.

4. The Community shall take cultural aspects into account in its action under other provisions of this Treaty.

In recent years, policies have been developed on matters that implicate archaeology directly. These policies include: legislation on the export of cultural goods and the return of cultural goods unlawfully removed from the territory of a Member State (OJ 92/L 395/1; OJ 93/L 74/74 and see e.g. Roberts 1993; Short 1993; Jernigan 1994; Vitrano 1994); Community action programmes such as 'Kaleidoscope' and 'Raphaël' (see OJ 94/C 227/11; OJ 95/C 287/161); and Council 'conclusions' on cultural networks and archives (OJ 91/C 314/01; OJ 94/C 235/03). The Regulation on the export of cultural goods and the Directive on the return of cultural objects make explicit reference to archaeological objects arising from discoveries and excavations underwater (OJ 92/L 395/1: Annex A. 1.; OJ 93/L 74/74: Annex A. 1.). Moreover, both the Environmental Assessment Directive (OJ 85/L 175/40) – which applies to coastal and water-based projects – and the Council resolution on future Community policy concerning the European coastal zone (OJ 92/C 59/01) make reference to cultural heritage. Furthermore, the Council conclusions of June 17 1994 on drawing up a Community Action Plan in the field of cultural heritage make specific reference to 'sub-aquatic heritage' (OJ 94/C 235/01) (see Firth 1992 b).

As in December 1994, a Committee of Experts met to discuss archaeology underwater in Europe in December 1995. Although many of the members of the committee were the same in 1995 as in 1994, in December 1995 the European Commission was the host; the Council of Europe's Committee of Experts has yet to meet for a second time. In a relatively short space of time, therefore, the European Union has become a significant institution in archaeology underwater and seems to have eclipsed the Council of Europe in this field. The success of the EU relative to the CoE might be taken to imply that the supra-national character of the former has superseded the inter-national character of the latter. The EU's cultural project should not, however, be embraced uncritically.

There is little doubt that such a cultural project is being pursued instrumentally – rather than emerging spontaneously – by the Commission, even though the Commission appears to vacillate between enthusiasm and reluctance in its instrumental rôle (see Shore 1993: 794; Shore and Black 1994: 287; Shore 1996). On the one hand, the attempt to create a 'new' heritage might be embraced, hence:

> ... there is a need to forge a new continental identity to replace that inherited from the now-crumbling post-war territorial settlement, without which the new Europe has little relevance and popular meaning. Only with such identification, shaped through a reinterpretation of the heritage of a European past, can a truly European future be created.
>
> (Ashworth and Larkham 1994: 5; see also Ashworth and Larkham 1994: 2; Ashworth 1994: 21)

On the other hand, it might be feared as precisely the same kind of identity creation that accompanied the emergence of the nation-state, but on a larger scale. The fear arises because – as with nationalism – the form of identity being advocated has unwelcome attributes:

> ... EC policy-makers tend to privilege a static, bounded and exclusivist definition of 'European identity' ... the Commission's representations of 'European identity' seem to reflect an essentialist model of identity as ...

something organic, fundamental, historically given and bounded.

(Shore 1993: 781, 792)

Not only is the form of identity unwelcome, but the specific components of the heritage that are invoked are reminiscent of the fantasies that form the basis of nationalist delusions. Shore and Black note that in failing to resolve what the identity of a new Europe might be, the Commission is leaving the door open for 'a highly selective definition of Europe that is politically biased and potentially racist, where "European culture" is equated with "Western Civilisation" (as opposed to "African barbarism" or "Oriental despotism", perhaps)' (Shore and Black 1994: 294). The similarity between new European identities and earlier nationalisms extends beyond the model and its components to include the same methods. Hence Shore argues that the Commission is constructing a new Europe on the same symbolic terrain as traditional nation-states, by way of flags, anthems, stamps, coins, histories, anniversaries and holidays (Shore 1993: 791; Shore 1996).

However, the parallels between the new Europe advocated by the Commission, and the nation-states that it promises to replace, are not as strong as Shore and others imply. Shore's own work demonstrates that the provisions on culture that have appeared in recent years suggest that the Europe Union places greater emphasis upon multiple identities and subsidiarity than on exclusivity (see Shore 1993: 782; 783–4; 792; 794). Furthermore, Ashworth and Larkham have noted that:

> The EC has been notably slow to develop the symbolism and trappings of a popular state. A second-hand flag ... and a second-hand anthem ... let alone the second-hand politicians ... are no substitute for the heroes and villains, battles and revolts, of most national founding mythologies.

(Ashworth and Larkham 1994: 4–5)

Earlier, they note that:

> Europe's long history of war, pogrom and persecution between nations, classes, races and religions has left its own legacies, which markedly contradict any theme of harmonious unity. Are these to be ignored, or somehow reinterpreted within the new European heritage product?

(Ashworth and Larkham 1994: 4)

Larkham offers an answer to this question later in the same volume:

> ... given the diversity of the continent, it would be impossible to prescribe a European heritage. The problem of the dispossessed in any such marketing is too great ... the 'nastiness' of a continent-wide history must be accepted, for it cannot be swept away.

(Larkham 1994: 270, 271)

The particular criticisms by Shore and others only hold so long as they assume that the development of the EU must follow the same path of identity-formation that has been followed by nation-states. While certain similarities might be anticipated – the EU, like nation-states, is an abstract system that has to inculcate the trust of individuals, where legitimacy is likely to arise in the construction of biographies of individuals and systems that are mutually constitutive – it does not follow that the particular relationship between identity and administration posited by the nation-state need be mimicked. I demonstrated in Sections 5.2 and 5.3 that disintegrative and integrative pressures at play in the world today can be addressed without resort to a singular association of nation with state.

Although the EU project is fundamentally integrative, it need not be considered as 'super-state building' that will create a homogenised European identity. It is the EU's project of a political organisation constituted through cultural diversity in particular – as set out in Article 128(1), quoted above – that marks its radical departure from the 'model' nation-state. Nonetheless, the EU is at an important juncture: references to 'unity in diversity' can be applied practically in an attempt to escape the model of the nation-state; alternatively, a flooding tide of easy nationalism can be allowed to set the agenda once more. In this respect, Shore and others are right to warn of the dangers attending the construction of European identities. There is a risk that ancient material will be used to support a chauvinistic, racist 'Europe' ring-fenced by immigration laws and intolerance to 'non-Europeans' within and outwith its borders (see Bunyan 1991; Pieterse 1991; Webber 1991).

This possibility is encouraged by the ambiguities of the term 'European', reflecting the ambiguity that afflicts 'national' and 'supranational' as outlined in Sections 5.1.1 and 5.3 (see Goddard, Llobera and Shore 1994: 25–26). References to 'Europe' in the EU's cultural policies are of uncertain import. For example, the Council and the Commission envisage action to conserve and safeguard 'cultural heritage of European significance' (OJ 94/C 235/01), but it is not clear whether a 'civil' or 'cultural' reading is implied. Are there certain monuments with which all those who would call themselves European can, or should, identify? Or does European significance merely imply that the problems facing these monument are most appropriately dealt with in concert at a 'European' level, with the Commission acting as executive on behalf of all citizens? Moreover, it seems impossible to contain 'Europe' within any territorial definition (see Hyde-Price 1993: 21; Macdonald 1993: 2; Buzan et al. 1990: 41–49; Schlesinger 1991:188–190; Goddard, Llobera and Shore 1994: 24). The range of formulations within which 'Europe' is juxtaposed with cultural policy in EU literature is considerable, but it is not my intention to pursue an analysis of the sort carried out in Chapters Two, Three and Four on this occasion. Rather, I highlight ambiguity in identity and territory in a European context to draw attention to the space such ambiguities leave for archaeologists to advance *their* views about how Europeanness can be interpreted, constructed and practised in relation to ancient material.

In this Chapter I have demonstrated the shortcomings of the nationalist model and shown that alternatives can be conceived of in domestic, international and European contexts; as Goddard, Llobera and Shore put it:

... to speak of a single, all constitutive 'Europe' becomes rather meaningless, or worse, encourages an essentialized vision of Europeannness as a quality that is somehow fixed, bounded, homogeneous and pure. Instead, we should recognize the plurality and diversity of the many Europes that exist, and have existed, in any given time or context...

(Goddard, Llobera and Shore 1994: 30)

Similarly, Larkham argues of ancient material that '... any new Europe will not actually require the subsuming of individual place-identities or national cultures; rather, perhaps, the acceptance of diversity and plurality' (Larkham 1994: 270). Broadening this point to include all aspects of archaeology as practised, I have to agree with the recent statement of Jones and Graves-Brown:

A theoretically-informed analysis of cultural identity in the present or the past illustrates that identity is dynamic and historically contingent, hence subjecting nationalist and ethnic claims about the permanent and inalienable status of identity and territory to continuous scrutiny. Thus, rather than reproduce monolithic notions of cultural unity and continuity in support of the 'New Europe', archaeology should be able to contribute to a critically informed view of the plurality of histories and cultures which make up European identities. Far from being a descent into relativism, such an approach is likely to bring archaeology into a closer alignment with the ways in which multiple narratives of the past are negotiated by communities themselves.

(Jones and Graves-Brown 1996: 19)

In contrast to Giddens' pessimism, with which I started this section, I have argued that new forms of community can be imagined. Such imagination is necessary if archaeologists are to overcome problems of managing archaeology underwater that have arisen from unimaginative practices in the UK and internationally. I finish by examining the relevance of archaeologists' imaginations to society and by concluding earlier points about archaeologists' involvement in social change.

6.   A SPANNER IN THE WORKS?

Insofar as management is susceptible to novel actions, notwithstanding institutional constraints, archaeologists can – in the course of their daily practices – intervene in the structuring of archaeology underwater and, therefore, in the transformation of the nation-state. There seems to be a way to start imagining the future, and for archaeologists to escape the previous complicity of their discipline in the maintenance of nationalism.

Such a conclusion might seem naive; it certainly contrasts with Slapsak's pessimistic summary of the relationship between archaeology and nationalism:

> The socio-political rôle for archaeology as advocated by post-modernists (explicit interpretative politics, autonomous, politically conscious social agency) is proven unrealistic the moment it is faced with real issues like dramatic political change, aggressive nationalism, war. Ideological agents involved in these processes are so powerful that the scholarly community stands no chance acting in opposition to them if defined by its ideological and political authority only: post-modernist archaeology risks either outright instrumentalisation by (integration into) political elites or complete social insignificance. A simple and cunning practitioner of mass manipulation will make use of history and archaeology much more effectively than someone burdened with knowledge, scientific method, and logic. So, while there is no doubt that archaeology is dependent on culture-bound conceptual tools and often ideology-laden research objectives, it can acquire respectability only through adequate implementation of disciplinary methods and logical procedures. It is this respectability, and not adherence to one or another socio-political goal, that permits archaeology to act as an independent social power.

(Slapsak 1993: 194–195)

I have confirmed that conceptual tools and research objectives are culture-bound and ideology-laden, but I question whether these 'failings' can be overcome by an attempted retreat into the respectability of blind method. I have also argued that it is inappropriate to presuppose that there is a passive mass awaiting manipulation, or that 'ideological agents' can be dismissed, however fearfully, as simple and/or cunning. My argument might well be characterised as 'post-modern'; it accepts that archaeologists are invariably subject to socio-political goals and I advocate explicitly interpretative, politically conscious archaeology. However, I would also contend that knowledge, scientific method, and logic need not be a burden if they are applied to archaeology as a practice in the present, as well as to remnants of the past. In short, archaeology should not aspire to being an independent social power; rather, archaeologists should use make use of meanings, resources and rules to emancipatory effect in the fields of culture and identity.

The capacity of archaeologists to instigate change arises from the duality of structure. As Giddens comments: 'every act which contributes to the reproduction of structure is also an act of production, a novel enterprise, and as such may initiate change by altering that structure at the same time as it reproduces it' (Giddens 1976 [1993]: 134) (see Section 1.4). Structuration theory indicates two ways in which archaeologists' activities may give rise to transformation, rather than reproduction.

First, the dialectic of control – whereby ' all forms of dependence offer some resources whereby those who are subordinate can influence the activities of their superiors' (Giddens 1984: 16) (see Section 3.2) – suggests that irrespective of constraints, archaeologists can always attempt a novel enterprise, even if it is simply to refuse an action that they believe to be nationalistic. In practice, archaeologists may feel that the level of constraint is such that they can hardly refuse the demands placed upon them. It should be recalled, however, that archaeologists are relatively well-educated, literate and articulate compared to many members of society, and are particularly privileged in respect of the creation of ancient material within the environment where it can have a practical impact upon everyday lives.

Second, as a social practice, archaeology exhibits Giddens' double hermeneutic; 'there is continual "slippage" of the concepts constructed in sociology, whereby these are appropriated by those whose conduct they were originally coined to analyse, and hence tend to become integral features *of* that conduct' (Giddens 1976 [1993]: 170). Although the terms used by archaeologists cannot be taken up by the dead people that they study, archaeologists' broader claims about the organisation of society and the character of humanity at various times in the past can be, and are, used in current debates. In this respect, Giddens further comment is important:

> ... in a social universe more and more pervaded by social reflexivity, in which possible futures are constantly not just balanced against the present but actively help constitute it, models of what could be the case can directly affect what comes to be the case.

(Giddens 1994: 249–250)

I am not arguing that archaeologists should deliberately falsify their interpretations in support of currently desired outcomes. Rather, I am suggesting that in abandoning the paradigm of the nation-state – along with homogenous identities and exclusive (coastal) boundaries as a pervasive interpretative framework – it may become easier for archaeologists to contribute to informed public debate about novel forms of social organisation.

Although archaeologists have a transformative potential, such capacity is constrained by the institutions within which they work. In order to mobilise meaning, power and trust in an effective manner, archaeologists have to comprehend the mechanics of those institutions. Against their wishes, perhaps, archaeologists need to recognise that their current practices are just as susceptible to analysis as the ancient practices that they are more accustomed to investigating. In the preceding chapters, I have elaborated interconnections between culture, identity and institutional frameworks (see Goddard, Llobera and Shore 1994: 29). I have also shown that archaeologists have to address management as an integral component of what they do; matters relating to 'law' and 'politics' have to be dealt with coherently rather than being relegated to particularist tirades. I have also made a case, by my own example, for management to be studied *by archaeologists* as well as by scholars in other disciplines. Although other disciplines can contribute substantially to an understanding of archaeology, non-archaeologists are unlikely to be sensitive to the structuring that occurs in some of the most mundane archaeological practices.

Among these mundane practices, I have shown how people – both archaeologists and public – can dwell in preconceptions about the past through their practical experience of ancient material. These preconceptions can affect the introduction of management provisions, so that they become thoroughly structured within implementation, even if the provisions themselves appear 'neutral'. Furthermore, I have shown that the institutionalisation of preconceptions within management can constrain archaeological research, thus inhibiting the emergence of fresh interpretations.

Having demonstrated that ancient material is an authoritative rather than allocative resource – that is to say, something that commands people not things – I showed that ancient material can be mobilised alongside other authoritative resources. In the case of the 1973 Act, the 'political' resources of parliamentarians, government and lobbyists were transformed into an 'archaeological' resource of protected wrecks. The character of the archaeological resource was, and still is, directly attributable to the mobilisation of resources in the legislative process of 1973. Whatever the source of specific terms in management, their institutionalisation within policy documents and, as I demonstrated, statutes in a range of countries impose particular characteristics upon the archaeological resource. Consequently, these words are not to be considered simply in terms of their consistency or adequacy, but also in terms of the presuppositions about the past embedded within them. Moreover, the institutionalisation of certain terms within management is not simply a nebulous interplay of multiple meanings; such terms are impressed physically upon popular environments by differential conservation of ancient material.

In addition, the terms and phrases used in managing archaeology underwater can play a significant rôle in inculcating – and failing to inculcate – archaeological norms in the behaviour of non-archaeologists. Similarly, the structuring of interaction between archaeologists and non-archaeologists by procedure and organisation can encourage or discourage rule-following behaviour, as was shown in respect of reporting. Furthermore, the way in which both positive and negative sanctions are formalised attests to the legitimacy of desired behaviour, even where those sanctions are implemented rarely. In the case of the Protection of Wrecks Act 1973 I demonstrated that the (in)effectiveness of management in trying to encourage non-archaeologists to behave archaeologically was a product of implementation in respect of individual licensees, attempts to bring various interests 'on board' in the course of legislating, and – in the absence of a formal arrangement – the constitution of ACHWS.

This analysis of managing archaeology underwater has been carried out by reference to the work of Anthony Giddens. His identification of different levels of integration – distinguishing between the practices of individuals, groups and systems while demonstrating their interaction – and of the different components of structure – meaning, power and trust – provided the matrix upon which Chapters Two, Three and Four were elaborated. His view of structure as both constraining and enabling has encouraged a realistic appraisal of the limitations within which archaeologists work, while facilitating recognition of the capacity of archaeologists to engage in social change. In this respect, Giddens' work on structuration complements his work on modernity, which is also demonstrably relevant to archaeology. In Chapter One, I showed that archaeologists were implicated in the development of trust between individuals and the abstract systems that administer their lives by way of the unspoken effect of ancient material on the construction of personal and collective identities. In Chapter Five, I demonstrated that the model of the nation-state that has beset relations between past and present in the last 100 years can be undermined by post-nationalist archaeological practices in domestic and international arenas. In this respect, I have tried to meet the challenge levelled by Goddard, Llobera and Shore:

> ... it is essential to persevere not only in locating the local within its wider context but in tackling the very institutions and practices which constitute the national and supra-national levels in question.
>
> (Goddard, Llobera and Shore 1994: 29)

Finally, Giddens' emphasis on the impact of time and space – as locale – upon practice has encouraged an account of managing archaeology underwater that gives due weight to ancient material as the focal point of interaction between archaeology and society.

In considering the potential for translating innovative imaginings into applied management of archaeology underwater through the institutions of the European Union, I drew attention to the dangers that attend the construction of a super-national identity. It is important, therefore, to look back to the analyses offered in Chapters Two, Three and Four, of the often-unintended consequences of nominally impartial institutions on interpretations, on the archaeological 'resource', and on behaviour towards ancient material. In trying to promote change in Europe, archaeologists should pay detailed attention to the processes through which change has occurred to archaeological institutions in various contexts in previous years. Furthermore, archaeologists should be mindful of the consequences not only of the alterations that they seek, but also of the manner in which those alterations are sought.

Although the mechanics and dynamics of managing archaeology underwater are complex I have demonstrated that they can be comprehended at all levels from individual to system. Comprehension begets manipulation, and I have shown that there are a number of opportunities for archaeologists to take a spanner to the works of management.

Such possibilities imply responsibility; if an opportunity, however limited, to take a novel action is declined, then responsibility for perpetuating inequalities of meaning, power and trust rests with the obstinate individual. Ancient material can be a powerful medium for the reproduction of repressive ideologies, but even though the coherence of the nation-state may be reinforced by appeals to ancient material, the 'message' does not inhere in the material but in the practice that comprehends it. Consequently, archaeologists have the capacity – and the responsibility – to use their privileged relationship with ancient material in a progressive manner. As Orwell noted, 'who controls the past controls the future'.

7. SOURCES

7.1 Books and Articles

Adams, J. (1986) 'Hull Structure' in Gawronski, J.H.G. (ed.) *Annual Report of the VOC-Ship "Amsterdam" Foundation 1985*, Amsterdam: Stitching VOC-Schip "Amsterdam", 22–28.

Addyman, P. (1989) 'The Stonehenge we deserve' in Cleere, H. (ed.) *Archaeological Heritage Management in the Modern World*, London: Unwin Hyman, 265–271.

Addyman, P. (1994) 'Reconstruction as interpretation: the example of the Jorvik Viking Centre, York' in Gathercole, P. and Lowenthal, D. (eds) *The Politics of the Past*, London: Routledge, 257–264.

Akehurst, M. (1982) *A Modern Introduction to International Law*, London: Allen and Unwin.

Anderson, B. (1983 [1991]) *Imagined Communities: reflections on the origins and spread of nationalism*, London: Verso.

Archaeological Diving Unit (1994) *Guide to Historic Wreck Sites Designated under the Protection of Wrecks Act 1973*, St. Andrews: University of St. Andrews.

Ascherson, N. (1987 [1988]) '"Tell the Children..."' in Ascherson, N. *Games with Shadows*, London: Radius, 10–13.

Ashworth, G.J. (1994) 'From History to Heritage: From Heritage to Identity: in search of new models' in Ashworth, G.J. and Larkham, P.J. (eds) *Building a New Heritage: tourism, culture and identity in the New Europe*, London: Routledge, 13–30.

Ashworth, G.J. and Larkham, P.J. (1994 b) 'A Heritage for Europe: the need, the task, the contribution' in Ashworth, G.J. and Larkham, P.J. (eds) *Building a New Heritage: tourism, culture and identity in the New Europe*, London: Routledge, 1–9.

Barrett, J.C. (1994) *Fragments from Antiquity*, Oxford: Berg.

Barrett, J.C. (1995) *Some Challenges in Contemporary Archaeology*, Oxford: Oxbow.

Barrowman, E. (1987) 'The Recovery of Shipwrecks in International Waters: a multilateral solution', *Michigan Yearbook of International Legal Studies*, 8: 231–246.

Barthes, R. (1972 [1957]) *Mythologies*, London: Vintage.

Beer, G. (1990) 'The Island and the Aeroplane: the case of Virginia Woolf' in Bhabha, H.K. (ed.) *Nation and Narration*, London: Routledge, 265–290.

Beix, R. (1989) *Rapport relatif aux biens culturels maritimes et modifiant la loi du 27 septembre 1941 portant reglementation des fouilles archeologiques*.

Belgrave, R. (1994) 'Black people and museums: the Caribbean Heritage Project in Southampton' in Gathercole, P. and Lowenthal, D. (eds) *The Politics of the Past*, London: Routledge, 63–73.

Binford, L.R. (1981) 'Behavioural Archaeology and the "Pompeii Premise"', *Journal of Anthropological Research*, 37, 3: 195–208.

Bingeman, J. (1985) 'Interim report on artefacts recovered from Invincible (1758) between 1978 and 1984', *International Journal of Nautical Archaeology*, 14, 3: 191–210.

Bingeman, J. (1990) 'Britain's Underwater Archaeological Heritage', *Mariner's Mirror*, 76, 2: 186–187.

Blackman, D.J. (ed.) (1973) *Marine Archaeology: proceedings of the Twentythird Symposium of the Colston Research Society*, London: Butterworths.

Bond, G.C. and Gilliam, A. (eds) (1994) *Social Construction of the Past: representation as power*, London: Routledge.

Bowman, G. (1994) '"A country of words": conceiving the Palestinian nation from the position of exile' in Laclau, E. (ed.) *The Making of Political Identities*, London: Verso, 138–170.

Breen, C. (1996) 'Maritime Archaeology in Northern Ireland: an interim statement' *IJNA*, 25, 1: 55–65.

Breeze, D.J. (1993) 'Ancient Monuments Legislation' in Hunter, J. and Ralston, I. (eds) *Archaeological Resource Management in the UK: An Introduction*, Stroud: Alan Sutton Publishing Ltd., 44–55.

Breuilly, J. (1990) 'The Nation-State and Violence: A Critique of Giddens' in Clark, J., Modgil, C. and Modgil, S. (eds) *Anthony Giddens: consensus and controversy*, London: Falmer Press, 271–288.

Brieur, F.L. and Mathers, C. (1996) *Trends and Patterns in Cultural Resource Significance: an historical perspective and annotated bibliography*, Alexandria, Virginia: US Army Corps of Engineers.

Brown, K.S. (1994) 'Seeing stars: character and identity in the landscapes of modern Macedonia', *Antiquity*, 68: 784–796.

Bryant, C.G.A. and Jary, D. (eds) (1991) *Giddens' Theory of Structuration: a critical appreciation*, London: Routledge.

Bunyan, T. (1991) 'Towards an authoritarian European state', *Race and Class*, 32, 3: 19–27.

Burton, I. and Drewry, G. (1974) 'Public Legislation: a survey of the session 1972/73', *Parliamentary Affairs*, 27: 120–158.

Buzan, B., Kelstrup, M., Lemaitre, P., Tromer, E. and Waever, O. (1990) *The European Security Order Recast: scenarios for the post-Cold War era*, London: Pinter.

Byrne, D. (1991) 'Western Hegemony in Archaeological Heritage Management', *History and Anthropology*, 5: 269–276.

Caflisch, L. (1982) 'Submarine antiquities and the International Law of the Sea', *Netherlands Yearbook of International Law*, XIII: 3–32.

Carman, J. (1990) 'Commodities, rubbish and treasure: valuing archaeological objects', *Archaeological Review from Cambridge*, 9, 2: 195–207.

Carman, J. (1993 a) 'The P is silent – as in archaeology', *Archaeological Review from Cambridge*, 12, 1: 39–53.

Carman, J. (1993 b) 'Valuing Ancient Things: archaeology and the law in England', *Unpublished PhD Thesis*.

Carman, J. (1995) 'The importance of things: archaeology and the law' in Cooper, M., Firth, A., Carman, J. and Wheatley, D. (eds) *Managing Archaeology*, London: Routledge.

Carver, M. (1996) 'On Archaeological Value' *Antiquity*, 70: 45-56.

Cederlund, C.O. (1994) 'The Regal Ships and Divine Kingdom' in Burstrom, M. and Carlsson, A. (eds) *Current Swedish Archaeology*, Stockholm: Swedish Archaeological Society, 47–85.

Champion, T. (1991) 'Theoretical archaeology in Britain' in Hodder, I. (ed.) *Archaeological Theory in Europe: the last three decades*, London: Routledge, 129–160.

Chapman, W. (1989) 'The organizational context in the history of archaeology: Pitt Rivers and other British Archaeologists in the 1860s', *Antiquaries Journal*, 69: 23–42.

Chippindale, C. (1983) 'The making of the first Ancient Monuments Act, 1882, and its administration under General Pitt-Rivers', *Journal of the British Archaeological Association*, 136: 1–55.

Churchill, R.R. and Lowe, A. V. (1988) *The law of the sea*, Manchester: Manchester University Press.

Clark, J., Modgil, C. and Modgil, S. (eds) (1990) *Anthony Giddens: consensus and controversy*, London: Falmer Press.

Cleere, H. (1989) 'Introduction: the rationale of archaeological heritage management' in Cleere, H. (ed.) *Archaeological Heritage Management in the Modern World*, London: Unwin Hyman.

Cleere, H. (ed.) (1989) *Archaeological Heritage Management in the Modern World*, London: Unwin Hyman.

Cleere, H.D. (1984) 'World cultural resource management: problems and perspectives' in H.F. Cleere (ed.) *Approaches to the archaeological heritage*, Cambridge: Cambridge University Press, 125–131.

Coastguard Agency (1994 a) *Where to Turn when you've Turned Something Up*, Southampton: The Coastguard Agency.

Coastguard Agency (1994 b) *Report of Wreck and Salvage*, Southampton: The Coastguard Agency.

Coastguard Agency (1994 c) *Historic Wreck Finds*, Southampton: The Coastguard Agency.

Cohen, I. (1989) *Structuration Theory: Anthony Giddens and the Constitution of Social Life*, Basingstoke: Macmillan.

Colley, L. (1992) *Britons: forging the nation 1707–1837*, London: Pimlico.

Confino, A. (1993) 'The Nation as a Local Metaphor: heimat, national memory and the German Empire, 1871-1918', *Memory and History*, 5, 1: 42–86.

Cooney, G. (1995) 'Theory and Practice in Irish Archaeology' in Ucko, P.J. (ed.) *Theory in Archaeology: a world perspective*, London: Routledge, 263–277.

Costall, A. and Still, A. (1989) 'Gibson's theory of direct perception and the problem of cultural relativism', *Journal for the Theory of Social Behaviour*, 19, 4: 433–441.

Council for British Archaeology (1994) 'All at Sea and Undefended', *British Archaeological News*, York: Council for British Archaeology, 16: 6–7.

Council for Nautical Archaeology (1973 a) 'Hand-written list of sites', *Unpublished document in CNA Archive*.

Council for Nautical Archaeology (1973 b) 'Schedulable Sites', *Unpublished document in CNA Archive*.

Council for Nautical Archaeology (1973 c) 'List of Sites Recommended for Immediate Designation being both of High Cultural Importance and at Risk', *Unpublished document in CNA Archive*.

Council for Nautical Archaeology (1974) 'The Future Organisation of British Nautical Archaeology', *Unpublished document in CNA Archive*.

Council of Europe (1992) *European Convention on the Protection of the Archaeological Heritage (revised): explanatory report*, Strasbourg: Council of Europe.

Couper, A. (ed.) (1989) *The Times Atlas and Encyclopedia of the Sea*, London: Times Books.

Craib, I. (1992) *Anthony Giddens*, London: Routledge.

Croome, A. (1988) 'Underwater archaeology in Britain: discussion meeting at The Royal Armouries, London, 30 January 1988', *International Journal of Nautical Archaeology*, 17, 2: 113–118.

Crumlin-Pedersen, O. (1990) 'Maritime Archaeology in Denmark', *Arkaeologiske Udgravninger i Danmark 1989*, 16–21.

Crumlin-Pedersen, O. and Rieck, F. (1993) 'The Nydam ships: old and new investigations at a classic site' in Coles, J., Fenwick, V. and Hutchinson, G. *A Spirit of Enquiry: Essays for Ted Wright*, Exeter: WARP, NAS, NMM, 39–45.

Cunningham, R.D. (1979) 'Why and How to Improve Archaeology's Business Work' *American Antiquity*, 44, 3: 572–574.

Darvill, T. (1993) *Valuing Britain's Archaeological Resource*, Poole: Bournemouth University.

Darvill, T. (1995) 'Value Systems in Archaeology', in Cooper, M., Firth, A., Carman, J. and Wheatley, D. (eds) (1995) *Managing Archaeology*, London: Routledge, 40–50.

Darvill, T., Saunders, A. and Startin, B. (1987) 'A question of national importance: approaches to the evaluation of ancient monuments for the Monuments Protection Programme in England', *Antiquity*, 61: 393–408.

Davies, P. (1973) 'The Mary, Charles II's Yacht: 1. the discovery of the wreck', *International Journal of Nautical Archaeology*, 2, 1: 59–60.

Davis, H.A. (1982) 'Professionalism in Archaeology' *American Antiquity*, 47, 1: 158–163.

Dean, M. (1988) *Guidelines on Acceptable Standards in Underwater Archaeology*, St. Andrews: Scottish Maritime Studies Development Association.

Dean, M., Ferrari, B., Oxley, I., Redknap. M., and Watson, K (1992) *Archaeology Underwater: The NAS Guide to Principles and Practice*, London: Nautical Archaeology Society/Archetype Publications Ltd.

Department of National Heritage (1996) *Press Release: Lord Inglewood announces new structure to the Advisory Committee on Historic Wreck Sites*, London: Department of National Heritage, 126/96.

Department of National Heritage (n.d. a) *Application for Designating a Site under the Protection of Wrecks Act 1973*, London: Department of National Heritage.

Department of National Heritage (n.d. b) *Application for a Licence to Survey a Site under the Protection of Wrecks Act 1973*, London: Department of National Heritage.

Department of National Heritage (n.d. c) *Application for a Licence to Excavate or Otherwise Disturb a Site under the Protection of Wrecks Act 1973*, London: Department of National Heritage.

Department of National Heritage (n.d. d) *Reports on Licensed Work on Protected Wreck Sites: reports required by the Advisory Committee on Historic Wreck Sites (ACHWS)*, London: Department of National Heritage.

Department of National Heritage/Welsh Office (1996) *Protecting Our Heritage: a consultation paper on the built heritage of England and Wales*, London: Department of National Heritage/Welsh Office.

Department of the Environment (1990 a) *Planning Policy Guidance: Archaeology and Planning*, London: HMSO.

Department of the Environment (1990 b) *The Government's Response to Heritage at Sea*.

Department of the Environment/Welsh Office (1993) *Development Below Low Water Mark: A review of regulation in England and Wales*, London: HMSO.

Department of Trade (Marine Division) (1975) 'United Kingdom: The Protection of Wrecks Act 1973', *International Journal of Nautical Archaeology*, 4, 2: 407–408.

Department of Trade (Marine Division) (1979) *Historic Wrecks: The Role of the Department of Trade*, London: Department of Trade (Marine Division).

Department of Trade (Marine Division) (1980) *Reports required by the Advisory Committee on Historic Wreck Sites*, London: Department of Trade (Marine Division).

Department of Trade (Marine Division) (1981) *Historic Wrecks: The Role of the Department of Trade – Developments in 1980*.

Department of Trade (Marine Division) (1982) *Historic Wrecks: The Role of the Department of Trade – Developments in 1981*.

Department of Trade (n.d. a) 'Application for a Designation Order to Protect an Historic Wreck Site', Form A, V3728.

Department of Trade (n.d. b) 'Application for a Licence to Survey an Historic Wreck Site', Form B, V3923.

Department of Trade (n.d. c) 'Application for a Licence to Excavate an Historic Wreck Site', Form C, V3924.

Department of Trade and Industry (1971 a) *unpublished note by the Secretary of the DTI Committee on Wreck*.

Department of Trade and Industry (1971 b) *unpublished note by the Solicitor's Department of the DTI*.

Department of Trade and Industry (1973 a) *Press Notice: wrecks of historical importance – committee of experts to designate sites and licence salvors*, London: Department of Trade and Industry.

Department of Trade and Industry (1973 b) *Press Notice: Mr Cranley Onslow names four historic wrecks to be protected*, London: Department of Trade and Industry.

Department of Trade and Industry (1973 c) *Press Notice: protection of historic wreck in Cattewater, Plymouth*, London: Department of Trade and Industry.

Department of Trade and Industry (1973 d) *Press Notice: increased rewards for treasure hunters*, London: Department of Trade and Industry.

Department of Trade and Industry (1973 e) 'Ancient Wrecks Reported to the Department of Trade and Industry', *Unpublished document in CNA Archive*, HWR(73)2/Annex.

Department of Trade and Industry (1974) 'News: British Isles', *International Journal of Nautical Archaeology*, 3, 1: 165.

Department of Trade, Committee on Wreck (1974) 'Revised Draft Report', *Unpublished document in CNA Archive*, WR(74)4.

Department of Transport (Marine Directorate) (1986) *Historic Wrecks: Guidance Note*, London: Department of Transport (Marine Directorate).

Department of Transport (Marine Directorate) (1988) 'A note on salvage legislation relating to historic wreck' in Dean, M *Guidelines on acceptable standards in underwater archaeology*, St Andrews: Scottish Institute of Maritime Studies.

Dietler, M. (1994) '"Our Ancestors the gauls": archaeology, ethnic nationalism, and the manipulation of Celtic identity in modern Europe', *American Anthropologist*, 96, 3: 584–605.

Division des Recherches Archeologiques Sous-Marines (1991) *Rapport D'activite 1990*, Marseille: Division des Recherches Archeologiques Sous-Marines.

Drewry, G. (1988) 'Legislation' in Ryle, M. and Richards, P. (eds) *The Commons under Scrutiny*, London: Routledge, 120–140.

Dromgoole, S. (1989) 'Protection of Historic Wreck: The UK Approach Part I: The Present Legal Framework', *International Journal of Estuarine and Coastal Law*, 4, 1: 26–51.

Dromgoole, S. (1993) 'Law and the Underwater Cultural Heritage: a legal framework for the protection of the underwater cultural heritage of the United Kingdom', *Unpublished PhD Thesis*.

Dromgoole, S. and Gaskell, N. (1993) 'Who has a Right to Historic Wrecks and Wreckage?', *International Journal of Cultural Property*, 2: 2: 217–273.

Edgeworth, M. (1990) 'Analogy as Practical Reason: the perception of objects in excavation practice', *Archaeological Review from Cambridge*, 9, 2: 243–251.

English Heritage (1991) *Management of Archaeological Projects*, London: Historic Buildings and Monuments Commission for England.

English Heritage/Royal Commission on the Historical Monuments of England (1996) *England's Coastal Heritage: a statement on the management of coastal archaeology*, London: English Heritage.

Eriksen, T.H. (1993) *Ethnicity and Nationalism: anthropological perspectives*, London: Pluto.

Fawcett, C. (1986) 'The politics of assimilation in Japanese archaeology', *Archaeological Review from Cambridge*, 5, 1: 43–57.

Fenton, P.C. (1993) 'The navigator as natural historian', *Mariner's Mirror*, 79, 1: 44–57.

Fenwick, V. (1993) 'Editor's note: the replication debate', *International Journal of Nautical Archaeology*, 22, 3: 197.

Ferrari, B. and Adams, J. (1990) 'Biogenic modifications of marine sediments and their influence on archaeological material', *International Journal of Nautical Archaeology*, 19, 2: 139–151.

Firth, A. (1988) 'The Council of Europe and the regulation of underwater cultural heritage', *unpublished B.A. dissertation*.

Firth, A. (1992 a) 'Archaeology Underwater in France', *International Journal of Estuarine and Coastal Law*, 7, 1: 57–63.

Firth, A. (1992 b) 'The Past in the Coastal Environment: European Perspectives', *SCOPAC Papers and Proceedings: The Regional Coastal Groups - After the House of Commons Report*.

Firth, A. (1995) 'Ghosts in the machine' in Cooper, M., Firth, A., Carman, J. and Wheatley, D. (eds) *Managing Archaeology*, London: Routledge.

Firth, A. (1996) 'Theorizing the management of archaeology underwater', *Historical Archaeology: journal of the Society for Historical Archaeology*, 30, 2: 85-92.

Fleury-Ilett, B. (1993) 'The Identity of France: the archaeological interaction', *Journal of European Archaeology*, 1, 2: 169-180.

Fleury-Ilett, B. (1996) '...' in Graves-Brown, P., Jones, S. and Gamble, C. (eds) *Cultural Identity and Archaeology: the construction of European communities*, London: Routledge.

Flinder, A. (1990) 'Re: Britain's Underwater Archaeological Heritage', *Mariner's Mirror*, 76, 3: 241.

Flinder, A. and McGrail, S. (1990) 'The United Kingdom Advisory Committee on Historic Wreck Sites', *International Journal of Nautical Archaeology*, 19, 2: 93–102.

Forster, W.A., and Higgs, K.B. (1973) 'The Kennemerland, 1971: An interim report', *International Journal of Nautical Archaeology*, 2, 2: 291–300.

Fotiadis, M. (1993) 'Regions of the Imagination: archaeologists, local people, and the archaeological record in fieldwork, Greece', *Journal of European Archaeology*, 1, 2: 151–170.

Fowler, D.D. (1987) 'The Use of the Past in the Service of the State', *American Antiquity*, 52: 229–248.

Fowler, P. (1987) 'What price the man-made heritage?', *Antiquity*, 61: 409–423.

Friel, I. (1993) 'Henry V's Grace Dieu and the wreck in the R. Hamble near Bursledon, Hampshire', *International Journal of Nautical Archaeology*, 22, 1: 3–20.

Gathercole, P. and Lowenthal, D. (eds) (1990 [1994]) *The politics of the past*, London: Unwin Hyman.

Gawronski, J.H. (1991) 'The Archaeological and Historical Research of the Dutch East Indiaman Amsterdam (1749)' in Reinders, R. and Paul, K. *Carvel Construction Technique: skeleton-first, shell-first*, Oxford: Oxbow, 81–84.

Gawronski, J.H.G. (1990) 'The Amsterdam Project', *International Journal of Nautical Archaeology*, 19, 1: 53–61.

Gawronski, J.H.G. (ed.) (1986) *Annual Report of the VOC-Ship "Amsterdam" Foundation 1985*, Amsterdam: Stitching VOC-Schip "Amsterdam".

Gawronski, J.H.G. (ed.) (1987) *Annual Report of the VOC-Ship "Amsterdam" Foundation 1986*, Amsterdam: Stitching VOC-Schip "Amsterdam".

Gellner, E. (1983) *Nations and Nationalism*, Oxford: Blackwell.

Gerth, H.H. and Wright Mills, C. (eds) (1991) *From Max Weber: essays in sociology*, London: Routledge.

Gibbins, D. and Chippindale, C. (1990) 'Special maritime section', *Antiquity*, 64: 334.

Gibson, J.J. (1979 [1986]) *The Ecological Approach to Visual Perception*, Hillsdale, New Jersey: Lawrence Erlbaum Associates.

Giddens, A. (1976 [1993]) *New Rules of Sociological Method: A Positive Critique of Interpretative Sociologies*, Cambridge: Polity Press.

Giddens, A. (1979) *Central Problems in Social Theory: action, structure and contradiction in social analysis*, London: Macmillan.

Giddens, A. (1981) *A Contemporary Critique of Historical Materialism: vol. 1 Power, property and the state*, London: MacMillan.

Giddens, A. (1984) *The Constitution of Society: Outline of the Theory of Structuration*, Cambridge: Polity Press.

Giddens, A. (1985) *The Nation-State and Violence: Volume two of a contemporary critique of historical materialism*, Cambridge: Polity Press.

Giddens, A. (1991) *Modernity and Self-Identity: Self and Society in the Late Modern Age*, Cambridge: Polity Press.

Giddens, A. (1994) *Beyond Left and Right: The future of radical politics*, Cambridge: Polity Press.

Giesecke, A.G. (1992) 'Historic Shipwreck Resources and State Law: a developmental perspective', *Unpublished PhD, Catholic University of America*.

Goddard, V.A., Llobera, J.R. and Shore, C. (1994) 'Introduction: the anthropology of Europe' in Goddard, V.A., Llobera, J.R. and Shore, C. (eds) *The Anthropology of Europe: identity and boundaries in conflict*, Oxford: Berg, 1–40.

Goodburn, D. (1993) 'Some further thoughts on reconstructions, replicas and simulations of ancient boats and ships', *International Journal of Nautical Archaeology*, 22, 3: 199–203.

Graves-Brown, P., Jones, S. and Gamble, C. (eds) (1996) *Cultural Identity and Archaeology: the construction of European communities*, London: Routledge.

Greenhill, B. (1988) 'Foreword' in Dean, M. *Guidelines on Acceptable Standards in Underwater Archaeology*, St. Andrews: Scottish Maritime Studies Development Association.

Gregory, D. (1995) 'Experiments into the deterioration characteristics of materials on the Duart Point wreck-site: an interim report', *International Journal of Nautical Archaeology*, 24, 1: 61–65.

Grenville, J. (1993) 'Curation Overview' in Hunter, J. and Ralston, I. (eds) *Archaeological Resource Management in the UK: An Introduction*, Stroud: Alan Sutton Publishing Ltd., 125–135.

Guilmartin, J.F. (1988) 'Early Modern Naval Ordnance and European Penetration of the Caribbean: the operational dimension', *International Journal of Nautical Archaeology*, 17, 1: 35–54.

Handler, R. (1988) *Nationalism and the Politics of Culture in Quebec*, Madison: University of Wisconsin Press.

Hareven, T.K. and Langenbach, R. (1981) 'Living places, work places and historical identity' in Lowenthal, D. and Binney, M. (eds) *Our Past Before Us? Why do we save it?*, London: Temple Smith, 109–123.

Harris, D.J. (1983) *Cases and Materials in International Law*, London: Sweet and Maxwell.

Hartley, T.C. (1994) *The Foundations of European Community Law: an introduction to the constitutional and administrative law of the European Community*, Oxford: Clarendon Press.

Hassner, P. (1990) 'Europe beyond partition and unity: disintegration or reconstitution?', *International Affairs*, 66: 461–475.

Hasted, R. (1990) 'Museums, racism and censorship' in Baker, F. and Thomas, J. (eds) *Writing the Past in the Present*, Lampeter: St David's University College, 152–162.

Heft, H. (1989) 'Affordances and the Body: An Intentional Analysis of Gibson's Ecological Approach to Visual Perception', *Journal for the Theory of Social Behaviour*, 19, 1: 1–30.

Held, D. and Thompson, J. B. (eds) (1989) *Social theory of modern societies: Anthony Giddens and his critics*, Cambridge: Cambridge University Press.

Helsinger, E. (1994) 'Turner and the Representation of England' in Mitchell, W.J.T. (ed.) *Landscape and Power*, Chicago: University of Chicago Press, 103–125.

Henderson, T. (1985) 'Shipwreck and underwater archaeology in Shetland' in Smith, B. (ed.) *Shetland Archaeology*, Lerwick, 175–212.

Hewison, R. (1987) *The Heritage Industry: Britain in a climate of decline*, London: Methuen.

Hildred, A. (1988) 'The King's Ship: A study in strategic ordnance', *International Journal of Nautical Archaeology*, 17, 1: 55.

Hobsbawm, E. (1983) 'Mass-Producing Traditions: Europe, 1870-1914' in Hobsbawm, E.J. and Ranger, T. *The Invention of Tradition*, Cambridge: Cambridge University Press, 263–307.

Hobsbawm, E.J. (1992) *Nations and Nationalism since 1780: programme, myth, reality*, Cambridge: Cambridge University Press.

Hodder, I. (1991) 'Archaeological theory in contemporary European societies: the emergence of competing traditions' in Hodder, I. (ed.) *Archaeological Theory in Europe: the last three decades*, London: Routledge, 1–24.

Hodder, I. (1992) 'Archaeology in 1984' in Hodder, I. *Theory and practice in archaeology*, London: Routledge, 122–134.

Holman, R.G. (1975) 'The Dartmouth, a British Frigate Wrecked off Mull, 1690: culinary and related items', *International Journal of Nautical Archaeology*, 4, 2: 253–265.

Hudson, K. (1981) *A Social History of Archaeology: the British experience*, London: Macmillan.

Hunter, J. and Ralston, I. (1993) *Archaeological Resource Management in the UK: An Introduction*, Stroud: Alan Sutton Publishing Ltd.

Hutchinson, G. (1991) 'The Early 16th-Century Wreck at Studland Bay, Dorset' in Reinders, R. and Paul, K. (eds.) *Carvel Construction Techniques: Fifth International Symposium on Boat and Ship Archaeology, Amsterdam 1988*, Oxford: Oxbow, 171–175.

Hutchinson, J. (1987) *The Dynamics of Cultural Nationalism: the Gaelic revival and the creation of the Irish ration state*, London: Allen and Unwin.

Hutchinson, J. and Smith, A. D. (1994) *Nationalism*, Oxford: Oxford University Press.

Hutt, S., Jones, E.W. and McAllister, M.E. (1992) *Archaeological Resource Protection*, Washington DC: The Preservation Press.

Hyde-Price, A.G.V. (1993) 'The System Level: the changing topology of Europe' in Wyn Rees, G. (ed.) *International Politics in Europe: the new agenda*, London: Routledge, 13–32.

Ingold, T. (1992) 'Culture and the perception of the environment' in Croll, E. and Parkin, D. *Bush base: forest farm – Culture, environment and development*, London: Routledge, 39–56.

Institute of Field Archaeologists (1988) *By-laws of the Institute of Field Archaeologists: Code of Conduct*, Birmingham: Institute of Field Archaeologists.

Institute of Field Archaeologists (1990) *By-laws of the Institute of Field Archaeologists: Code of Approved Practice for the Regulation of Contractual Arrangements in Field Archaeology*, Birmingham: Institute of Field Archaeologists.

Institute of Field Archaeologists (1994) *Draft Standard and Guidance for Archaeological Excavations*, Birmingham: Institute of Field Archaeologists.

Jary, D. and Jary, J. (1995) 'The Transformations of Anthony Giddens: the continuing story of structuration theory', *Theory, Culture and Society*, 12: 141–160.

Jernigan, C.G. (1994) 'Protecting National Treasures in a Single-Market EC', *Boston College International and Comparative Law Review*, 17: 153–164.

Johnson, N. (1995) 'Cast in Stone: monuments, geography and nationalism', *Environment and Planning D: society and space*, 13: 51–65.

Joint Nautical Archaeology Policy Committee (1989) *Heritage at Sea: Proposals for the better protection of archaeological sites underwater*, London: National Maritime Museum.

Joint Nautical Archaeology Policy Committee (1995) *Code of Practice for Seabed Developers*, London: Joint Nautical Archaeology Policy Committee.

Jones, B. (1984) *Past Imperfect: The Story of Rescue Archaeology*, London: Heinemann.

Jones, D.C. (1978) 'The Pwll Fanog Wreck: A slate cargo in the Menai Strait', *International Journal of Nautical Archaeology*, 7, 2: 152–159.

Jones, S. (1994) 'Archaeology and Ethnicity: constructing identities in the past and the present', *unpublished PhD thesis, University of Southampton*.

Jones, S. and Graves-Brown, P. (1996) 'Introduction' in Graves-Brown, P., Jones, S. and Gamble, C. (eds) *Cultural Identity and Archaeology: the construction of European communities*, London: Routledge.

Jones, S. and Pay, S. (1994) 'The legacy of Eve' in Gathercole, P. and Lowenthal, D. (eds) *The Politics of the Past*, London: Routledge, 160–171.

Jordan, A.G. and Richardson, J.J. (1987) *Government and Pressure Groups in Britain*, Oxford: Clarendon Press.

Kellermann, P. (1992) 'Current European Transformations', *Innovation*, 5, 1: 5–10.

King, T.F. (1983) 'Professional Responsibility in Public Archaeology', *Annual Review of Anthropology*, 12: 143–164.

Knudson, R. (1982) 'Basic Principles of Archaeological Resource Management', *American Antiquity*, 47, 1: 163–166.

Kohl, P. (1993) 'Nationalism, Politics, and the Practice of Archaeology in Soviet Transcaucasia', *Journal of European Archaeology*, 1, 2: 181–188.

Kristiansen, K. (1992) '"The Strength of the past and its Great Might": an essay on the use of the past', *Journal of European Archaeology*, 1: 3–32.

Larkham, P.J. (1994) 'A New Heritage for a New Europe: problem and potential' in Ashworth, G.J. and Larkham, P.J. (eds) *Building a New Heritage: tourism, culture and identity in the New Europe*, London: Routledge, 260–273.

Layton, R. (ed.) (1989) *Conflict in the Archaeology of Living traditions*, London: Unwin Hyman.

Lindbloom, S.J. (1986) 'Historic Shipwreck Legislation: rescuing the Titanic from the law of the sea', *Journal of Legislation*, 13: 92–111.

Lowenthal, D. (1994) 'European and English Landscapes as National Symbols', in Hooson, D. (ed.) (1994 b) *Geography and National Identity*, Oxford: Blackwell, 15–38.

Lund, C. (1987) 'Protection of Historic Shipwrecks and Ancient Monuments on the Danish Sea Bed' in Skov-og Naturstyrelsen *Fortidsminder og Kulturhistorie*, 149–150.

Lyon, J.M. (1994) 'The Herder syndrome: a comparative study of cultural nationalism', *Ethnic and Racial Studies*, 17, 2: 224–237.

Maarleveld, T.J. (1995 a) 'Type or Technique: some thoughts on boat and ship finds as indicative of cultural traditions', *International Journal of Nautical Archaeology*, 24, 1: 3–7.

Maarleveld, T.J. (1995 b) 'Environment Factors in Underwater Heritage Management: a reflection on the Dutch situation' in Olsen, O., Madsen, J.S. and Rieck, F. (eds) *Shipshape: essays for Ole-Crumlin Pedersen*, Roskilde: Viking Ship Museum, 313–328.

Maarleveld, T.J. and Stassen, P. (1993) 'An exceptionally huge rider-mast-step from the Brouwershavensche Gat', *International Journal of Nautical Archaeology*, 22, 3: 283–285.

Mac Giolla Chriost, D. (1996) 'Material Culture and Ethnic Conflict in Northern Ireland', *Transcript of paper presented at TAG Conference December 1995, University of Reading*.

Macdonald, S. (1993) 'Identity Complexes in Western Europe: social anthropological perspectives' in Macdonald, S. (ed.) *Inside European Identities: ethnography in Western Europe*, Oxford: Berg, 1–26.

Mackay, D. (1990) 'Images in a landscape: Bonnie Prince Charlie and the Highland clearances' in Baker, F. and Thomas, J. (eds) *Writing the Past in the Present*, Lampeter: St David's University College, 192–203.

Mackay, D. (1993) 'Scottish Rural Highland Settlement: preserving a people's past' in Hingley, R. (ed.) *Medieval or Later Rural Settlement in Scotland: management and preservation*, Edinburgh: Historic Scotland, 43–51.

Marsden, P. (1972) 'The wreck of the Dutch East Indiaman Amsterdam near Hastings, 1749: an interim report', *International Journal of Nautical Archaeology*, 1: 73–96.

Marsden, P. (1973) 'The investigation of the wreck of the "Amsterdam"' in Blackman, D.J. (ed.) *Marine Archaeology: proceedings of the Twentythird Symposium of the Colston Research Society*, London: Butterworths, 483–492.

Marsden, P. (1974) *The Wreck of the Amsterdam*, London: Hutchinson.

Marsden, P. (1978) 'A reconstruction of the treasure of the Amsterdam and the Hollandia, and their significance', *International Journal of Nautical Archaeology*, 7, 2: 133–148.

Marsden, P. (1986) 'The origin of the Council for Nautical Archaeology', *International Journal of Nautical Archaeology*, 15. 3: 179–183.

Marsden, P. (1990 a) 'Britain's Underwater Archaeological Heritage', *Mariner's Mirror*, 76, 1: 2–4.

Marsden, P. (1990 b) 'Britain's Underwater Archaeological Heritage', *Mariner's Mirror*, 76, 2: 187–188.

Marsden, P. (1990 c) 'Re: Britain's Underwater Archaeological Heritage', *Mariner's Mirror*, 76, 3: 242.

Marsden, P. (1993) 'Replica versus Reconstruction', *International Journal of Nautical Archaeology*, 22, 3: 206–207.

Marsden, P. (1994) 'A comparative look at records of twenty years of wreck archaeology', *International Journal of Nautical Archaeology*, 23, 2: 155–158.

Marsden, P. and Lyon, D. (1977) 'A wreck believed to be the warship Anne, lost in 1690', *International Journal of Nautical Archaeology*, 6, 1: 9–20.

Marsh, D. (1988) *Private Members' Bills*, Cambridge: Cambridge University Press.

Martin, C. (1975) *Full Fathom Five: wrecks of the Spanish Armada*, London: Chatto and Windus.

Martin, C. (1978) 'The Dartmouth, a British frigate wrecked off Mull, 1690: 5. The ship', *International Journal of Nautical Archaeology*, 7, 1: 9–58.

Martin, C. (1995) 'The Cromwellian shipwreck off Duart Point, Mull: an interim report', *International Journal of Nautical Archaeology*, 24, 1: 15–32.

Martin, P. F. de C. (1977) 'The Dartmouth, a British frigate wrecked off Mull, 1690: 4. The clay pipes', *International Journal of Nautical Archaeology*, 6, 3: 219–223.

Mary Rose Trust (1993) *Annual Report*, Portsmouth: Mary Rose Trust.

Mary Rose Trust (n.d.) *Mary Rose: Henry VIII's warship and the exciting exhibition of her treasures*, Portsmouth: Mary Rose Trust.

Massey, D. (1993) 'Politics and Space/Time' in Keith, M. and Pile, S. *Place and the Politics of Identity*, London: Routledge, 141–161.

Matz, E. (n.d.) *Vasa*, Stockholm: Vasa Museum.

Mayall, J. (1990) *Nationalism and International Society*, Cambridge: Cambridge University Press.

McBride, P. (1976) 'The Dartmouth, a British frigate wrecked off Mull, 1690: 3. The guns', *International Journal of Nautical Archaeology*, 5, 3: 189–200.

McBride, P.W.J. (1973) 'The Mary, Charles II's Yacht: 2. her history, importance and ordnance', *International Journal of Nautical Archaeology*, 2, 1: 61–70.

McCann, W.J. (1994) 'Volk und Germanentum: the presentation of the past in Nazi Germany' in Gathercole,

P. and Lowenthal, D. (eds) *The Politics of the Past*, London: Routledge, 74–88.

McDonald, J.D., Zimmerman, L.J., McDonald, A.L., Tall Bull, W. and Rising Sun, T. (1991) 'The Northern Cheyenne Outbreak of 1879: using oral history and archaeology as tools of resistance' in McGuire, R.H. and Paynter, R. (eds) *The Archaeology of Inequality*, Oxford: Blackwell, 64–78.

McGrail, S. (1989) 'Maritime Archaeology in Britain', *The Antiquaries Journal*, 69: 10–22.

McGrail, S. (1992) 'Replicas, reconstructions and floating hypotheses', *International Journal of Nautical Archaeology*, 21, 4: 353–355.

McGrail, S. (1993) 'The future of the Designated Wreck site in the R. Hamble', *International Journal of Nautical Archaeology*, 22, 1: 45–52.

McGrail, S. (1995) 'Training Maritime Archaeologists' in Olsen, O., Madsen, J.S. and Rieck, F. (eds) *Shipshape: essays for Ole Crumlin-Pedersen*, Roskilde: Viking Ship Museum, 329–334.

McGuire, R.H. (1991) 'Building power in the cultural landscape of Broome County, New York 1880 to 1940', in McGuire, R.H. and Paynter, R. (eds) (1991) *The Archaeology of Inequality*, Oxford: Blackwell, 102–124.

McKee. A. (1968) 'Progress Report: First year of Mary Rose (1967) Committee, prepared for Co-ordinating Committee on Maritime Archaeology', *Unpublished document in CNA Archive*.

McKee. A. (1982) *How we found the Mary Rose*, London.

McMahon, J.A. (1995) *Education and Culture in European Community Law*, London: Athlone.

Meacham, J.A. (1993) 'Where is the Social Environment? A commentary on Reed' in Wozniak, R.H. and Fischer, K.W. *Development in Context: acting and thinking in specific environments*, Hillsdale, New Jersey: Lawrence Erlbaum, 255–267.

Mikolaczyk, A. (1994) 'Didactic presentations of the past: some retrospective considerations in relation to the Archaeological and Ethnographical Museum, Lodz, Poland' in Gathercole, P. and Lowenthal, D. (eds) *The Politics of the Past*, London: Routledge, 247–256.

Miller, R. (1994) 'Charting the Future of Historic Shipwreck Legislation in California: application of the English model in the salvage of the Brother Jonathan', *Hastings International and Comparative Law Review*, 17: 793–817.

Morris. R. (1979) *HMS Colossus*, London: Hutchinson.

Muckeroy, K. (1976) 'The Integration of Historical and Archaeological Data Concerning an Historic Wreck Site: The Kennemerland', *World Archaeology*, 7: 280–289.

Muckeroy, K. (1978) *Maritime Archaeology*, Cambridge: Cambridge University Press.

Muckelroy, K. (1980) 'Two Bronze Age Cargoes in British Waters', *Antiquity*, LIV: 100–109.

Muckelroy, K. (1981) 'Middle Bronze Age Trade between Britain and Europe', *Proceedings of the Prehistoric Society*, 47: 275–297.

Mulhern, F. (1993) 'A European Home?' in Bird, J., Curtis, B., Putnam, T., Robertson, G. and Tickner, L. (eds) *Mapping the Futures: local cultures, global change*, London: Routledge, 199–204.

Murray, T. (1989) 'The history, philosophy and sociology of archaeology: the case of the Ancient Monuments Protection Act (1882)' in Pinsky, V. and Wylie, A. (eds) *Critical Traditions in Contemporary Archaeology: essays in the philosophy, history and socio-politics of archaeology*, Cambridge: Cambridge University Press, 55–67.

Naevestad, D. (1992) *Kulturminner under vann*, Oslo: FOK.

Naevestad, D. (1993) *Kulturminner under vann: vurdering av nye titak i fortvaltningen*, Oslo: Norsk Sjofartsmuseum.

Nairn, T. (1977 [1981]) *The Break-Up of Britain: crisis and neo-nationalism*, London: Verso.

Neumann, I.B. and Welsh, J.M. (1991) 'The Other in European self-definition: an addendum to the literature on international society', *Review of International Studies*, 17: 327–348.

Noble, W. (1993) 'Meaning and the "Discursive Ecology": further to the debate on ecological perception theory', *Journal for the Theory of Social Behaviour*, 23, 4: 375–398.

Noble, W.G. (1981) 'Gibsonian Theory and the Pragmatist Perspective', *Journal for the Theory of Social Behaviour*, 11, 1: 65–85.

Nordquist, M.H., Rosenne, S. and Sohn, L.B. (1989) *United Nations Convention on the Law of the Sea, 1982: a commentary*, Dordrecht: Martinus Nijhoff.

Norges Dykkeforbund (n.d.) *Protection of Cultural Monuments in the Sea*, Oslo: Norges Dykkeforbund.

O'Keefe, P. J. and Prott, L. V. (1984) *Law and the cultural heritage vol. 1: Discovery and excavation*, London: Professional Books Ltd.

O'Keefe, P.J. and Nafziger, J.A.R. (1994) 'The Draft Convention on the Protection of the Underwater Cultural Heritage', *Ocean Development and International Law*, 25: 391–418.

Oliver, P. (1982) *Free Movement of Goods in the EEC under Articles 30 to 36 of the Rome Treaty*, London: European Law Centre.

Olsen, B. (1986) 'Norwegian archaeology and the people without (Pre-)history: or how to create a myth of a uniform past', *Archaeological Review from Cambridge*, 5, 1: 25–42.

Orwell, G. (1949 [1983]) *Nineteen Eighty-Four*, London: Penguin.

Owen, N.C. (1988) 'HMS Hazardous wrecked 1706. Predisturbance survey report', *International Journal of Nautical Archaeology*, 17, 4: 285–293.

Owen, N.C. (1991) 'Hazardous 1990-1991 interim report', *International Journal of Nautical Archaeology*, 20, 4: 325–334.

Oxley, I. (1995) 'The Role of the Protection of Wrecks Act 1973 in Integrated Management of the Marine Archaeological Heritage: a personal view' in A. Berry and Brown, I.W. (eds) *Managing Ancient Monuments: An integrated approach*, Mold: Clwyd County Council, 169–180.

Oxman, B.H. (1980) 'The Third United Nations Conference on the Law of the Sea: the Eighth Session (1979)', *American Journal of International Law*, 74, 1: 1–47.

Oxman, B.H. (1981) 'The Third United Nations Conference on the Law of the Sea: the Ninth Session (1980)', *American Journal of International Law*, 75, 2: 211–256.

Palsson, G. (1994) 'Enskilment at Sea', *Man*, 29, 4: 901–927.

Papadakis, Y. (1994) 'The national struggle museums of a divided city', in (1994) *Ethnic and Racial Studies*, 17, 3: 400–419.

Parker, A.J. (1995) 'Maritime Cultures and Wreck Assemblages in the Graeco-Roman World', *International Journal of Nautical Archaeology*, 24, 2: 87–95.

Parthesius, R. (1987) 'Fusion of the Two Disciplines: the historical-archaeological research of the "Amsterdam"' in Gawronski, J.H.G. (ed.) *Annual Report of the VOC-Ship "Amsterdam" Foundation 1986*, Amsterdam: Stitching VOC-Schip "Amsterdam", 31–36.

Piccini, A. (1996) 'Prehistory and the Landscapes of Heritage in Wales', *Transcript of paper presented at TAG Conference December 1995, University of Reading*.

Pieterse, J.N. (1991) 'Fictions of Europe', *Race and Class*, 32, 3: 3–10.

Pinsky, V. and Wylie, A. (eds) (1989) *Critical Traditions in Contemporary Archaeology: essays in the philosophy, history and socio-politics of archaeology*, Cambridge: Cambridge University Press.

Polanyi, M. (1967) *The Tacit Dimension*, London: Routledge and Keegan Paul.

Preece, C. and Burton, S. (1993) 'Church Rocks, 1975-83: a reassessment', *International Journal of Nautical Archaeology*, 22, 3: 257–266.

Price, R. and Muckelroy, K., and (1974) 'The second season of work on the Kennemerland site, 1973: an interim report', *International Journal of Nautical Archaeology*, 3, 2: 257–268.

Price, R. and Muckelroy, K., and (1977) 'The Kennemerland Site: the third and fourth seasons 1974 and 1976. An interim report', *International Journal of Nautical Archaeology*, 6, 3: 187–218.

Price, R., Muckelroy, K. and Willies, L. (1980) 'The Kennemerland Site: a report on the lead ingots', *International Journal of Nautical Archaeology*, 9, 1: 7–25.

Priestman, K. (1973) 'The Mary, Charles II's Yacht: 3. conservation of finds', *International Journal of Nautical Archaeology*, 2, 1: 70–73.

Prott, L.V. (1992) 'A Common Heritage: the World Heritage Convention' in Macinnes, L. and Wickham-Jones, C.R. *All Natural Things: archaeology and the green debate*, Oxford: Oxbow, 65–86.

Redknap, M. (1984) *The Cattewater Wreck*, Oxford: BAR.

Redknap, M. (1985) 'The Cattewater Wreck: A Contribution to 16th Century Maritime Archaeology' in Cederlund, C.O. *Post Medieval Boat and Ship Archaeology*, Oxford: BAR, 39–60.

Reed, E.S. (1993) 'The Intention to Use a Specific Affordance: a conceptual framework for psychology' in Wozniak, R.H. and Fischer, K.W. *Development in Context: acting and thinking in specific environments*, Hillsdale, New Jersey: Lawrence Erlbaum, 45–76.

Renfrew, C. (1994) 'The Identity of Europe in Prehistoric Archaeology', *Journal of European Archaeology*, 2, 2: 153–173.

Richards, P.G. (1977) 'Private Members' Legislation', *The Commons in the Seventies*, 113–128.

Roberts, E.L. (1993) 'Cultural Policy in the European Community: a case against extensive national retention', *Texas International Law Journal*, 28: 191–228.

Roberts, O.T.P. (1979) 'Pwll Fanog Wreck, Menai Straits, North Wales: An interim report on the ship's remains revealed during the 1978 exploratory excavation of the slate cargo mound', *International Journal of Nautical Archaeology*, 8, 3: 249–254.

Roper (ed.) (1978) *The Underwater Cultural Heritage: report of the Committee on Culture and Education*, Strasbourg: Council of Europe.

Roskams, S. (1988) 'Giving meaning to the past: political perspectives in archaeology' in Bintliff, J. (ed.) *Extracting Meaning from the Past*, Oxford: Oxbow, 65–68.

Roth, R. (1996) 'The Cannon from Dunwich Bank, Suffolk', *IJNA*, 25, 1: 21–32.

Rowlands, M. (1994) 'The Politics of Identity in Archaeology' in Bond, G.C. and Gilliam, A. (eds) *Social Construction of the Past: representation as power*, London: Routledge, 129–143.

Royal Commission on the Historical Monuments of England/Nautical Archaeology Society (n.d.) *Dive into History*, Southampton: Royal Commission on the Historical Monuments of England.

Royal Ministry of Foreign Affairs (1990) *Mini-Facts about Norway 1990-91*, Oslo: Royal Ministry of Foreign Affairs.

Ruffman, A., Townsend Gault, I. and VanderZwaag, D. (1988) 'Legal Jurisdiction over the Titanic', *Lighthouse*, 37: 23–39.

Said, E.W. (1978 [1995]) *Orientalism: western conceptions of the Orient*, London: Penguin.

Sanger, C. (1986) *Ordering the Oceans: the making of the law of the sea*, London: Zed Books.

Saunders, A. (1994) 'Twenty Years of the Historic Wrecks Committee', *Antiquaries Journal*, LXXIV: 315–319.

Saussure, F. (1916 [1983]) *Course in General Linguistics*, London: Duckworth.

Schiffer, M.B. and Gumerman, G.L. (eds) (1977) *Conservation Archaeology: a guide for cultural resource management studies*, New York: Academic Press.

Schlesinger, P. (1991) *Media, State and Nation: political violence and collective identities*, London: Sage.

Searing, D.D. (1995) 'Backbench and Leadership Roles in The House of Commons', *Parliamentary Affairs*, 48, 3: 418–437.

Shanks, M. (1992) *Experiencing the Past: On the character of archaeology*, London: Routledge.

Shanks, M. and Tilley, C. (1992) *Re-Constructing Archaeology*, London: Routledge.

Shehadeh, R. (1982) *The Third Way: a journal of life in the West Bank*, London: Quartet Books.

Shore, C. (1993) 'Inventing the "People's Europe": critical approaches to European Community "cultural policy"', *Man*, 28: 779–800.

Shore, C. (1996) 'Imagining the New Europe: identity and heritage in European Community discourse' in Graves, P. and Jones, S. *European Communities*, London: Routledge.

Shore, C. and Black, A. (1994) 'Citizens' Europe and the Construction of European Identity' in Goddard, V.A., Llobera, J.R. and Shore, C. (eds) *The Anthropology of Europe: identity and boundaries in conflict*, Oxford: Berg, 275–298.

Short, K.A. (1993) 'Preventing the Theft and Illegal Export of Art in a Europe without Borders', *Vanderbilt Journal of Transnational Law*, 26: 633–665.

Slapsak, B. (1993) 'Archaeology and the Contemporary Myths of the Past', *Journal of European Archaeology*, 1, 2: 191–195.

Smith, A.D. (1991) *National Identity*, London: Penguin Books.

Smith, L. (1993) 'Towards a Theoretical Framework for Archaeological Heritage Management', *Archaeological Review from Cambridge*, 12, 1: 55–75.

Solli, B. (1996) 'Narratives of Veøy: on the poetics and scientifics of archaeology' in Graves-Brown, P., Jones, S. and Gamble, C. (eds) *Cultural Identity and Archaeology: the construction of European communities*, London: Routledge, 209–227.

SouthWest Trains (1995) *Outlook: SouthWest Trains' complimentary magazine*.

Startin, B. (1991) 'The Monuments Protection Programme: archaeological records' in Larsen, C.U. (ed.) *Sites and Monuments Records: National Archaeological Records*, Copenhagen: National Museum of Denmark, 201–206.

Startin, B. (1995) 'MPP: protecting what, how and for whom?' in Cooper, M., Firth, A., Carman, J. and Wheatley, D. (eds) *Managing Archaeology*, London: Routledge, 137–145.

Stenuit, R. (1969) 'Ireland's rugged coast yields priceless relics of the Spanish Armada', *National Geographic*, 135, 6: 745–777.

Strati, A. (1991) 'Deep Seabed Cultural Property and the Common Heritage of Mankind', *International and Comparative Law Quarterly*, 40: 859–894.

Sutcliffe, S. (1972) *Martello Towers*, Newton Abbot: David and Charles.

Taylor, B. (1995) 'Amateurs, Professionals and the Knowledge of Archaeology', *British Journal of Sociology*, 46, 3: 499–508.

Tilley, C. (1989) 'Excavation as Theatre', *Antiquity*, 63: 275–280.

Tilley, C. (1994) *A Phenomenology of Landscape: places, paths and monuments*, Oxford: Berg.

Tilly, C. (1992) 'Futures of European States', *Social Research*, 59, 4: 705–717.

Tomalin, D., Cross, J. and Motkin, D. (1988) 'An Alberghetti bronze minion and carriage from Yarmouth Roads, Isle of Wight', *International Journal of Nautical Archaeology*, 17, 1: 75–86.

Trigger, B.G. (1984) 'Alternative archaeologies: nationalist, colonialist, imperialist', *Man*, 19: 355–370.

Trigger B.G. (1989) *A History of Archaeological Thought*, Cambridge: Cambridge University Press.

Ucko, F. (1987) *Academic Freedom and Apartheid: the story of the World Archaeological Congress*, London: Duckworth.

Ucko, P. (1989 a) 'Foreword' in Cleere, H. (ed.) *Archaeological Heritage Management in the Modern World*, London: Unwin Hyman, ix–xiv.

Ucko, P. (1989 b) 'Foreword' in Layton, R. (ed.) *Conflict in the Archaeology of Living traditions*, London: Unwin Hyman, ix–xvii.

Ucko, P. (1990 [1994]) 'Foreword' in Gathercole, P. and Lowenthal, D. (eds) *The Politics of the Past*, London: Routledge, ix–xxi.

Ucko, P.J. (1995) 'Introduction: archaeological interpretation in a world context' in Ucko, P.J. (ed.) *Theory in Archaeology: a world perspective*, London: Routledge, 1–27.

Ucko, P.J., Hunter, M., Clark, A.J. and David, A. (1991) *Avebury Reconsidered: from the 1660s to the 1990s*, London: Unwin Hyman.

UNESCO (1995) *Preliminary Study on the Advisability of Preparing an International Instrument for the Protection of the Underwater Cultural Heritage*, Paris: UNESCO, 28 C/39.

United Nations (1982) *Third United Nations Conference on the Law of the Sea: official records – summary record of meetings (resumed Ninth Session: Geneva, 28 July - 29 August 1980)*, New York: United Nations, XIV.

United Nations (1995) 'Archaeological and Historical Object under the United Nations Convention on the Law of the Sea: note by Division for Ocean Affairs and the Law of the Sea, Office of Legal Affairs, UN', *Transcript of paper presented at National Maritime Museum Conference on Protection of Underwater Cultural Heritage January 1995, Greenwich*.

van de Noort, R. and Davies, P. (1993) *Wetland Heritage: an archaeological assessment of the Humber Wetlands*, Hull: Humber Wetlands Project.

Veit, U. (1989) 'Ethnic Concepts in German Prehistory: a case study on the relationship between cultural identity and archaeological objectivity' in Shennan, S.J. (ed.) *Archaeological Approaches to Cultural Identity*, London: Unwin Hyman.

Visram, R. (1990) 'Black history, whose history? Black perspectives on British History' in Baker, F. and Thomas, J. (eds) *Writing the Past in the Present*, Lampeter: St David's University College, 163–171.

Vitrano, V.J. (1994) 'Protecting Cultural Objects in an Internal Border-Free EC: the EC Directive and Regulation for the protection and return of cultural objects', *Fordham International Law Journal*, 17: 1165–1201.

Wainwright, G. (1993) 'Exploring Our Past', *Transcript of public lecture, University of Southampton*, 2 November 1992.

Walka, J.J. (1979) 'Management Methods and Opportunities in Archaeology', *American Antiquity*, 44, 3: 575–582.

Wallace, W. (1991) 'Foreign policy and national identity in the United Kingdom', *International Affairs*, 67, 1: 65–80.

Warner, 1985 (1985) *Monuments and Maidens: the allegory of the female form*, London: Weidenfeld and Nicolson.

Waterman, C. (n.d.) *The Dover Bronze Age Boat*, Dover: Dover Bronze Age Boat Trust.

Watters, D.R. (1983) 'The Law of the Sea Treaty and Underwater Cultural Resources', *American Antiquity*, 48, 4: 808–816.

Wæver, O., Buzan, B. Kelstrup, M. and Lemaitre, P. (1993) *Identity, Migration and the New Security Agenda in Europe*, London: Pinter.

Weatherill, S. and Beaumont, P. (1993) *EC Law: the essential guide to the legal workings of the European Community*, London: Penguin.

Webber, F. (1991) 'From ethnocentrism to Euro-racism', *Race and Class*, 32, 3: 11–17.

Weber, M. (1968) *Economy and Society: an outline of interpretive sociology*, New York: Bedminster Press.

Wenban-Smith, F. (1995) 'Square Pegs in Round Holes' in Cooper, M., Firth, A., Carman, J. and Wheatley, D *Managing Archaeology*, London: Routledge.

Westerdahl, C. (1992) 'Review of J.F. Coates, S.K. Platis and J.T. Shaw, The Trireme Trials 1988, Report on the Anglo-Hellenic Sea Trials of Olympias', *International Journal of Nautical Archaeology*, 21, 2: 183–184.

Westerdahl, C. (1993) 'The trireme – an experimental form?', *International Journal of Nautical Archaeology*, 22, 3: 205–206.

Westerdahl, C. (1994) 'Maritime Cultures and Ship Types: brief comments on the significance of maritime archaeology', *International Journal of Nautical Archaeology*, 23, 4: 265–270.

Wheatley, D. (1995) 'The impact of information technology on the practice of archaeological management' in Cooper, M., Firth, A., Carman, J. and Wheatley, D *Managing Archaeology*, London: Routledge.

Wignall, S. (1973) 'The Armada shot controversy' in Blackman, D.J. (ed.) *Marine Archaeology: proceedings of the Twentythird Symposium of the Colston Research Society*, London: Butterworths, 463–481.

Wignall, S. (1975 a) 'The "Grey Dove" Affair' in Martin, C. *Full Fathom Five: wrecks of the Spanish Armada*, London: Chatto and Windus, 233–246.

Wignall, S. (1975 b) 'Armada Shot: a possible reason for failure' in Martin, C. *Full Fathom Five: wrecks of the Spanish Armada*, London: Chatto and Windus, 247–261.

Wittop Koening, D.A. (1986) 'Medical Treatment Aboard' in Gawronski, J.H.G. (ed.) *Annual Report of the VOC-Ship "Amsterdam" Foundation 1985*, Amsterdam: Stitching VOC-Schip "Amsterdam", 88–90.

Woodman, P.C. (1995) 'Who Possesses Tara? politics and archaeology in Ireland' in Ucko, P.J. (ed.) *Theory in Archaeology: a world perspective*, London: Routledge, 278–297.

World Archaeological Congress (1991) 'First Code of Ethics: member's obligations to indigenous peoples', *World Archaeological Bulletin*, 5: 22-23.

Wright, E. (1990) *The Ferriby Boats: seacraft of the Bronze Age*, London: Routledge.

Wright, P. (1985) *On Living in an Old Country: the national past in contemporary Britain*, London: Verso.

Wylie, A. (1989) 'Introduction: socio-political context' in Pinsky, V. and Wylie, A. (eds) *Critical Traditions in Contemporary Archaeology: essays in the philosophy, history and socio-politics of archaeology*, Cambridge: Cambridge University Press, 93–95.

Wyn Rees, G. (ed.) (1993) *International Politics in Europe: the new agenda*, London: Routledge.

7.2 Newspapers

The Daily Telegraph Magazine, 28/04/72, 'Charade on the Seabed', Angela Croome, p. 7.

The Guardian, 18/04/72, 'Don't forget the diver', Peter Fiddick.

The Observer, 16/01/72, '"Pirates" safe from the Navy', Richard Walter.

The Times, 30/11/74, 'Treasure in shipwrecks' (letter), Peter Marsden.

The Times, 12/06/87, [Archaeological Diving Unit] (letter), Edward Wright.

The Times, 25/06/87, [Archaeological Diving Unit] (letter), Robert Prescott.

7.3 Cases

Anglo-French Continental Shelf arbitration XVIII ILM 397 (1979)

Anglo-Norwegian Fisheries case [1951] ICJ Rep 116

Commission of the European Communities v Italian Republic [1968] ECR 423

Corfu Channel case [1949] ICJ Rep 1

Hoveringham Gravels Ltd. v. Secretary of State for the Environment [1975] 1 QB 754

Post Office v. Estuary Radio case [1968] 2 QB 740

Morris v. Lyonesse Salvage *The Association and The Romney* [1970] 2 Lloyd's Rep 59

The Tubantia [1924] P 78

Webb v. Ireland [1988] IR 353

7.4 Statutes

All statutes other than those in English are in translations supplied by the authorities of the country concerned, unless stated otherwise. Legislative sources were principally collated in January 1992 and were correct at that time. Where possible, amendments that are more recent have been included.

4319 C-080.22/91 HKH/HS	Fylkeskommunenes rolle i saker om skipsfunn etter Lov om Kulterminner s. 14	Letter, Riksantikvaren to Fylkeskommunene, De arkeologiske landesmuseer, Sjofartsmuseene	Norway
ACAMF 1942	Act Concerning Ancient Monuments and Finds 1942	Act of 12 June 1942 (No. 350, Reprinted 1976 No. 442) concerning ancient monuments and finds	Sweden
ACAMF 1988	Act Concerning Ancient Monuments and Finds 1988	An Act concerning ancient monuments and finds, promulgated 30th June 1988	Sweden
ACMCP 1989	Act Concerning Maritime Cultural Property 1989	Act No. 89-874 of 1 December 1989 concerning Maritime Cultural Property and Amending the Act of 27 September 1971 Regulating Archaeological Excavations	France
AM 1984 [1989]	Act on Museums 1984	Act no. 291 of June 6, 1984 concerning museums, etc. with amendments pursuant to Act no. 592 of December 19, 1985, Act. no. 948 of December 23, 1986 and Act no. 380 of June 7, 1989	Denmark
AMA 1931	Ancient Monuments Act 1931	1931	UK

Sources

AMAA 1979	Ancient Monuments and Archaeological Areas Act 1979	1979	UK
AMCA 1913	Ancient Monuments Amendment and Consolidation Act 1913	1913	UK
Arrete du 4 janvier 1996	Arrete du 4 janvier 1996 portant creation et organisation du department des recherches archeologiques subaquatiques et sous-marines	Arrete du 4 janvier 1996	France
Constitution of Ireland 1937		1937	Ireland
CHA 1979	Cultural Heritage Act 1979	Act of 9 June No. 50 concerning Cultural Heritage entered into force 15 February 1979	Norway
CHPA 1984	Cultural Heritage Protection Act 1984	Cultural Heritage Protection Act of 1 February 1984	Netherlands
Decret 91–1226	Decret 91–1226 du 5 decembre 1991 pris pour l'application de la loi no. 89-874 du 1 decembre 1989 relative aux biens culturels maritimes ...	Decret 91–1226 du 5 decembre 1991	France
HBAMA 1953	Historic Buildings and Ancient Monuments Act 1953	1953	UK
IA 1978	Interpretation Act 1978	1978	UK
LGA 1972	Local Government Act 1972	1972	UK
MHBA 1988	Monuments and Historic Buildings Act 1988	The Act providing for the Preservation of Monuments and Historic Buildings of Historic and Artistic Importance, published 30 December 1988	Netherlands
MMA/Mc-1497	Ontdekking scheepswrak met lading met grote intrensieke waarde	Letter, Ministerie van Welzijn, Volksgezondheid en Cultuur to Monumentenraad	Netherlands
MSA 1894	Merchant Shipping Act 1894	57 & 58 Vict.	UK
MSA 1993	Merchant Shipping (Registration, etc.) Act 1993	1993	UK
MSA 1995	Merchant Shipping Act 1995	1995	UK
NHA 1983	National Heritage Act 1983	1983	UK
NMA 1930	National Monuments Act 1930	Number 2 of 1930	Ireland
NMA 1930 [1987]			Ireland
NMA 1930 [1994]			Ireland
NMA 1987	National Monuments (Amendment) Act, 1987	Number 17 of 1987	Ireland
NMA 1987 [1994]			Ireland
NMA 1994	National Monuments (Amendment) Act, 1994	Number 17 of 1994	Ireland
OPW 1995	Underwater Heritage Order 1995	Underwater Heritage Order made by the Commissioners of Public Works in Ireland pursuant to Section 3(1) of the National Monuments (Amendment) Act, 1987	Ireland
PMRA 1987	Protection of Military Remains Act 1986	1986	UK
PNA 1992	Protection of Nature Act 1992	Act No. 9 of 3 January 1992	Denmark
PWA 1973	Protection of Wrecks Act 1973	1973	UK
RMA 1991	Raw Materials Act 1991	Act No. 357 of June 6, 1991	Denmark
Territorial Waters (Amendment) Order in Council 1979		1979 p. 2866	UK

7.5   Statutory Instruments (Protection of Wrecks Act 1973)

1979 No. 6	The Protection of Wrecks (Revocation) Order 1979	04/01/79	*Dartmouth*
1984 No. 802	The Protection of Wrecks (Revocation No. 2) Order 1984	14/06/84	Frenchman's Rocks
1984 No. 2	The Protection of Wrecks (Revocation) Order 1984	05/01/84	*Colossus*
1986 No. 1020	The Protection of Wrecks (Revocation) Order 1986	18/06/86	*Admiral Gardner*

7.6   International Conventions

DCPUCH 1995	Draft Convention on the Protection of Underwater Cultural Heritage 1995
ECC 1955	European Cultural Convention 1955
ECPAH 1992	European Convention on the Protection of the Archaeological Heritage 1992
LOSC 1982	UN Convention on the Law of the Sea 1982
Recommendation 848	Recommendation 848 (1978) of the Parliamentary Assembly of the Council of Europe on the underwater cultural heritage
WHC 1972	Convention concerning the Protection of the World Cultural Heritage 1972
	Montevideo Convention on Rights and Duties of States 1933

7.7   European Union Documents

85/L 175/40	27/06/85	Council	Council Directive on the assessment of the effects of certain public and private projects on the environment.
91/C 314/01	14/11/91	Council	Resolution of the Council and the Ministers of Culture meeting within the Council of 14 November 1991 on European cultural networks
92/C 191	07/02/92		Treaty on European Union
92/C 59/01	25/02/92	Council	Council Resolution on the future Community policy concerning the European coastal zone
92/L 395/01	09/12/92	Council	Council Regulation (EEC) No 3911/92 of 9 December 1992 on the export of cultural goods (EEC) No 3911/92
93/C 42/173	21/01/93	European Parliament	Resolution on the Commission communication entitled 'New prospects for Community cultural action' A3-0396/92
93/L 74/74	15/03/93	Council	Council Directive 93/7/EEC of 15 March 1993 on the return of cultural objects unlawfully removed from the territory of a Member State 93/7/EEC
94/C 227/11		Commission	Programme 'Kaleidoscope Scheme' organized by the Commission of the European Communities: conditions of participation
94/C 235/01	17/06/94	Council	Council Conclusions of 17 June 1994 on drawing up a Community Action Plan in the field of cultural heritage
94/C 235/03	17/06/94	Council	Council conclusions of 17 June 1994 concerning greater cooperation in the field of archives
95/C 287/161	12/10/95	European Parliament	Proposals for a European Parliament and Council Decision establishing a Community action programme in the field of cultural heritage – the Raphaël Programme.

7.8   Parliamentary Reports (Hansard)

06/04/67	Commons	Fifth	vol. 744 col. 71w	Merchant Shipping Act, 1898 (Salvage Rules), NB. Q's on Torrey Canyon; Mr. Nott to President of the Board of Trade
04/03/70	Commons	Fifth	vol. 797 col. 415–417	Historic Wrecks Bill, First reading
06/03/70	Commons	Fifth	vol. 797 col. 868	Historic Wrecks Bill, Second reading deferred
11/03/70	Commons	Fifth	vol. 797 col. 1362–1377	Merchant Shipping Bill, Amendment on historic wreck, introduced and withdrawn
13/03/70	Commons	Fifth	vol. 797 col. 1815	Historic Wrecks Bill, Second reading deferred
20/03/70	Commons	Fifth	vol. 798 col. 932	Historic Wrecks Bill, Second reading deferred
10/04/70	Commons	Fifth	vol. 799 col. 983	Historic Wrecks Bill, Second reading deferred
14/04/70	Lords	Fifth	vol. 309 col. 317	Protection of Historic Wrecks; Lord Ilford to Her Majesty's Government
14/04/70	Lords	Fifth	vol. 309 col. 317–318	Protection of Historic Wrecks; Lord Ilford to Her Majesty's Government
01/05/70	Commons	Fifth	vol. 800 col. 1715	Historic Wrecks Bill, Second reading deferred
08/05/70	Commons	Fifth	vol. 801 col. 787	Historic Wrecks Bill, No instruction
20/01/72	Commons	Fifth	vol. 829 col. 212w	Charles II Royal Yacht "Mary"; Mr. Faulds to Minister of State for Defence
10/04/72	Commons	Fifth	vol. 834 col. 860–985	Debate on Royal Navy
20/07/72	Commons	Fifth	vol. 841 col. 171w	m.s. "Amsterdam" (Wreck); Mr. Faulds to Secretary of State for Foreign and Commonwealth Affairs
04/12/72	Commons	Fifth	vol. 847 col. 293w	Historic Wreck Sites; Sir Bernard Braine to Secretary of State for trade and Industry
02/03/73	Commons	Fifth	vol. 851 col. 1848–1879	Protection of Wrecks Bill, Second reading

14/03/73	Commons	Fifth	vol. 852 col. 363–364w	Underwater Salvages (Conservation); Mr. Faulds to Secretary of State for Education and Science
13/04/73	Commons	Fifth	vol. 854 col. 1756	Protection of Wrecks Bill, Committed to a committee of the whole House
04/05/73	Commons	Fifth	vol. 855 col. 1694	Protection of Wrecks Bill, Reported
04/05/73	Commons	Fifth	vol. 855 col. 1695–1707	Protection of Wrecks Bill, Third reading
04/05/73	Commons	Fifth	vol. 855 col. 1656–1694	Protection of Wrecks Bill, Committee
08/05/73	Lords	Fifth	vol. 342 col. 256	Protection of Wrecks Bill, Brought from Commons, first reading (Lords)
17/05/73	Lords	Fifth	vol. 342 col. 914–935	Protection of Wrecks Bill, Second reading (Lords)
08/06/73	Lords	Fifth	vol. 343 col. 306–317	Protection of Wrecks Bill, Committee of whole House
28/06/73	Lords	Fifth	vol. 343 col. 2173–2176	Protection of Wrecks Bill, Report received
09/07/73	Lords	Fifth	vol. 344 col. 509	Protection of Wrecks Bill, Third reading, passed
18/07/73	Lords	Fifth	vol. 344 col. 1161	Protection of Wrecks Bill, Royal Assent
18/07/73	Commons	Fifth	vol. 860 col. 494	Protection of Wrecks Bill, Royal Assent
04/03/76	Commons	Fifth	vol. 906 col. 708–709w	Wreck Committee (Report); Mr. Bean to Secretary of State for Trade
28/02/78	Commons	Fifth	vol. 945 col. 151w	Wrecks. N.B. Next question is by Wm. Ross, about oil pollution; Mr. Wm. Ross to Secretary of State for Trade
04/04/79	Commons	Fifth	vol. 965 col. 1360–1375	Ancient Monuments Bill, Third reading, committed to Cttee of the whole House
02/12/81	Commons	Sixth	vol. 14 col. 207–208w	Quangos; Mr. Holland to Secretary of State for Trade
09/12/81	Commons	Sixth	vol. 14 col. 412w	Quangos; Mr. Holland to Secretary of State for Trade
08/03/88	Commons	Sixth	vol. 129 col. 155w	Merchant Shipping Act 1894; Mr. Wallace to Secretary of State for Transport
24/05/88	Commons	Sixth	vol. 134 col. 150w	Historic Wrecks Advisory Committee; Mr. Onslow to Secretary of State for Transport
25/07/88	Commons	Sixth	vol. 138 col. 29–30w	Historic Warship Wrecks; Mr. Onslow to Secretary of State for Defence
29/07/88	Commons	Sixth	vol. 138 col. 770w	HMS Invincible (Antiquities); Mr. Onslow to Secretary of State for Transport
15/10/90	Commons	Sixth	vol. 177 col. 636w	Nautical Archaeology; Mr. Onslow to Prime Minister
06/03/91	Commons	Sixth	vol. 187 col. 197w	Wrecks; Sir Gerrard Neale to Secretary of Sate for the Environment
06/03/91	Lords	Fifth	vol. 526 col. 73WA	Wrecks: Abolition of Commission Payments to Receivers; Lord Norrie to Her Majesty's Government
20/04/93	Commons	Sixth	vol. 223 col. 71–72w	Marine Archaeology; Mr. Dalyell to Secretary of State for Transport

7.9 Letters

04/01/68	P.N. Davies to J. du P. Taylor (CNA)	Holyhead cannon	CNA 470*
10/12/69	J. Mr. Nott to B. Greenhill		CNA 230
02/08/71	D. Byrne, DTI to A. Croome (CNA)	Wreck Law Review	CNA 519
15/11/71	S. Wignall to A. Croome (CNA)	Interim legislation	CNA 494
18/11/71	L. Leicester (DTI) to A. Croome (CNA)	Documents via Duke of Edinburgh	CNA 355
15/03/72	A. Croome (CNA) to P. Kirk, Under Secretary of State for Defence	*Mary*	CNA 596
29/03/72	MoD to A. Croome (CNA)	*Mary*	CNA 595
16/05/72	P. Kirk, Under Secretary of State for Defence, to D. Dr. Owen, MP	Protection of *Mary* following Navy Debate	CNA 99
31/03/93	Caithness, Minister for Aviation and Shipping, to T. Dalyell, MP	Merchant Shipping Bill	L/PSO/6890/93‡

* 'CNA' denotes letter in the archive of the Council for Nautical Archaeology, held by RCHME

‡ Copy held in the Library of the House of Commons

7.10 CNA Minutes

All CNA Minutes are from the CNA Archive, held by RCHME.

12/10/64	British Nautical Archaeological Research Committee	Minutes of a meeting held at the Institute of Archaeology, London
06/11/68	Committee for Nautical Archaeology	Minutes of a meeting held at the Institute of Archaeology, London

05/02/69	Committee for Nautical Archaeology	Minutes of a meeting held at the Institute of Archaeology, London
19/11/69	Committee for Nautical Archaeology	Minutes of a meeting held at the Institute of Archaeology, London
24/02/71	Committee for Nautical Archaeology	Minutes of a meeting held at the Institute of Archaeology, London
16/09/71	Council for Nautical Archaeology	Minutes of a meeting held at the Institute of Archaeology, London
09/11/71	Council for Nautical Archaeology	Minutes of a meeting held at the Institute of Archaeology, London
06/02/72	Council for Nautical Archaeology	Minutes of a meeting held at the Institute of Archaeology, London
15/03/72	Council for Nautical Archaeology	Minutes of a meeting held at the Institute of Archaeology, London
10/05/72	Council for Nautical Archaeology	Minutes of a meeting held at the Institute of Archaeology, London
20/07/72	Council for Nautical Archaeology	Minutes of a meeting held at the Institute of Archaeology, London
01/11/72	Council for Nautical Archaeology	Minutes of a meeting held at the Institute of Archaeology, London
05/12/72	Council for Nautical Archaeology	Minutes of a meeting held at the Institute of Archaeology, London
17/01/73	Council for Nautical Archaeology	Minutes of a meeting held at the Institute of Archaeology, London

7.11 List of Interviewees

UK

Andrew Burr, Department of Transport, London	13 December 1991

Netherlands

Thijs Maarleveld, Afdeling Archeologie Onder water, Alphen aan den Rijn	20 January 1992
Reinder Reinders, University of Groningen	3 February 1992

Denmark

Flemming Rieck, IMA - Skibshistorisk Laboratorium, Roskilde	22 January 1992
Henrik Christiansen, Forhistorisk Museum, Moesgard & Jan Larsen, Bangsbo Museet, Fredrickshavn	23 January 1992
Birger Thomsen, Skov -og Naturstyrelsen, Horsholm	24 January 1992

Norway

Johan Klosters, Norsk Sjofartsmuseum, Oslo	28 January 1992
Dag Naevestad, Norsk Sjofartsmuseum, Oslo	
Marek Jasinski, University of Trondhiem	29 January 1992

Sweden

Carl Olaf Cederlund, University of Stockholm - Sjohistoriska Museet, Stockholm	30 January 1992
Bert Westenberg, Sjohistoriska Museet, Stockholm	31 January 1992
Birgitta Johansen, Riksantikvarambetet, Stockholm	31 January 1992

France

Eric Rieth, CNRS - Musee de la Marine, Paris	17 February 1992

Ireland

Eamonn Kelly, National Museum, Dublin	15 February 1992

www.ingramcontent.com/pod-product-compliance
Lightning Source LLC
Chambersburg PA
CBHW0€I002030426
42334CB00033B/3334